# Women and Religion in Early America, 160Ω 185Ω

*Women and Religion in Early America, 1600–1850* explores the first two centuries of America's religious history, examining the relationships between the sociopolitical environment, gender politics, and religion.

Drawing its background from women's religious roles and experiences in England during the Reformation, the book follows both British and African-American women through colonial settlement, the rise of evangelicalism with the "Great Awakening," the American Revolution, and the second flowering of popular religion in the first half of the nineteenth century.

*Women and Religion in Early America, 1600–1850* traces the female spiritual tradition through the Puritans, Baptists, Methodists and Evangelical reformers, arguing that religion was both an oppressive and an empowering force for women in early America.

**Marilyn J. Westerkamp** is Professor of History at the University of California, Santa Cruz.

# Christianity and society in the modern world
General editor: Hugh McLeod

Also available:

**The Reformation and the visual arts: the Protestant image question in Western and Eastern Europe**
*Sergiusz Michalski*

**European religion in the age of great cities**
*Hugh McLeod*

**Women and religion in England, 1500–1720**
*Patricia Crawford*

**The reformation of ritual: an interpretation of early modern Germany**
*Susan Karant-Nunn*

**The Anabaptists**
*Hans-Jürgen Goertz*

**Calvinism and society**
*Philip Benedict*

**The clergy in modern Europe**
*Gregory Freeze*

**Religion and social change in industrial Britain**
*David Hempton*

**Religion and revolution, 1400–1650**
*Michael Baylor*

**The British missionary movement, 1700–1950**
*Jeff Cox*

**Representing witchcraft**
*Charles Zika*

**Christianity and sexuality, 1450–1750**
*Merry E. Wiesner-Hanks*

**War and religion in Britain**
*Michael Snape*

# Women and Religion in Early America, 1600–1850

## The Puritan and Evangelical Traditions

Marilyn J. Westerkamp

London and New York

First published 1999
by Routledge
11 New Fetter Lane, London EC4P 4EE

Simultaneously published in the USA and Canada
by Routledge
29 West 35th Street, New York, NY 10001

Typeset in Palatino by Routledge
Printed and bound in Great Britain by
Clays Ltd, St Ives PLC

*British Library Cataloguing in Publication Data*
A catalogue record for this book is available from the British
Library

*Library of Congress Cataloging in Publication Data*
Westerkamp, Marilyn J.
Women and Religion in Early America, 1600–1850 / Marilyn J.
Westerkamp
p.cm. (Christianity and society in the modern world)
Includes bibliographical references and index.
1. Women in Christianity–United States–History.
2. United States–Church History. I Title. II Series.
BR520.W4741999
277.3'07' 082–dc21 98–30837 CIP

ISBN 0 415–09814–9 (hbk)
ISBN 0 415–19448–2 (pbk)

For my family,
Claire, Hugh, and, especially, Cynthia

# Contents

# Acknowledgements

This work on Puritan and Evangelical women has depended upon the assistance and support of many institutions and individuals. The research undergirding the three Puritanism chapters was supported in part by a travel grant and a summer stipend from the National Endowment for the Humanities as well as faculty research funds granted by the University of California, Santa Cruz. My engagement with the increasingly rich scholarship in the field surely indicates my dependence upon the Interlibrary Loan Department of the University of California, Santa Cruz library, and I am grateful for their searching skills and astonishing efficiency.

I acknowledge deeper debts to my students whose comments upon my lectures and presentations have helped me refine my arguments and, occasionally, called me to expand my research in order to fill out undeveloped or scantily supported conclusions. I thank especially teaching assistants who have been hearing and commenting perceptively upon my lectures for many years now, although I realize this is poor recompense for being required to listen over and over again to stories of Anne Hutchinson, Zilpha Elaw, the Great Awakening, and the Salem Witch Trials. More specifically, I thank my research assistants, Jennifer Cullison, for her initial bibliographic work, and Tiffany Wayne. Tiffany was an invaluable aide as I crafted and revised the manuscript. She performed the standard responsibilities of research assistants with speed and skill, but she also sat with me for hours as I worked through the construction of key arguments. Our conversations help me clarify my thoughts and refine my writing; sections of chapter six, on evangelicalism and national identity, are especially indebted to her criticisms and suggestions.

I wish, too, to thank readers Hugh McLeod and Susan Juster, as well as anonymous commentators, whose reactions to the text were encouraging and challenging. While I did not agree with all of their recommendations, there is no question but that the book is better for their intervention. I am also indebted to the staff of Routledge, especially Claire L'Enfant, Heather McCallum, and Ruth Jeavons, who tended this project through from origin to completion. Their nudges always gentle, their patience infinite, it has been a pleasure to work with them. Finally, I want to express my great gratitude to and respect for Bob Scribner, who died before this project was completed. It was he who, seven years ago, first broached the possibility of this book with me, and he who encouraged the work and kept me on track. I much regret that he could not see the end of his beginning, but his influence on this project has remained strong.

I gratefully acknowledge permission for the use of portions of my essays published in the following journal and anthology: "Engendering Puritan Religious Culture in Old and New England," in *Empire, Society, and Labor: Essays in Honor of Richard S. Dunn*, a special issue of *Pennsylvania History* 64 (1997), 105–122. and "Anne Hutchinson, (Congregational)" and "Mary Dyer, (Quaker)," in George H. Shriver, ed., *Dictionary of Heresy Trials in American Christianity* (Westport, Ct.: Greenwood Press, 1997), 177–187; 121–130, an imprint of the Greenwood Publishing Group, Inc., Westport Ct.

# 1   Women, the Spirit, and the Reformation

> I will pour out my spirit upon all flesh; and your sons and your daughters shall prophesy; your old men shall dream dreams; your young men shall see visions:
> And also upon the servants and upon the handmaids in those days will I pour out my vision.
>
> (Joel 2:28–29)

Throughout the history of Christianity, leaders and followers have looked to a variety of authorities to understand the divine and structure their relationships with God. Different communities have focused upon different sources of truth – church tradition, reason and learning, popular practice, and the scriptures; yet most affirm that the significance of each authority has been mediated by the Holy Spirit. In some groups, the Spirit's grace merely hangs as a plumb line against which to measure the unchanging legacy of scripture or tradition. For others, the Holy Spirit plays an active, vital role in the personal lives of believers, directing spiritual journeys and mandating personal and social change. The stronger a church's belief in the immanence of the Spirit , the more difficult it is for a church's magisterium to control its members. For centuries, Christians have remained convinced that God moved in arbitrary, unpredictable ways, sometimes gifting the least of humanity while ignoring the most powerful. Surely, if a man or woman acted under divine commission, no earthly church institution could justify countermanding that person or controlling actions or speech.

This book explores the theological beliefs and spiritual careers of Puritan and evangelical women during the first 200 years in what became the United States. These women, socially and politically subordinate according to custom and law, experienced the Holy Spirit during their lives and discovered their own charismatic authority. Largely descendants of British and West African forebears, these women were members of Christian movements that envisioned the Holy Spirit as a powerful, immediate force in the world. Their history began during the sixteenth century, the century of Protestant Reformation, with the intensely pietistic and strictly reformed English Puritan community. At the beginning of the seventeenth century, many Puritans emigrated to New England to create a godly community that maintained its integrity for almost a hundred years. During the century that followed, women of different ethnicities across the North American colonies became involved in an expanded, diversified pietism. This reconstruction of Puritans' introverted spirituality has come to be known as evangelicalism, a religiosity that owed much to community ritual even as it retained the primary goal of the individual sinner's salvation. Once established, evangelicalism prospered throughout the eighteenth and early nineteenth centuries, counting extraordinary numbers of women among its strongest adherents. This book examines the ways these religious systems defined, understood, and constrained women, and the various ways that women responded to these restrictions and to the urgings of God in their hearts.

Such work of the Spirit was not unknown to English women before the Reformation. The fourteenth-century mystic Margery Kempe received several visions and experienced a close communion with Christ, recording her earthly travels and mystical experiences in the *Book of Margery Kempe*. Although married and the mother of fourteen children, she and her husband pursued a spiritual lifestyle that included a fairly ascetic regimen, vows of chastity, and pilgrimages to Canterbury and the Holy Land. Her prayers and meditations seem to have been influenced by her visits to Julian of Norwich, a woman known to Margery (and to others) as an expert in spiritual guidance.[1]

Julian, too, is easily described as a mystic, but unlike Margery she had taken vows early in her life. She spent most of her adult career as an anchoress, a woman who lived an ascetic, solitary life confined to her cell, or anchorhold. At the age of 30, Julian received a series of sixteen revelations over two days, and she devoted the next twenty years to meditation and prayer in an effort to understand what had been revealed to her. Her revelations focused primarily upon the Trinity and the sufferings of Christ, and her writings reflected a continuous concern for the trials of human experience and the struggle of the soul to be united with the divine. At one point she spoke of the presence and absence of the Spirit in the life of the soul. "To experience well-being is to be touched and illumined by grace, and with true certainty of endless joy." This joy, however, might quickly disappear in the absence of God, to be followed by the dejection and weariness that would come with the sense of abandonment.

> And then presently God gave me again comfort and rest for my soul, delight and security so blessedly and so powerfully that there was no fear, no sorrow, no pain, physical or spiritual, that one could

suffer which might have disturbed me. And then again I felt the pain, and then afterwards the delight and the joy…And in the time of joy I could have said with St. Paul: Nothing shall separate me from the love of Christ; and in the pain I could have said with St. Peter: Lord, save me, I am perishing.

In a beautiful exposition that foreshadows the Puritan belief in the unconditional freeness of the Holy Spirit's grace, Julian added that neither the sorrow nor the happiness were deserved:

> For in this time I committed no sin for which I ought to have been left to myself, for it was so sudden. Nor did I deserve these feelings of joy, but the Lord gives it freely when he wills, and sometimes he allows us to be in sorrow, and both are one in love.[2]

Such early records of revelations and union with the divine are scarce indeed, and from women they are even rarer. It will never be known how many women actually experienced the supreme joys described by Julian and Margery; but, even for those not inspired, the medieval church provided support. Convents offered a home and a discipline for those few women who felt called to take Jesus as their immediate bridegroom. Women who wished to avoid marriage and dependence upon an individual man could also join one of these female communities. For women who chose marriage, there were multitudes of saints and devotions to the Virgin Mary, the Mother of God. Yet, while marriage was a respectable choice, and the choice of most Christians, the Church placed a premium upon chastity for men and, especially, women. In their vows of celibacy and poverty, nuns were thought to overcome their feminine bodies and, in consequence, achieve heightened spiritual awareness, holiness, and authority.[3] Men, too, benefited from the chastity of women, since chaste women would no longer lure men into the trap of sensuality and away from their spiritual purposes.

The Reformation arrived in England in 1533 and proceeded at a rather slow pace. Until the accession of Elizabeth in 1558, the progress of reforming bishops was haphazard, tied as it was (for good or ill) to the will of monarchs, who from reign to reign changed the direction of the church. Politically, the English Reformation removed the institutional church from the purview of the papacy by placing it in the hands of English bishops under the headship of the monarch. Religiously, this process worked to distance the English Church from much of the theology and practice of the Church of Rome. The Reformation removed or undermined many of the emotionally satisfying rituals of the medieval church, and priests were no longer recognized as an especial, sacred caste with particular access to God. The veneration of Mary and the saints was attacked, and many special festivals and feast days were eliminated. In essence, all mediation between the individual soul and God was replaced with the priesthood of all believers, a belief acted out with direct prayer to God, the father, and Jesus Christ, his son and the savior of humanity. Sociologically, the reformers challenged the conviction that celibacy was superior to marriage, and marriage was now valued for its role in promoting divine providence. All persons, including ministers, were to marry.

It might be argued that the Reformation brought little change to the lives of English men and women. In 1600 as in 1500, most adults in all classes married, bore children, and supported their families as best they could. However, the Reformation did change the ideological touchstone of holiness. Not only was the superiority of celibacy discounted; celibacy was barely an acceptable choice. Reformed theologians agreed that man was duty-bound to marry and follow the example of the patriarchs (though stopping short of their multiple wives). New Testament caveats invoked by Roman Catholics were explained away. Paul's preference for celibacy, "It were good for a man not to touche a woman," was clarified: "...because mariage, through mans corruption, and not by Gods institution, bringeth cares and troubles." Later in the same chapter, when Paul argued with vehemence for the superiority of virginity, the Calvinist commentator explained that "He doeth not preferre singleness as a thing more holie than mariage, but by reason of incommodities, which the one hathe more than the other."[4]

The first century of reform saw the publication of detailed domestic manuals that filled hundreds of pages with descriptions of utopian households. The vocation of spouse and parent was spiritually elevated. The family became the most sacred of humane institutions: "the familie is a little Church, and a little commonwealth."[5] Undoubtedly, many aspiring young ministers were pleased that the unhappy demands of the chaste life would no longer be required. In place of the special spiritual status granted to a few men and women by virtue of their celibacy and consecration, the mandate for marriage gratified all men. Each became a patriarch, to follow in Abraham's footprints, he who "was a King, a priest, a Prophet in his owne Family."[6]

But what of women? The destruction of the Catholic Church was followed by the destruction of those few institutions that provided some opportunity, however limited, for female autonomy. The anchoress, bricked into her hermitage, nevertheless lived autonomously through her own choice. If she was not free to move about the countryside, she was also not required to attend to the demands of male "protectors." Gone were the convents, sneered at by men of distinction, but nonetheless a haven from male restriction and interference. Medieval convents may have required a male priest to perform sacramental rituals, but these were female communities, governed by women for the comfort and encouragement of women.[7] Protestant women were destined to be married, to labor in the household, and to subject themselves to the rule of their husbands. This calling was lodged in women's natural inferiority: their intellectual weakness, making them unable to distinguish between good and evil, and their spiritual weakness, rendering them unable to assert their wills to follow the good.

With the rising importance of the family as a spiritual unit, and the central role played by the housewife, Amanda Porterfield has argued that the status of women improved.[8] While the anchoress or nun may have enjoyed greater autonomy than her married peer, might even have exercised some power or influence, this independence and authority grew out of a holiness possible only in her celibacy. In other words, by denying her sexuality and overcoming her femaleness, the "genderless" individual claimed spiritual power. After the Reformation, this argument continues, women were honored in their femaleness as essential members of the family. This vision articulated in the domestic manuals was also reflected in countless eulogies and memorials.

> Here lies,
> A worthy matron of unspotted life,
> A loving mother and obedient wife,
> A friendly neighbor, pitiful to poor,
> Whom oft she fed and clothed with her store;
> To servants wisely awful, but yet kind,
> And as they did so reward did find.
> A true instructor of her family,
> The which she orderd with dexterity.[9]

So Anne Bradstreet praised her late mother Dorothy Dudley, praise that echoed across the seventeenth century and beyond, as sons, husbands, and pastors praised mothers, wives, and widows. Loving, charitable, kind, and wise, she ordered her family.

Yet, this argument seems rather narrowly drawn and shortsighted. Seclusion and celibacy seem an extraordinary price to pay for what many twentieth-century scholars judge extremely limited power. In medieval eyes, the price may not have been so dear, nor the power so limited. In disbelieving the satisfaction that some women claimed to find within monastic lives, scholars are accepting the reformers' limited definition of female fulfillment instead of hearing and believing women's own words. Consider what was meant by housewife: a superior laborer, a middle manager who, in the best circumstances, governed her female servants and young children under the headship of her spouse. Wives may have been honored for their sterling qualities and valued for their skills; some exercised considerable influence over their households. Still, however great the honor and value, housewifery did not bring autonomy. As Margaret Newcastle mourned: "Men, that are not only our Tyrants, but our Devils, keep us in the Hell of Subjection, from whence I cannot Perceive any Redemption...."[10] The worthy Dorothy Dudley was also an obedient wife.

The Reformation returned all women to a life that most women had lived anyway; it reconfirmed old lines of patriarchy within household and family – a case of new language for old structures. Religiously, however, there was a change for the ordinary believer. The medieval conviction that an individual could reach union with the Holy Spirit remained, but Protestant reformers, committed as they were to the elimination of a special, sacred caste of priests, monks, and nuns, believed that this experience was available to everyone. When reformers looked to the Bible for exemplary women, they found Bathsheba the housekeeper, Susannah the chaste wife, and Mary the submissive. They also found in Paul's Epistles and the Acts of the Apostles the names of many women honored as preachers and community leaders. In the final chapter of his Epistle to the Romans, Paul explicitly addressed and commended nine women in his long list of salutations. Try as they might, reformers could not deny that among women the "gifts of miracles and tongues were common to many as well as the gift of Prophecy."[11] The best they could do was dismiss prophesying women to the specific, miraculous years of the early Christian church, the years during which God actively revealed his scriptural word.

Most English reformers were content with this solution to the problem, but not all. Puritans and their evangelical descendants did not want to dismiss such knowledge out of hand. They were deeply interested in the strength of such seemingly ordinary persons; they envied their charisma and marveled at the power of their speech. In such individuals, Puritans and evangelicals found promise in the ability of ordinary persons like themselves to reach God, and they revelled in the hope of that astonishing moment when God would touch their lives. This conviction in the mystical ability of the individual soul to experience God stood at the center of Puritans' and evangelicals' spiritual strength. Male religious leaders would be committed to patriarchal structures based upon an understanding of gender that regarded women as essentially inferior – physically, intellectually, and emotionally – to men. However, the value placed upon order (and its reward of male power) frequently competed with an ethos that embraced the sacred potential of all individuals, women as well as men, to discover God and attain union with the divine.

Puritans and evangelicals will be discussed in some detail in subsequent chapters, but at this point it is important to clarify the paradoxical nature of the religiosity that these two communities shared. Both seventeenth-century Puritans and their evangelical descendants judged the work of the Spirit of paramount importance among believers. All individuals sought to hear and feel God in their souls, and pastors led their congregants toward that mystical communion. However, each cultural system also engaged competing demands to establish order amidst the swirling chaos of society and sin. Whether that order was grounded in the seventeenth-century belief in divine providence, the eighteenth-century Enlightenment system of natural philosophy, or the nineteenth-century romantic vision of separate spheres, women were consistently placed in a subordinate position to men. Moreover, the elite men who controlled positions of secular and religious authority were not disinterested interpreters of scripture and the Spirit in light of providence or natural philosophy. Surely, at some level, magistrates, ministers, and (in the later period) white men generally wanted to maintain their power. The only way that women could overcome their disabilities was through the intervention of the Holy Spirit; and the voice of the Spirit was so powerful that the only way male leaders could maintain their patriarchal headship was to silence, or at least limit, that voice.

The following chapters explore the ideological, ritual, and institutional structures that promoted and constrained women's spiritual authority within religious cultures whose spirituality was explicitly connected to personal experience of the Holy Spirit. Chapters 2, 3, and 4 discuss New England Puritans during their first century of settlement, with each chapter focusing upon one facet of the relationship among women, the Spirit, and the church. Chapter 2 addresses the nature of Puritanism, the social and political dynamics surrounding women's lives, and the religious ideology constructing women's identity. While this chapter ends with an exploration of the ordinary woman's piety, the third moves to a detailed analysis of charismatically gifted women whose exercise of those gifts challenged the Church and State. The fourth chapter examines the construction and gendering of evil, with attention paid to the witch persecutions. Although the Puritans represented a small segment of the North American colonists, their society merits such attention. The detailed information available about New England society as well as Puritan theology and practice provides a terrific opportunity to examine the intricate workings of such a pietistic system firsthand. More importantly, in their intense personal piety and dedication to a life of total adherence to divine law, Puritans are the literal and metaphorical forebears of American evangelicals of the eighteenth and nineteenth centuries.

Chapters 5 to 8 turn to the rise of evangelicalism during the Great Awakening of the eighteenth century, the arrival and prosperity of the Methodist movement in the new United States, particularly the western frontier, and the appearance of a less dramatic evangelicalism in the eastern states. In these chapters the lens expands as evangelical revivalism swept through the colonies and traveled south and west. As evangelicalism developed and changed from 1740 to 1850, the leadership of women changed as well. In the Awakening decades, women assumed leadership of small prayer groups and, in some communities, served on lay committees directing congregational affairs. During the early decades of the nineteenth century, a few women, including several especially gifted African-American women, followed the Spirit's call and built reputations as lay preachers and exhorters. Moving to mid-century, some women sought explicitly pastoral or public roles, and they found their vocations in the fields of overseas missions, the Holiness movement, and reform. Throughout these decades the progress of individual churches was tied to the democratic, economic, and geographic expansion of the nation; and women's status within the new denominations was tied to politics and the frontier. In other words, while evangelicals believed in their favored connection with the Spirit, the innovations and excitement of their movement owed as much to the changing political and intellectual environment as to the effects of the Spirit.

In each chapter, I have provided background information to contextualize the exploration of each religious culture; in the four evangelicalism chapters I have focused upon one or two communities as exemplars of the social and cultural dynamics at work. When possible, I have used biography to personalize the narrative and demonstrate the ways that these religious systems affected and worked themselves out through individuals. Because information on individuals is generally available only for extraordinary persons, the women who are discussed in detail were extraordinary for their time and place. They were not necessarily members of society's ruling elite, but if they were not well-known, and some were, they were signally important to their own communities.

Finally, I note that this book is not concerned with what many, in a rationalist world, want to know. That is, I do not ask if women had delusions brought on by rye fungus, saw visions during migraines, or heard voices out of their own personal psychoses. Those seeking scientific explanations for supernatural phenomena must go elsewhere. I am content to explore the spirituality of Puritans and evangelicals from the position that for most residents of the seventeenth, eighteenth, and early nineteenth centuries, the supernatural world did exist, and God (and, it might be added, Satan, angels, and evil spirits) was personally involved in their lives. Interactions between the natural and supernatural world were real; for most, the only question was whether the experience was divine, demonic, or delusional. Yes, they acknowledged delusions a possibility, but this was certainly not assumed. Puritan and evangelical women and men believed that they heard the voice of the Spirit, felt themselves attacked by demons, and had visions of themselves embracing Jesus as their lover. The important question is not whether such things actually happened, but how women and the surrounding society judged the validity of their experiences and discovered the meanings of the providence, visions, and voices that they knew to be the breath of God.

# Part I
# The Puritan heritage

# 2 Wives and mothers in the colonial New England landscape

On Easter Monday, 1630, John Winthrop, governor of the Company of Massachusetts Bay, set sail aboard the *Arbella*, the flagship of a fleet carrying colonists to their newly chartered colony in New England. The men, women, and children who embarked upon this venture hoped to build villages and towns, churches and governments that reflected their own vision of godliness and order. Winthrop's well-known exhortation, that they were to be a "City on a Hill," a shining example to England and the world, was reflected in plans for a biblical commonwealth to be grounded in laws and principles gleaned from the Scriptures. The colonizers were mostly Puritans, and their identity as Puritans would come to define not only the religious organization but also the cultural climate, social environment, and political structures of New England through the next century. Historians have told the story so often that it has become a simple one: united, dedicated religionists governed by wise, astute leaders always in control of their harmonious society together met challenges posed by the natural environment, the native Americans, as well as troublesome, sometimes antagonistic European outsiders. This oft-told story involved men of intense piety, committed laymen as well as clerics, who had defied the established church and its bishops and left their homes to construct a new Israel in the wilderness. It is a story of governors, ministers, merchants, artisans, and farmers – a story of men.

Yet the story is not so simple, for the people were frequently at odds with each other and with their leaders. The leaders themselves were sometimes pushed beyond their political abilities by spiraling growth and disruptive religious diversity. Additionally, the New England experiment involved as many women as men, as silent participants certainly, but also as actors effecting change in their own right. The very nature of Puritan culture, its focus upon religious and political reform and the intensity of Puritan spirituality, opened the doors of religious power and authority to all persons, poor and wealthy, lowly and highly ranked, illiterate and educated, female and male.

By the end of the sixteenth century, the social, political, and ideological forces that would unite English dissenters into a self-conscious religious and political coalition were in place. During its first twenty-five years, the English Reformation had produced institutional insecurity, inconsistency, even chaos under the rules of the barely Protestant Henry VIII, the devoted reformer child-king Edward VI, and the equally resolute Roman Catholic Mary. Following Mary's death in 1558, the Elizabethan Reformation firmly established a Protestant Church of England as the state church, a *via media*, or middle way, between closeted Roman Catholics and less well-hidden Puritans who struggled to continue the work of reformation.

Initially, Puritans were set apart by their opposition to the relics of Roman Catholicism that continued, in their minds, to corrupt the English Church. Formal rituals, vestments, holy days, even church architecture were denounced as superstitious, idolatrous, sometimes pagan. They soon added to their grievances the character of the Anglican clergy, who, Puritans complained, frequently lacked erudition and even respectability. Puritans called for a return to clerical accountability, to godly conduct, and to the plain preaching and plain worship outlined in the Scriptures.

Many Puritans were also deeply spiritual and, increasingly disgusted with the legalism and formal emptiness of Anglican services, felt justified turning to private religious meetings to satisfy their spiritual cravings. Lay persons gathered weekly, sometimes more frequently, to pray, to study, and to preach, finding among themselves the piety, inspiration (and even learning) absent on Sundays. They also spread word of reliable, reformed ministers, graduates of Cambridge, known for their learning and piety as well as their criticism of the established church. Yet even the presence of reliable ministers did not relieve laypersons from their own spiritual responsibilities to educate themselves, to pray, to study, and to follow after Christ. In fact, in their understanding of the believer's spiritual quest, reformers posited a direct relationship between God and the soul. God offered grace, the soul was transformed, and salvation was realized. Among Puritan congregations, a clergyman might have assisted individuals on their spiritual quest through teaching, counseling, and exhortation, but he could not intervene with God on the soul's behalf. In the end, each person was his or her own priest. It was an awesome responsibility, yet Puritan men and women embraced it as their own.

Upon the accession of James I in 1603, Anglican bishops launched the first of several attacks against the Puritan movement, removing hundreds of clerics from their livings for their refusal to follow prescribed Anglican ceremonies. In 1605 many Brownists – radical, separatist Puritans who judged the established church irredeemably corrupt – fled to escape Anglican persecution and found, in the Netherlands, space and toleration for their beliefs and practices. As the Anglican Church, with the support of the monarch, strengthened its restrictions upon clergy and congregational practices, Puritans grew increasingly hostile to bishops. Power battles in the religious realm soon overlapped battles in the civil arena, and many Puritans and their sympathizers found themselves bound by political interests. Generally members of the rising bourgeoisie, either merchants or lesser landed gentry, they opposed not only bishops but also aristocracy and king as they struggled to establish their own economic and political power base within Parliament, especially the House of Commons. As the seventeenth century progressed, King James I and, later, his son Charles I, had increasing difficulty maintaining authority as religious and political strife intensified. In fact, the Puritan/Parliamentary party grew so strong and so angry that, within forty years of the death of Elizabeth, England was plunged into civil war.

As king, James faced a heavy disadvantage in his predecessor: Elizabeth was remarkably successful, extremely popular, and exceptionally long-lived. Only the most gifted of politicians could have comfortably followed a reign noted for domestic stability, economic prosperity, and, of course, the imperial victory over the Armada. Still, to some extent James carried forward Elizabeth's religious policies of moderation towards individual dissenters even as he promoted the expansion of institutional church authority. He proved able to maintain an uneasy truce with nation and Parliament; not so Charles. Charles assumed extensive royal prerogatives, justifiable by law but unwise in practice, and dismissed Parliament when the assembly would not accede to his demands.

Under the guidance of his chaplain (and later Archbishop of Canterbury), William Laud, Charles confirmed and expanded significant changes in the Anglican Church already begun during his father's reign. Ceremonies became more complex, formalized, and, to Puritan sensibilities, artificial as preaching was displaced by sacramentalism in Anglican worship. Moreover, the Laudian party had moved away from a strict Calvinist predestinarian theology of humanity's complete depravity and dependence upon God toward an Arminian posture that encouraged individuals to work toward their salvation. Charles also grew less tolerant of Puritan clerics and congregants, and he began an initially haphazard, but soon systematic, effort to force conformity to the progressively catholic Church of England. Episcopal visitations to congregations became arenas for major displays of conflict, disobedience, and challenge. As a result of their own (or their congregations') stances, ministers lost their livings; some were defrocked; congregants were fined for not attending services; and many influential Puritans, especially clerics, were arrested and imprisoned.

As early as 1628, only three years after Charles succeeded to the throne, a large company of Puritans found itself able to gather adequate resources for a colonizing enterprise and began to explore the possibility of emigration. Dissatisfied and troubled by the growing estrangement between Parliament and king as well as the rising power of Laud, many sought to escape the monarch's control and Laud's influence in an overseas colony. Additionally, some Puritans feared that the increased decadence, corruption, and the "popishness" of Laud were harbingers of the impending apocalypse foretold in Revelation. Envisioning themselves as the saved remnant, some were following a millennialist impulse to leave God's terrible vengeance in England and build a godly commonwealth that would continue the necessary work begun in the Reformation. For others focused upon secular affairs, the seventeenth century had brought a decline in the quality of life – decreased opportunity, increased criminality, burdensome taxation, and a surfeit of corrupt bureaucrats, court officers, and lawyers driving people more deeply into poverty.[1] Yet whether fleeing persecution, escaping divine wrath, embracing the responsibilities (and rewards) of the saved remnant, or seeking the mundane goals of economic opportunity and justice, a significant number of English men and women embarked upon a holy experiment to build a godly community in the wilderness – under royal sponsorship but beyond Charles's interference.

On 7 April 1630 seven hundred settlers embarked for the new colony. During the next twelve years, New England would annually absorb hundreds, sometimes thousands of immigrants fleeing economic and political instability and seeking prosperity and piety. Unlike other British colonial enterprises, where most settlers were young, unmarried men, New England immigrants arrived in families. In her study of the passengers of seven ships, Virginia DeJohn Anderson found that nearly half the immigrants were women, and almost a third of the passengers were under 15 years of age. These were not, by and large, adventurers seeking great fortunes, but husbands and wives with their children, relatives, and servants planning to settle and build a permanent, thriving commonwealth.[2] During this "Great Migration," between 15,000 and 20,000 people risked the crossing. Most, about 13,000, would stay in Massachusetts Bay, but many others, finding opportunities limited or the government restrictive, would move to other settlements – Rhode Island, Providence, New Haven, Connecticut, and New Hampshire – all founded between 1634 and 1637 by dissatisfied Massachusetts residents.

In addition to Plymouth, six New England colonies were founded beyond the political purview of Massachusetts within ten years. Some Puritans, like Thomas Hooker and his congregation, left in search of more land, better economic opportunities, and freedom from the colonial government. Their settlement in Connecticut, and the later colonists of New Haven, remained friendly with Massachusetts though protective of their autonomy. However, the three settlements that would constitute Rhode Island, as well as the western settlement of New Hampshire, were founded by religious outcasts, banished from Massachusetts on charges of heresy or blasphemy. With the exception of Plymouth (united with

Massachusetts in 1691) these smaller settlements remained politically independent of Massachusetts. Yet, despite their separate organizations, they were deeply connected through extensive cultural and social similarities and by the joint enterprise of colonization.

New England society was an English society, and, while Puritans planned to construct a biblical nation, at the core of their culture lay a family/household structure grounded within a complex of English common law and custom founded upon assumptions of marital unity and male superiority. The ideal of female subjection was partially realized in the concept of coverture, through which the legal personhood of a woman was completely subsumed under her husband's identity, her property under his ownership. A wife's dependence became not only a matter of cultural, social, and legal restrictions, but necessarily of concrete economics as women moved from the households of fathers to husbands. Even widows, though legally permitted to act on their own behalf, often found the lessons of dependency overwhelming and thus sought the financial and emotional support of adult sons or another male relative.[3]

The theology of Puritan leaders reaffirmed the hierarchical nature of their society. The great Hebrew patriarchs and kings became role models for leaders, and their recorded wisdom, reinforced by Pauline pronouncements, guided the pious toward an ordered society. While some few persons were called to exercise power as magistrates and ministers, and many more as husbands and fathers, most, and certainly all women, were called to subject themselves to the authority of others. The Holy Scriptures had ordained a clear, ordered family system that arranged all members of society into dichotomous power relationships: master–servant, parent–child, husband–wife. Within this domestic system the father assumed the central role as head of household. Their God was a God of order, and out of their religious convictions and experiences Puritan leaders found divine sanction for a firm, clear hierarchy. Together religion, law, and custom constructed and upheld an ostensibly scriptural, but certainly English, patriarchy.

Of course, Massachusetts was not England, nor even ancient Israel, and women in this frontier environment often found themselves in positions demanding effective, independent action. The housewives' duties, including food and clothing production, childbearing and rearing, and family health, set burdensome demands upon women, and New England, at least during the first decades of settlement, lacked the markets, fairs, traveling artisans, and peddlers that eased work in English villages. Here women found that trading for food and other necessities – knowing where to find the goods, how to judge them, and how to bargain – required an additional collection of skills. English women had usually been entrusted with the family stores, but in the colonies women often controlled all family business for prolonged periods. Although the primary occupation of most men was farming, men pursued business in neighboring colonies, England, and the Caribbean. They fished, captained, and manned ships on the seas; they engaged in trade throughout the British empire; they fought wars against American natives and other European colonizers. In other words, husbands absented themselves for weeks or months at a time, and wives had to be trusted not only with all household affairs, but with their spouse's public business as well.[4]

Additionally, women living at the edge of settlement shared direct risks with their husbands and fathers. They reconstructed new, colonial identities partly out of their response to the frontier environment, partly by comparing themselves with the native American communities, and always in fear of natural disaster and war. During the native uprising of 1675–1676 and the wars against the French and their native American allies at the end of the century, many women lost their homes, sometimes their husbands, occasionally their own lives. Others endured and triumphed victorious. Hannah Dunston, Mary Neff, and a boy named Samuel Lennardson, captured during an attack against the town of Haverhill, escaped by killing their captors. When they returned to Boston, they brought grisly proof of their accomplishment: ten scalps, including those of six children. The survival of other captives through guile and submissive endurance seems less spectacular, yet such women, in meeting this challenge, stood as symbols for the courage and autonomy of Puritan women. Perhaps Mary Rowlandson, a minister's wife, best exemplified the strength of godly women to meet the threats posed by the frontier. Under Rowlandson's pen, her captivity and redemption became a metaphor for her spiritual journey, a metaphor that ministers would expand analogically to all of New England in its final victory over the united native American nations.[5]

Mary Rowlandson's interpretation of her captivity in terms of her relationship with God reflects the intensely religious and inward focus of New England's Puritan culture. This piety is probably the most important quality linking the New England colonies. They shared an economy of subsistence agriculture, maritime enterprise, and merchant trade; they shared a need to accommodate or conquer the native populations; but they also shared a Puritan ancestry characterized by a deep commitment to pursuing piety. Although the centrality of religion in New England has been challenged by historians who emphasize the economic drives of colonists, one cannot deny the extensive (and successful) recruitment of ministers, the organization of so many churches, and the founding of Harvard colleges (1636) and Yale (1715) as institutions for training clergymen. And, while it would be wrong to claim that all Puritans were like-minded, they were descended from and had been nourished by the same culture of dissent. Even recalcitrant Rhode Island revealed this deeply religious core. Viewed by others as the sewer of New England because of a policy of religious toleration and an acceptance of any banished from other colonies, Rhode Island proved a hotbed of radical sectarians, including Baptists and Quakers, both sharing a history with the more demure congregationalists of Massachusetts.

Within all of these colonies the family remained at the center of organized religion. The household was a little church, and while the housewife should work to promote the spiritual health of her servants and children, the householder remained its spiritual as well as legal head. Each town's families were gathered together in an independent congregation led by a minister and lay elders chosen by the membership. With no overarching church hierarchy holding authority, congregations retained almost complete control of their affairs, accountable only to the State in terms of maintaining orthodoxy and order. Like families, churches were characterized by an odd mixture of shared responsibilities and rewards along with a clear, hierarchical line of authority. Far from an open membership, individuals applied to join a New England church. Membership was granted only to visible saints who had demonstrated to other saints, through their sanctified behavior and their testimony about their personal relationship with God, the likelihood of their election to salvation. Membership was open to all men and women, and early records of the Boston church show that equal numbers of women and men did join the churches.[6] However, in conducting the affairs of the congregation, only male members voted. Moreover, once a minister and elders were in place, they retained comprehensive control over their flock. Still, the church, like the family, was merely a support for an individual saint who necessarily sought her or his salvation alone, a situation that held an implicit threat of subversion in a society that had so carefully organized itself along patriarchal power lines.

Puritans actively supported the idea that all believers could interpret scripture for themselves, pray directly to God, and struggle with their own souls on the pathway to salvation. All persons were held to high moral standards of chastity, justice, honor, industriousness, and all were equally likely to fail. Additionally, men of rank or office might be held accountable for the work and faith of those under their care as well as themselves, but as descendants of Adam they were born in sin and constantly falling into temptations. Yet, amidst their unswerving conviction of human depravity, Puritans embraced an optimistic faith in the ability of all persons to understand scripture and grasp basic theological truths.

Puritans urged all believers towards literacy as a necessary condition for following their pathway to God. They knew that the Bible, as the word of God, was a difficult text, and they believed that most laypersons, lacking formal education, were unable to grasp without (or even with!) assistance many abstruse points of theology. Nonetheless, the guidance of a highly educated ministry enabled all to approach the unknowable. In addition to their faith in ordinary human reason, Puritans discovered in scripture ample evidence that God engaged the individual soul directly. God may have been a God of majesty and power, but through grace and the Holy Spirit he was also accessible to the least of his children. Every person was able to interpret God's word as revealed in the Bible, and each was spiritually capable of forming a relationship with God independently; that is, without mediation.

In other words, although Puritans expressed diverse opinions on a wide range of theological issues, they shared two common ideological convictions. The first was the emphasis placed upon learning: the Puritan movement demanded erudition of its clergy and actively encouraged literacy and learning among the laity. Believers were thinking Christians, responsible for their own knowledge and behavior. The second commonality characterizing Puritans' spirituality was a certainty that each saint enjoyed a direct, personal relationship with God. This relationship would be reflected in a conversion experience expected of every believer, and taken much further by some. It provided a mystical counterpoint to the extraordinarily strong emphasis upon learning, and stood, I would argue, as the more important common thread tying Puritan dissenters together.[7]

For many New England Puritans, the focus upon learning joined with a common understanding of spirituality to fulfill the need of faithful individuals to control their own spiritual destinies. In a theological climate characterized by election and, by extension, predestination, many found themselves anxiously crossing a dangerous spiritual landscape. True Calvinists risked fatalism and depression, or, perhaps, arrogance and hedonism. The problem lay in an understanding of sin, damnation, and salvation grounded in the total depravity of humanity and the omnipotence and omniscience of God. Calvinism held that the human soul, naturally depraved, could achieve salvation only through faith possible by means of divine grace. God offered this grace to a few chosen for arbitrary, unpredictable reasons, and these elect had been predestined for salvation (and the rest of humanity for damnation) from the beginning of time. If the membership of the elect had been predetermined, then why should anyone attempt holiness? Upon what grounds could a pastor encourage scriptural study and holy behavior?

Of course, the truly elect did not require rewards for godly behavior; the saint pursued perfection in order to glorify God. In preaching about this sanctification of behavior, ministers focused their audience upon the visible fruits of the Spirit, reinforcing individual and community commitments to holiness. For those anxious individuals worried about their gracious states, sanctification provided reassuring evidence of election. Yet, while striving Christians might be encouraged by their own personal holiness, no one could be certain of election on this basis alone. The worst hypocrites could read scripture, follow the law, and model their behavior after a Gospel example. For this reason, Puritans looked toward the additional, some would say superior, evidence of the witness of the Spirit.

Divine grace transformed the believer's heart, mind, and will through an intensive conversion experience, an exhaustive, never-ending process recognized and sought by all Puritans, from the most highly educated theologian to the least of the congregants. The nature of this experiential conversion was discussed and debated, chronicled in diaries, and related in church testimonies with such monotonous consistency that scholars have been able to reconstruct its morphology in astonishing detail. In the early stages, the struggling soul, mortified by his or her own sins, was terrified by the specter of eternal punishment that awaited. The believer would grow desperate in the knowledge that the penalty was deserved and become humiliated by the inability to follow God's law. During the middle, climactic, stages the saint acknowledged complete dependence upon God, opened the self up to divine grace, came to hope in Christ's atonement, and realized the assurance of salvation. In the final phase, the saint's thoughts and actions were sanctified, and, while ongoing doubts might have remained, divine grace continued to reassure.[8]

In demanding that church members articulate their convictions, New England churches subtly altered the meaning and import of the conversion experience for many believers. If the actual experience was private and personal – an emotional confrontation between soul and Spirit, witnessing to this confrontation seems excruciatingly public. Such testimonies became expressive performances that pastor, elders, and congregants could judge and, perhaps more importantly, manipulate. If the narrative was too short or the path described unrecognizable, clarifying questions could elaborate the briefest account or wrestle the most puzzling tale into a comfortable pattern. In one case, despite extensive, elaborate testimony replete with biblical quotations, elders found it necessary to fit Mary Angier's confession into the mold. They asked "whether she had closed with the person of Christ," and later "whether she had assurance."[9] Such leading questions benefited both applicant and congregation. Clearly, if able to answer the questions, the candidate would be accepted into membership, and the congregation would hear reinforced the orthodox construction of conversion. Still, by forcing the narrative into a mold, pastors and elders transmuted what may have been diverse human–divine encounters into homogeneous, well-trodden tales of terror and redemption.[10]

As they dissected further the character of these stages of conversion the New England clerics disagreed. A few believed that the human soul was merely an empty vessel to be filled with the oil of divine grace, completely passive in the face of God. Others encouraged their hearers to prepare for that moment when the Spirit would arrive. The very word "preparation" pointed up the paradoxical relationship Puritans found between God and humanity. While accepting that a sinner could not move a single step toward faith and salvation without grace, most proclaimed the need of believers to prepare for that grace. At one level, the preparation required was described in the vaguest of terms. Hooker counseled his readers to "come to him" and to "yeeld to the Lord Jesus Christ to be at his disposing and carving." Others called upon sinners to seek out God. If such evidences as prayer and brokenness of heart did not convince a person that he was saved, "he is to lament his unbelief, and to seek to the Lord to persuade his heart as the man in the Gospel did."[11] Many offered explicit instructions, including Bible reading, prayer, sermons, and meditations. Such actions guaranteed nothing; they could not be read as evidence of election. Nevertheless, they were "guides to leade us to Christ, so they are meanes to convey grace, mercy and comfort from Christ to our soules." The sinner should strive in this preparation, avoid "vaine, joviall" company, and "labour to acquaint your selves throughly with God and with his law, and to see the compasse and breadth of it; the words of the Commandements are few, but there are many sinnes forbidden in them, and many duties required."[12] Despite theologians' affirmation that all was in God's hands, the language of preparation was a language of action. The sinner should submit, yield, seek, labor, study, pray.

In the end, efforts to reassure anxious Puritans provided believers with some sense of control over their spiritual destinies. Also, a concentration upon sanctification was profoundly helpful to the Puritan leaders' commitment to order, for outward behavior could be controlled and sanctified behavior emulated. Additionally, much of the mystery of the conversion experience was countered by a delineation of its development phase by phase, and the implication that at least the initial stages involved conscious activity. While Puritans would have insisted, with Paul, that "there is nether male nor female: for ye are all one in Christ Jesus," their intense engagement with sanctification and preparation belied this.[13] The means toward grace, including sermons, catechizing, and the sacraments, were controlled by a male clergy. And, while prayer was certainly available to all, only private prayer remained a genderless occupation. Women were expected to pray publicly along with the congregation, but they were not permitted to lead public prayer. Even in private circles women were to lead prayers only for other women.

So, too, the emphasis placed upon studying scripture reinforced the gender hierarchy. Although Puritan leaders urged all believers to read the Bible for themselves, they understood that most people needed assistance. The text was difficult, often abstruse and obscure. Only with formal training in languages, logic, rhetoric, and theology was a man truly prepared to interpret scripture. In New England, about half as many women as men could read, and in both old and New England women were absolutely excluded from university education.[14] By privi-

leging erudition as a primary source of religious authority, Puritans effectively disfranchised women religiously.

Salvation came through grace, and knowledge of salvation through
conversion. The conversion experience itself came to be defined by the
preparatory steps of reading, study, and prayer; the sanctification
following conversion; and the performance involved in testifying to the
soul's conversion. The experience may have been available to all regardless of gender, but men witnessed publicly before the congregation while
women generally related their experiences privately and stood silently
before the congregation as their testimonies were read. In other words,
women's voices were subsumed under a male representative's report, as
if women could not understand or interpret the work of the Spirit in
their own souls. Without the power to articulate their experiences,
women lost some of the power to determine their own religiosity.

I find this focus upon erudition, preparation, and sanctification to be a
game attempt to reconstruct an essentially mystical spirituality as a
developmental one. Since Puritan leaders basically agreed with other
Englishmen that men boasted superior strength of will and mind, a
developmental understanding favored men by privileging men's intellectual and moral superiority as defined by seventeenth-century science
and theology. Yet the fact that a reconstruction was necessary at all
reflected the basic conflict inherent in Puritan religiosity. The very nature
of mysticism – a direct, intense relationship with the divine, a relationship available to anyone, depending only upon the arbitrary choice of
God – established a core egalitarian spirituality that empowered the individual in relation to society.

Women and other disfranchised believers often refused to accept the
limits of that developmental reconstruction. Despite their emphasis upon
learning, preparation, and sanctification, Puritan clerics granted that
God's grace came freely to each believer. God had a personal relationship
with each individual, and this relationship was understood to be a direct
communion between the believer and the Holy Spirit, unmediated by
anyone. "To works of creation there needeth no preparation; the
almighty power of God calleth them to be his people, that were not his
people." 1 *Peter* 2.10. "And by calling them to be so, hee maketh them to
be so." *Rom.* 9.25, 26.[15] Once called to God, the soul experienced a miraculous transformation, "The *beleever* being once engrafted into *Christ* his
*nature* is thereby changed...Changed in his *Affections, Motions,
dispositions*: having *divine nature*." However, until that moment, the
believer was passive and dependent:

> in the first act they are merely passive; Onely *receiving* of Jesus
> Christ...Neither can they do this of themselves; this being a work of
> the Spirit of God in them, which is to them a *Spirit of Revelation*, and

a *Spirit of Faith*: Revealing Christ to them, and in them: inclining and perswading their hearts to close with Jesus Christ.[16]

Because God offered his grace freely and unconditionally and because, in the end, learning and preparation merited nothing, the gracious experience of conversion came to be recognized as the key sign of election as well as the centerpiece of the Puritan's spiritual journey. Whether clerical or lay, gentleman or laborer, male or female, Puritans looked forward (or back) to that point when they would experience the grace of God in their lives. Divine grace brought spiritual gifts of faith and repentance, replaced the inevitability of damnation with the hope of paradise, and freed the will to embrace glad obedience to God's commands.

Understandably, the core of Puritan religiosity was revealed most clearly not in the esoteric debates and discourses of theologians but in the words of the converts themselves. When she testified before the congregation, Alice Stedman reported that she had been convinced "not to build my faith on duties but on freeness of God's love in Christ." Many applying for membership in the Newtown congregation said that they had followed all the preparatory rules. They had studied, prayed, heard sermons, participated in private prayer meetings, and attended the ordinances. Over and over, they noted the failure of such efforts. Here, self-reliance proved both fruitless and sinful. Until a believer had fallen into the depths of despair, until she could say, as Barbary Cutter did, "[I] saw nothing but vileness. And could say nothing but – Lord I am vile," the struggling Christian would wander amidst confusions and doubts. It was God who brought hope to sinners like Stedman: "by John 3:16 – that whoever believes – the Lord was pleased by that word to overcome my heart and to show me the freeness of His love, not only to them that be in greater, but in a lesser measure humbled."[17]

Aspiring church members appeared as ambivalent toward preparatory means as the clergy, perhaps more so. Stedman spoke for many when she declared her inability to discover God through duties or ordinances rather than looking toward divine grace. Sister Crackbone found that "means did not profit me…"; likewise Joanna Sill, "though she did not neglect duties, yet she found no presence of God there as at other times," while Elizabeth Olbon finally understood "how duties could not help her because a man in prison must be always paying his debts."[18] Those depending upon such strategies were often, perhaps unconsciously, hoping that they would somehow be able to reach God through their own efforts. In laying claim to some self-sufficiency they were pretending to control God. On the other hand, those open to the work of the Holy Spirit could find themselves blessed. Utter dependence upon God was the key, and it was only after the coming of grace that the ordinances became meaningful and fruitful for the believer.

The person who opened himself or herself to grace would reap an awesome reward. Swept up by the Spirit and carried into light, sinners captured by divine grace found joy in ordinances and sermons, duties and prayers, a joy that elevated the experience beyond comprehensibility. True, theologians had constructed a clear outline of a believer's gracious progress that enabled preachers to explain the experience and lead their listeners through distinct, identifiable stages. Lay congregants could grasp and evaluate a convert's testimony and, if the narrative was unintelligible or puzzling, elicit an orderly presentation. A substantial amount of reasoning and analysis was spent defining, describing, and categorizing the experience. Yet the language of conversion was not a rational language cataloguing spiritual growth, but rhapsodic poetry struggling to express the incommensurable joy and strength felt in a union with God.

Converts did not proceed through a logical, cumulative, intellectual exercise but were attacked, overwhelmed by the onrush of grace. Elizabeth Olbon "witnessed the Lord's love to her. Sometime a heart to run and sometime to sit still in the Lord's way." Robert Holmes heard a sermon on "*Zechariah* 12:10 – spirit of mourning – and hence heart melted and I had joy." Nathaniel Sparrowhawk seemed taken completely by surprise: "the Lord revealed Himself so as never before with abundance of sweetness of Himself, which rejoicing made me break out to weeping and hardly could I refrain from speaking to others to let them see what the Lord had done." As Sister Moore so beautifully summarized, "when the Lord filled the temple I found the Lord had filled my soul with glorious apprehensions of Himself."[19]

Preachers often turned to marriage in their metaphorical attempts to elucidate that nature of God's love for his people, perhaps because that was the way that converts had experienced and interpreted their union with the Spirit. As one woman candidly explained,

> *Hosea* 2 – I'll betroth thee to me – and setting out spiritual marriage of a king, making suit to a poor silly maid do but give thy consent and then care not for other things and Christ would be better than earthly husband. No fear there of widowhood so I took Christ then upon His own terms.

These expressions were not intellectual exercises in analogical argument, but deep, open struggles to grasp their feelings. "And hearing of the freeness of the love of the bridegroom and speaking that all things were ready in Christ," John Fessenden declared, "the Lord affected myself with it. And the Lord made me willing to take the Lord Jesus." This was a sensual, passionate love that aroused the soul in instinctive responses. Before her heart ran in the Lord's way, Olbon realized that "she must come to a naked Christ and that she found the hardest thing in the world to do. Yet by this Scripture out of Isaiah and Matthew He let her feel His love." It was a passion that inflamed layperson and clergyman alike, drawing each convert into the loving whirlwind that was grace.

> Thy Saving Grace my Wedden Garment make:
> Thy Spouses Frame into my Soul Convay.
> I then shall be thy Bride Espousd by thee
> And thou my Bridesgroom Deare Espousde shalt bee.[20]

The importance of this mystical experience to Puritan religiosity cannot be overstated. Conversion represented God's struggle with one particular saint, a passionate exchange through which a sinner was brought into the warmth of divine love. In their understanding of conversion, many Puritans acknowledged the profound possibility of a divine–human relationship of great personal intimacy, almost a mystical, ecstatic, transcendent union with God.

> Here is a *spiritual Coalition* betwixt *Christ* and the Believer; an *union*, and that a very near one. Not only like that of the *Ivie* and the *Oake*, which are one by Adhesion, the one cleaving to the other; but like the *Graft* and the *Stock*, which are made by one *Insition*; both one *Body*, one *Tree*.[21]

Even as God was understood to have established a covenanted relationship with the community as a whole, mandating communal ideology and commitment, he had, paradoxically, developed a private, personal relationship with each believer. Much more than erudition or moral behavior, this conviction in the ability of individual souls to touch God and their own achievement of communion with the divine provided a sense of spiritual superiority that stood at the center of Puritans' strength, self-confidence, and identity as a chosen people. With this power of spiritual knowledge they could stand against the powers of a corrupt church, confound a cunning, degenerate monarch, and establish an overseas colony.

Yet this conviction was also the source of ideological confusion in the face of New Englanders' struggle to create the perfect patriarchal community. Puritans were deeply concerned with familial relations, including those of husbands and wives, fathers and daughters, and mothers and sons. As writers constructed a rigid system of gender relations, they also mapped out a model of female virtue determined, in part, by their own construction of women's weaknesses as well as their desire and need to sustain male authority from the household outward. Puritan leaders wrote and behaved as if women were potent forces that needed to be restrained and restricted lest they destroy themselves, their families, and the society. Yet they also accepted and embraced the sacred potential of all individuals, women as well as men, to discover God and attain salvation.

For Puritan men, elect women would be model wives and mothers. Within the little church of the household, women guided children and servants, always acknowledging their husband's headship. Domestic manuals, sermons, and broadsides all displayed the paradoxical convictions that women were weak and in great need of male protection, dangerous and able to drag men down after them, and yet capable of great piety and strength as they performed their duties under the direction of men. The best women followed along the lines of Eve and Bathsheba. Two legendary mothers, to be sure, but they had also brought the sexual temptations that seduced Adam, father of the race, and David, the favored king, into sin. One writer reminded women that they were "all the Daughters of *Eve*, who was the Author of much more evil to mankinde, in seducing her Husband to eat of the forbidden Fruit, [than] *Judas* was in betraying our Saviour...." However, such transgressions could be forgotten, and these women could be justifiably honored because each had submitted herself to marriage and the restrictive control of a great patriarch.[22]

The chastity of Susanna, the loyalty of Ruth toward her mother-in-law Naomi, and the subservience of Abigail to King David were all praised and, in Ruth's and Abigail's case, rewarded with marriage. Piety, too, was proclaimed, particularly if accompanied by a complete surrender to God, as in the cases of Hannah, Anna, and Elizabeth, all of whom had accepted the blight of barrenness. Paradoxically, God rewarded such submission with children: Anna's sight of the Christ child and sons born to Hannah and Elizabeth. Mothering itself was honored in Mary, Sarah, and Rebecca, acclaimed particularly for tricking Esau out of his blessing in order to benefit younger son Jacob. As docility and submission were demanded of all women regardless of rank, the writers took particular pleasure in the humility of the Queen of Sheba. Among the most popular was Queen Esther, delicate and beautiful, courageous and pious. Exploiting her own beauty to achieve her goals, Esther followed her uncle's guidance and exhibited a gratifyingly feminine cunning, yet she neither led individuals into sin nor insisted upon her own judgment. She came before her husband to defend her people, fainted at his expression of displeasure, and triumphed over her enemy by submitting her own views to her husband's decision.[23] In effect, the glory that was woman could predictably be summarized in two characteristics: pliable acquiescence and extraordinary love and devotion.

In placing great importance upon the family as a spiritual unit and recognizing the central role played in that domus by the housewife, Puritans honored godly wives and mothers among them. This vision articulated in the domestic manuals was also reflected in countless eulogies and memorials. Thomas Foxcroft lamented that the "Death of a tender and gracious Mother infers the Loss of a great and comprehensive Blessing," and he decried the "Ungodliness...Unrighteousness ...Contention...Intemperance, and other foolish Lusts" that would afflict families after the death of a "Pious Mother; whose grave Presence and prudent Counsels and Reproofs, together with Her Holy Example, had kept a Check on the vicious Dispositions of the Children and Others...." Cotton Mather had privately noted three commonalities among ministers' blessed wives: "Much Constancy and Fervency of Devotion with study to improve in the Knowledge of the great Savior, and in Communion with God...Ingenuity with Assiduity, in the Instructing of their Families and Instilling of Piety into their Domestics...Compassion and Helpfulness and Benignity...."[24] Like the good wife of Proverbs, her husband praised her, and her children rose up and called her blessed.

While domestic piety did sit at the center of the prescriptive literature, and women were lauded for passively filling subservient spiritual roles, Puritans also celebrated a tradition of extraordinarily godly women who, empowered by the Spirit, stood firm (and often alone) against powerful forces. In John Foxe's *Acts and Monuments*, an almost sacred account of the origins of the English reformation, pious women, as well as men, demonstrated courage and faith. Anne Askew, for example, left her husband and home in order to maintain her religious principles, and she endured torture and was executed in 1546 for her beliefs. At the stake, she brought to her three compatriots "greater comfort in that so painful and doleful kind of death; [they], beholding her invincible constancy, and also stirred up through her persuasions, did set apart all kind of fear."[25] Overall, in his accounts of the Marian persecutions, Foxe identified more than eighty women among the hundreds of martyrs. Such women fought against the demands of fathers and husbands, intellectually outmaneuvered their examiners, endured sexual insults and brutal tortures, and frequently died at the stake.[26]

Puritan theologians certainly thought that women courted heresy and blasphemy, and they lamented women's intellectual weakness. However, the honor accorded these female martyrs countermanded traditional perceptions of women's inferiority. Perhaps the female example was even more startling and had greater impact because women were expected to be weak and easily led. Surely women like Anne Askew, staunch in their faith and their refusals to submit to their husbands' religious leadership, were models of mixed messages. Yet John Bale, Askew's publisher, had concluded that in Askew "the strength of God is here made perfyght by weakenesse."[27] It was as if the Holy Ghost used her quintessential female weakness as a counterpoint against which to display the overwhelming power of the Spirit.

The sufferings and stoicism of the women taught important lessons about the strength of the weak, affirming for female believers the potential of feminine spirituality and warning against spiritual pride men who, supposedly stronger in body and mind, had yet to be asked to accept the pain and humiliation women silently endured. Still, the Marian years were a heroic era, and during the latter half of the sixteenth century women served important (but less visible) roles as correspondents and hosts of private house meetings. Devout widows opened their presses and bookshops; women of wealth and rank, such as Lady Anne Bacon and Lady Elizabeth Russell, became honored patrons of the Puritan clergy.[28] Yet even beyond the financial support (and courtly influence) that such noblewomen could provide, women brought the movement to their community and hearths. Many reformers knew that women had great persuasive powers over fathers, husbands, and sons. Anglican Richard Hooker once complained that Puritans labored most to convert female members, for their judgments were "weakest by reason of their sex" and yet they were "propense and inclinable to holiness...[T]he eagerness of their affection, that maketh them, which way soever they take, diligent in drawing their husbands, children, servants, friends and allies the same way," would lead pastors to value women as invaluable spiritual resources and recruiters.[29]

Theologians, clerics, and magistrates recognized and admired the stalwart religiosity of the martyred women; they attended the spiritual lessons taught in the stoical suffering of the weak. Yet such figures were extraordinary inhabitants of extraordinary times; in the end, the true ideal for ordinary women returned to domestic piety. Certainly after the New England emigration, where the sacred and secular establishments were built by the Puritans (rather than their enemies), in support of (rather than opposition to) true religion, there was little space for individual, heroic testimony to divine truth. It was not that such strong, Spirit-directed women did not exist. Women like Anne Hutchinson, Mary Dyer, and Lady Deborah Moody continued to lead and resist in the tradition of Anne Askew. However, seventeenth-century Massachusetts magistrates found their presence intolerable and drove them from the colony.[30] For the most part, Puritan culture honored virtuous women who, like Cotton Mather's *Daughters of Zion*, exemplified great piety, family devotion, and passivity and subservience to their husbands, fathers, and pastors.[31]

In their passivity and self-abnegation, the unexceptional quality of their lives, their very ordinariness, these women, however central to their families and communities, are almost hidden from the historians' view. Hannah Sewall, Sarah Cotton, and Katherine, Hannah, and Abigail Mather are all seen through the eyes of husbands or fathers. The conversion narratives recorded by Thomas Shepard included those of many women, but they stand more as a testimony (and a manipulated one) to a singular moment of spiritual crisis than a reflection of the religiosity of those saints. Occasional memorials, diaries, and letters provide some glimpses into the complex religious journeys of Puritan women; certainly

Margaret Winthrop's letters to husband John, in their very concern with daily affairs, reflect the interlacing of spirituality with the mundane cares of a Puritan wife.[32] However, one of the best portraits of "unexceptional" women's spiritual experience can be found in the amazing poetry of one of New England's early writers, Anne Bradstreet.

Anne Bradstreet was born in 1612, daughter of Dorothy Yorke Dudley and Thomas Dudley, a man active in Massachusetts government, serving as its second governor. At 16 she married Simon Bradstreet, and while the two joined her parents on board the *Arbella*, arriving in New England in 1630, the Bradstreets moved northward, first to Ipswich and later Andover. Simon followed his father-in-law in colonial politics, rising to the rank of governor in 1679, seven years after Anne's death. She lived to be 60, had eight children, and seven survived her. Her early years must have been filled with pressures brought by nonconformity, the duties of early marriage, and the emigration and settlement: "I found a new world and new manners, at which my heart rose."[33] Her New England life was occupied with her responsibility for a large household of children and servants, often as the primary authority figure, since her husband regularly governed in Boston.

Amidst such ordinary duties, Bradstreet found time to write poetry judged worthy of publication by contemporary as well as twentieth-century standards. Although claiming, as convention dictated, that she had no such objective, a large group of poems, all published in *The Tenth Muse, Lately Sprung Up In America* (1650) seemed intended for print. Derivative in subject and structure, poems like *The Four Elements*; *The Four Seasons*; and *The Four Monarchies* tracked standard themes in standard rhyme and meter, accomplishing this with impersonal competence, if not brilliance.

A second group of poems, however, were not intended for publication. She wrote these personal poems for her husband, her children, or herself as she contemplated crises of her own life. None of this poetry appeared in print during her lifetime; some verses were appended to a second, posthumous edition of her works, others appeared only in the nineteenth century. Of a radically different quality and nature, these verses reflected a depth of emotional involvement and personal engagement that made for intimate, touching, and essentially better poetry. The verses ponder the particular concerns of a Puritan woman of faith, touching upon individual moments experienced and expressed through the prism of her religious world. The poetry exemplifies the patterns in which women may have consciously reconstructed their experiences for themselves, but it also discloses, almost unintentionally, hints of at least one woman's uncensored reactions to the life and culture in the new colonies. In Bradstreet's poetry, four themes predominate – childbirth, sickness and death, family members, and engagement with God – each represented in the more haphazard writings of other women.

Bradstreet, and many other women, claimed childbearing and nurturing as their own, perhaps because they alone fully appreciated and accepted the risks.[34] The female community was thoroughly familiar with the pains of travail, and folk remedies of herbs and charms were passed down through female generations along with birthing stools and childbed linens. Bradstreet memorialized women's sufferings in her *Four Ages of Man*:

> My mother's breeding sickness I will spare,
> Her Nine months weary burthen not declare.
> To show her bearing pains, I should do wrong,
> To tell those pangs which can't be told by tongue:
> With tears into the world I did arrive;
> My mother still did waste as I did thrive,
> Who yet with love and all alacrity,
> Spending, was willing to be spent for me.[35]

The specter of death hovered over childbirth, and every woman knew that her pregnancy could well end in death, her infant's death or her own. Even within the relatively healthy environment of New England, the infant mortality rate was high. Many women lost half their children in infancy, and most women had experienced the death of at least one baby.[36] Additionally, mothers feared for their own lives. A woman might die giving birth to her first child, and one who had survived the birth of eight children might die giving birth to the ninth. Historians have estimated that as many as 20 percent of New England women died in childbirth.[37] Any woman facing childbirth was likely to have known more than one woman who had died giving birth. Healthy Puritans frequently spoke in general terms about death looming over everyone, but expectant women confronted directly their own mortality.

Bradstreet and other women who wrote revealed a preoccupation with death in childbirth. As she neared the end of one pregnancy, Bradstreet bid farewell to her husband.

> All things within this fading world hath end,
> Adversity doth still our joys attend;
> No ties so strong, no friends so dear and sweet,
> But with death's parting blow is sure to meet.
> The sentence past is most irrevocable,
> A common thing, yet oh, inevitable.[38]

Sixty years later, Jerusha Oliver displayed the same fears, noting that she would use her time to "prepare for my Lying in, and would therefore prepare for Death."[39] For a Puritan woman, the possibility of death could transport her to a special, intense spiritual awareness. In her ninth pregnancy, Sarah Goodhue grew convinced that she would die in childbirth, and she wrote the pious *Valedictory and Monitory Writing*, which she hoped would help her husband and children cope with her death.[40] Among her poems, Bradstreet memorialized a daughter-in-law who died in childbirth, as well as three grandchildren who all died before reaching the age of 4. In all cases she writes of grief at the loss, combined with self-recrimination for such a selfish sorrow.

> Blest babe, why should I once bewail thy fate,
> Or sigh thy days so soon were terminate,
> Sith thou art settled in an everlasting state.[41]

She knew that death was inevitable, and she believed that death was good in that it freed the individual from this earth to go to heaven. Bradstreet also understood that the death of a child, grandchild, or spouse remained tragic for the survivors. In her memorial to her daughter-in-law, Bradstreet uses such language as wailing, woe, griefs, and misery: "My bruised heart lies sobbing at the root, That thou, dear son, hath lost both tree and fruit." Urging her son to take comfort in God, Bradstreet revealed, in the construction of her theological sentiment, a resignation both angry and confused.

> Cheer up, dear son, thy fainting bleeding heart,
> In Him alone that caused all this smart;
> What though thy strokes full sad and grievous be,
> He knows it is the best for thee and me.[42]

The connection that Bradstreet felt to her family was reflected in the inspirations for the poems. Of the thirty-six poems in the private corpus, more than half were explicitly focused upon her children, grandchildren, and especially her husband. Excepting memorials, these poems were written to express her anxiety about her children and husband – fears for their health and voyages, gratitude for homecoming and healing. Like Margaret Winthrop, whose letters always blessed God and expressed acceptance of his will, Bradstreet tried to temper her deep love for her spouse with resignation to his assembly duties and to God's will. But also like Winthrop, who poured out her anxieties for her absent husband and children, Bradstreet's longing and resistance sometimes shined through.

> If two be one, as surely thou and I,
> How stayest thou there, whilst I at Ipswich lie?
> ...
> In this dead time, alas, what can I more
> Than view those fruits which through thy heat I bore?[43]

In this "Letter to Her Husband," Bradstreet envisioned herself as the earth and her husband as the sun, an image often used to portray a divinity. This rhetorical connection of her husband with divinity works in tandem with her knowledge of the Spirit, revealing that Bradstreet's understanding of God was assisted by her experience of marriage.

> First, Thou art my Creator, I Thy creature, Thou my master, I Thy servant. But hence arises not my comfort, Thou art my Father, I Thy child; "Ye shall be My sons and daughters," saith the Lord Almighty. Christ is my brother, I ascent unto my Father, and your Father, unto my God and your God; but lest this should not be enough, thy maker is thy husband. Nay more, I am a member of His body, He my head.[44]

As connected as Bradstreet revealed herself to her family, she was not oblivious to herself: ten poems were composed in response to her own illness. While the birth of eight healthy children, and her own survival of those births, suggest robust health, the evidence of the poems indicates that Bradstreet suffered from fevers and fainting fits. In these texts Bradstreet expressed not so much fear as the expectation of death and salvation. In one of her earliest verses, she had concluded: "My race is run, my thread is spun, lo, here is fatal death...Yet live I shall this life's but small, in place of highest bliss...." Bradstreet lamented the pain and tedium of her illness, and she regretted her husband's absence during these times, yet she found comfort in God. Her sickness was "so much the sorer...to me because my dear husband was from home (who is my chiefest comforter on earth) but my God, who never failed me, was not absent but helped me and graciously manifested his love to me."[45] Moreover, while she may have suffered physical pain, she seemed to have no mental anguish; she understood why. Within Bradstreet's world, sickness and hardship (such as the fire that destroyed her house) were sent by God either to chastise the believer or to call backsliders to attention.

> [God] hath never suffered me long to sit loose from Him...I have no sooner felt my heart out of order, but I have expected correction for it, which most commonly hath been upon my own person in sickness, weakness, pains, sometimes on my soul, in doubts and fears of God's displeasure and my sincerity towards Him; sometimes He hath smote a child with a sickness, sometimes chastened by losses in estate, and these times (through His great mercy) have been the times of my greatest getting and advantage; yea, I have found them the times when the Lord hath manifested the most love to me.[46]

For Bradstreet, the harsh realities of her world were understood and eased through a full knowledge of God. Her theology of salvation and spiritual journey explained such troubles as trials, needed punishments, and gifts of grace. And, while sending such difficult trials, God also provided the strength and comfort to endure.

In constructing her relationship with illness, Bradstreet revealed one face of her relationship with God, namely wayward and troubled child corrected and consoled by nurturant parent. " 'Ye shall be My sons and daughters,' saith the Lord Almighty." These paternal images are important ones, and they appear more frequently than others, possibly because so much of her writing concerns afflictions or anxieties. Still, there is an alternative image of God that stands out, especially in the brief spiritual autobiography written for her children. This image neither replaces nor even competes with God as father, but stands side by side the paternal in Bradstreet's spiritual experience. Within this second construction God moves as husband and lover, and the relationship described is one of ecstatic communion: "thy maker is thy husband. Nay more, I am a member of His body, He my head."[47]

When Bradstreet "found my heart through His goodness enlarged in thankfulness to Him," she was speaking not only of grace, faith, and assurance, but of a personal and intense relationship with God himself. Although not easy to describe, the poet managed to find some words to express her sense of joy.

> I have often been perplexed that I have not found that constant joy in my pilgrimage and refreshing which I supposed most of the servants of God have, although He hath not left me altogether without the witness of His holy spirit, who hath oft given me His word and set to His seal that it shall be well with me. I have some-times tasted of that hidden manna that the world knows not ...

Her love for God was such that she would endure hell itself in order to find it: "were I in hell itself and could there find the love of God toward me, it would be a heaven. And could I have been in heaven without the love of God, it would have been a hell to me, for in truth it is the absence and presence of God that makes heaven or hell." Throughout these few pages, Bradstreet portrayed herself a believer disturbed by the doctrinal hairsplitting of theologians, even briefly questioning the condemnation of Roman Catholics who, after all, follow the same God, the same Christ, the same Bible. And while she could reassure herself about rejecting Catholics who, after all, did persecute Protestants, she seemed unable to work up any hatred or even contempt for them.[48]

Other people and other churches were not her concern. She worried about her children's physical and spiritual health, about her husband. Yet, in the end, Bradstreet found comfort in her trust in God, looking, at the end of her life, towards her final union with God.

> Then soul and body shall unite
>   And of their Maker have the sight.
> Such lasting joys shall there behold
>   As ear ne'er heard nor tongue e'er told.
> Lord, make me ready for that day,
>   Then come, dear Bridegroom, come away.[49]

Despite the wealth and learning that placed her among the privileged, in the importance of childbirth, sickness, and death in forming her earthly and spiritual career, Bradstreet's life could stand for the experience of any New England woman. Even though she engaged in the "masculine" endeavor of composing poetry, her submission to her fate, her attachment to her father and husband, and her devotion to her children marked her as a model for all women. In her poetry, Bradstreet employed two analogical images of God in relation to the individual believer, images that satisfied different intellectual and emotional needs. On one side, she wrote of God as a devoted, protective, yet stern parent chastising his child through afflictions of estate, body, and spirit. From this perspective she could maintain her Calvinist conviction in a benevolent, divine providence yet still account for the hardships she and her family members had endured. Suffering had a purpose, and God remained good and loving. An alternative analogy suggested a more intensely personal connection with God. Language envisioning a male God as the husband and lover of the female saint expressed a rapturous spiritual experience whose intimacy and ecstasy seemed beyond the boundaries of theological language. While clerics undoubtedly approved Bradstreet's perception of God as strict parent, reflecting as it did a traditional understanding of God's relationship to the believer, her engagement with God as lover would not have been completely alien to their sensibilities. They, too, knew that the Spirit brought not only guidance and care but also great, exciting joy.

Puritan men often invoked the erotic language of the *Song of Solomon*, the Old Testament love poem that described the "love of Jesus Christ, the true Salomon and King of peace, and the faithful soule...." John Cotton had delivered (and published) a series of sermons upon these canticles, using the sensuous language as a means of enticing his listeners toward God. Just as Bradstreet's contemporary Anne Hutchinson had heard the "voice of my beloved," Thomas Hooker assured believers that they were spouses of Christ, while Thomas Shepard longed to accept Christ as "Lord and Savior and Husband."[50] The most graphic, illustrious example of such emotional outpourings remains the poetry of Edward Taylor who, in his meditations upon Canticles, recorded his experience of the excitement and joys of spirituality as the thrills and pleasures of the marital sexuality.

In light of the tremendous spiritual authority lodged in the saint's relationship with God, the gendered nature of that experience created an uneasy balance of spiritual power within Puritan society. In the developmental religiosity of education and preparation, God was father, and the believer was his son or daughter. Men might seem more godlike, have more of the image of God in the same way that sons identified with fathers and daughters with mothers.[51] However, in the mystical language of conversion, God was the bridegroom, the believer the bride, and rather than strive to uncover the image of God in one's own soul, the believer sought ecstatic union with God. The extension of conversion to saints regardless of gender, education, or rank deeply threatened male leaders who hoped to maintain a hierarchical order with themselves at its top. That conversion was sometimes expressed in language of sexual intimacy, with God as male and the believer as female, raised the possibility that women's female nature opened them more quickly to the workings of the Spirit. God's grace and divine love fulfilled women spiritually, but the inexpressible joy and power to be found in Puritan mysticism was not always in line with submission to male husbands, ministers, and governors.

# 3 Prophesying women
## Pushing the boundaries of patriarchy

Puritan theology, church rituals, and devotional practices applied and reinforced patriarchal goals and assumptions within and through religious ideas and institutions, particularly in terms of an emphasis upon erudition and sanctification in the face of their mystical convictions. Man, with his superior intellect, would far surpass woman in his ability to interpret the Bible, understand God through the natural world, and grasp the intricacies of theological debate. So, too, man's superior strength of will, rooted, like his intellect, in his biological nature, was far better equipped to control his behavior and traverse the pathways of preparation in hopes of divine grace and salvation. Still, despite these intellectual efforts, spiritual and political leaders found themselves and their arguments caught by the spiritual foundations of Puritan religiosity. They recognized that within Puritan mysticism lay sources of charismatic power not only for the patriarchs, but also for those very inferiors that patriarchs had hoped to control.

Most women appeared satisfied with a destiny of housewife, childbearer, and passive, silent saint, although even Anne Bradstreet, in many ways the quintessential Puritan woman described by theologians, wanted to use her own voice, if only to express her ultimate satisfaction with her world. Some women, however, found themselves called by the Holy Spirit to speak out and lead. So Anne Hutchinson explained her right to conduct religious meetings in her home: "It is said, I will poure my Spirit upon your Daughters, and they shall prophesie, &c. If God give mee a gift of Prophecy, I may use it."[1] Here was reflected the paradoxical nature of God's relationship to humanity. New England leaders were certain that God had created a world ordered by gender and rank, mandating male leadership of Church and State. Yet they also knew, and in fact flourished in the knowledge, that the spirit moved within individuals, and that God was no respecter of persons. Each person met God individually, and divine favor had little to do with rank, wealth, education, or gender.

Still, the patriarchs were not completely defenseless when meeting the claims of charismatic women. Theologians had explored the nature of the female soul and discovered within a problematic personality, weak character, even inferior spiritual capacity, all the natural outgrowth of woman's inferior biology. Many ministers and magistrates had concluded that women were not merely inferior to men, but essentially evil, or at least congenitally inclined toward evil. Women were burdened with a range of character flaws that could be summarized as passionate and uncontrolled, incapable of reason, supremely credulous, and, thus, easily led astray. They needed the controls of subservience for their own protection, as well as that of society, and any dissatisfaction that women felt and expressed merely proved their incapacity to reason and judge. Circular as it was, this argument was ideally suited to confront the challenges posed by spiritually empowered women, for it turned women's claims back upon themselves as proof of their unfitness. Although begrudgingly granting the possibility that the spirit might speak through a woman, most Puritan leaders could easily conclude that any speech or action which threatened the divinely created patriarchal order could not, by definition, come from God. Considering their nature, women were far more likely to be deluded than inspired, and any such claims to spiritual power could be reconfigured as confirmation of women's spiritual weakness.

Historians have no way of knowing whether women were satisfied or the prescriptive literature was in any way influential, whether eulogies reflected the real trajectory of female saints or simply wishful thinking. The evidence is largely negative, and the failure of women to register grievances could indicate a range of attitudes, from joyful acceptance of women's allotted role to resentful resignation to the inevitable power play to the forceful suppression of dissent. Yet, while the generality of contented, or at least resigned, women went unremarked except in abstract terms, several moments of discontent and dissent were recorded in some detail. Scolds, unwed mothers, and witches, all deemed flagrantly evil, appeared before church and civil courts to be judged and punished in the effort to construct the perfect, godly commonwealth. Additionally, Puritan leaders struggled against the equally troublesome collection of exceptionally spiritual women, women whose spiritual charisma led leaders to classify them with the extremely evil.

As has already been discussed, Puritan women arrived in New England with an assurance of their own importance to their religious community. They had served as patrons, publishers, and popularizers; they had died for the faith in the sixteenth century and opened their homes to private prayer meetings in the seventeenth. In England, they had been honored for choosing a reformist position, upholding nonconformist reform, and leading others in resistance to the established church. Many had undoubtedly seen themselves as independent religionists capable of discerning the truth; some as spiritual leaders. Suddenly they were members of the established church and their religious stance was expected to move from dissent to acceptance, from challenge to quiescence.

While many shifted easily into their new role of passive congregant, some continued to speak out and demonstrate an independence and spirituality apart from that offered by the church congregation. Lady Deborah Moody, "a wise and anciently religious woman," came to reject infant baptism and was admonished and later excommunicated by the church at Salem. She maintained her views, but voluntarily removed herself to the Dutch colony of New Netherlands along with others "infected with anabaptism."[2] In Boston, the church disciplined Sister Hogg "for her disorderly singing and her idleness and for saying she is Comanded of Christ so to do" and Sarah Keayne for "irregular prophesying in mixt Assemblies and for Refusing ordinarily to heare in the Churches of Christ."[3] In Malden, female congregants had supported the men in delivering a call to Marmaduke Mathews, a clergyman, that the General Court, the legislative assembly of Massachusetts Bay, had judged unsound. Far from allowing the men to handle the congregation's response, the women contributed their own opinion, believing that they should be heard and seriously considered: "god in great mercie to our souls as we Trust hath after many prayers Indeavors & long wayting brought Mr. Mathews Among us & putt him into the worke of the Ministrie." They implied that if Malden found that by his "pious life & labour the Lord hath Afforded [them] Many Saving convictions...and Consolations," the Court had no business to refuse their requests.[4]

Causing disturbance over a longer term was Mary Oliver of Salem, a woman who had already suffered in England for refusing to bow at the name of Jesus. After her arrival in New England, she was astonished and angry that even among her coreligionists she would not be admitted to Communion unless she testified to her faith and joined in covenant with the congregation. On the day that the church celebrated the sacrament, she publicly demanded Communion, argued her right to admission, and refused to be silent until the magistrate threatened to have the constable throw her out. Charged with disturbing the peace of the church, she was imprisoned until she acknowledged her fault. Five years later, she was whipped for reproaching the magistrates, saying that the governor was unjust, corrupt, and a wretch, a punishment she bore "with a masculine spirit, glorying in her suffering." Eventually, she too left Massachusetts' jurisdiction.[5]

These brief encounters reflect two interconnected trends – the continuation of women's spiritual self-sufficiency and strength and the efforts of the magistrates and clergy to keep women under control. New England congregations denied female church members a vote in congregational affairs, and most denied them any public voice. Even when testifying to their conversion, aspiring female candidates related their experiences privately to the minister and elders, who then read these testimonies to the congregation. As one minister explained, the churches had

> such a tender respect [for] the weaker sex (who are usually more fearefull and bashfull) that we commit their triall to the Elders & some few others in private, who upon their testimony are admitted into the Church, without any more adoe.[6]

In general, the only women who did speak publicly in church were those called to answer for their sins; women's speech was being transformed into a symbol of sin and disorder. Governors and clerics tried hard (and eventually would triumph), but among the first generation of colonizers the tradition of dissent was too strong. Too many women of the first generation had nurtured and thus been supported by the Puritan network in England, and they were not prepared to step meekly into a passive relationship with their pastor and their community.

There were two particular moments in Massachusetts' early history when the charisma of spiritual women deeply threatened the establishment. Not only have extensive records of the trials survived, but both cases were memorialized in the polemical literature. The first woman to disturb the peace was a member of that colonizing generation pursuing piety and godliness in the new Israel. Anne Hutchinson arrived in 1634, was quickly recognized as a spiritual leader who had garnered so much authority – and appeared at the center of so much disorder – that the government banished her in 1637. She and her husband would move to Newport, in what became Rhode Island, and, after his death, she continued southward to Long Island, where she was killed during a native uprising in 1643. Among those who followed Hutchinson to Newport was Mary Dyer. She remained there comfortably for fifteen years until accompanying her husband to England, where she was converted to the Quaker movement. When, in 1656, the Quaker itinerants came to Massachusetts, frightening the clergy and magistrates with seeming blasphemies and social disruption, Dyer was prominent among them. The government response to the Quakers was initially less expeditious but in the end more ruthless: Dyer and three other male Quakers were hanged, and countless others were tortured or whipped. However, unlike the Hutchinsonians, the Quakers never completely disappeared from the colony. Together, the Hutchinsonian and the Quaker crises provide extraordinary insight into the social and cultural workings of seventeenth-century New England. Both communities aroused fears regarding male weakness, female power, the gendered social order; both were countered with the same set of patriarchal assumptions and legal tools; both were judged blasphemers; yet both had discovered their spiritual power from the same point as the Puritan leaders: divine union with God.

Wife of a prominent merchant, Anne Hutchinson easily found a respectable position among Boston's women, a place reinforced by her gifts as healer and midwife. Moreover, as the daughter of learned clergyman, Francis Marbury, she had been carefully educated, and her scriptural knowledge and theological sophistication were greatly admired. At some point, it is not known precisely when, Hutchinson instituted private religious meetings for Boston's women, an opportunity for scriptural study and spiritual explorations. The natural leader in this venue, Hutchinson quickly moved beyond explicating ministers' sermons to delivering her own. Soon, women brought their husbands; these meetings became so successful that Hutchinson held two each week, one for women only and one for both women and men. Hutchinson's enemies estimated the general attendance at sixty to eighty persons – that is, most of the town.

By spring 1636, word of aberrant theology reached the clergy. The primary issue was the relationship between human endeavor and salvation. Hutchinson, and her mentor John Cotton, stressed the futility of human action and the passivity of the believer in an absolute dependence upon God. Most New England clergy, however, found in such arguments dangerous tendencies toward irreligion and anarchy. While granting the arbitrary and unconditional nature of God's actions, these ministers also understood the anxiety of believers; thus they emphasized the hope that lay in sanctification as a sign of election and urged congregants to prepare for grace through scripture study, attendance at sermons, guarding their conduct, and prayer. The Hutchinsonians judged preparationism as salvation through works and attacked the clergy for legalism, while the clergy labeled Hutchinsonians fanatical and antinomian, or anarchic.

Although two conferences involving Hutchinson and the clergy seemed to reconcile theological differences, the laity, along with minister John Wheelwright, Hutchinson's brother-in-law, continued to discredit ministers, including Boston's own pastor, John Wilson. Wheelwright publicly attacked the New England churches as the antichrist, while Hutchinsonian laymen refused to serve in the militia organized to fight the Pequots because the militia's chaplain was John Wilson. Through the spring and summer of 1637, Hutchinson's opponents, led by Governor John Winthrop, convinced the General Court to limit and restrict Hutchinsonian behavior, condemning efforts to dispute doctrine with the preacher. More explicitly, the Court banned Hutchinson's meetings, granting that while

women might meet (some few together) to pray and edify one another; yet such a set assembly, (as was then in practice at Boston,) where sixty or more did meet every week, and one woman (in a prophetical way, by resolving questions of doctrine, and expounding scripture) took upon her the whole exercise, was agreed to be disorderly, and without rule.[7]

Finally, Winthrop moved against individuals: Wheelwright was banished; Hutchinsonians were disarmed, disfranchised, fined, and/or banished; and, lastly, on 7 November, Hutchinson herself, "the breeder and nourisher of all these distempers...a woman of haughty and fierce carriage, of a nimble wit and active spirit," was brought to trial.[8]

The trial lasted scarcely two days, yet during those two days the essence of the conflict became startlingly clear in the charges of the Court and Hutchinson's formidable self-defense. For one and a half days she ran exegetical circles around her opponents. They quoted Scripture; she quoted back. They interpreted a verse against her; she responded with a second text and a valid interpretation. Winthrop first charged her with breaking the Fifth Commandment because she countenanced those who had signed a seditious petition on behalf of Wheelwright. She noted that she might entertain the petitioners as children of God without countenancing their sin. Hutchinson herself had signed nothing, so the Court had no direct evidence. After a quick thrust and parry, a frustrated Winthrop asserted that she did adhere to the petitioners, she did endeavor to promote their faction, she had thus dishonored the magistrates – her parents, and the Court did "not mean to discourse with those of your sex...."[9]

Winthrop next turned to her private meetings. Scripture forbade women to teach publicly, but, answered Hutchinson, her home was not public. She cited texts proclaiming the duty of elder women to instruct the younger; members of the Court retorted that she was known to instruct men. She explained that at mixed meetings only men spoke, though she believed that if a man came to her, she was permitted to instruct him as Priscilla had guided Apollo. When Winthrop refused to grant that her biblical citations provided a guiding rule, she asked if she must "shew my name written therein?" In a second display of authority Winthrop announced that the meetings must end because he said so: "We are your judges, and not you ours and we must compel you to it." Hutchinson acquiesced. "If it please you by authority to put it down I will freely let you for I am subject to your authority."[10]

This did not satisfy, for, as Deputy Governor Thomas Dudley complained, the colony had once been at peace, but from the moment Hutchinson landed, she was the fount of great disturbances. They wanted her gone, and to this end Winthrop turned to her criticism of the clergy. When she compared the clergy unfavorably to Cotton, implying that they did not preach the true pathway to salvation, she undermined the colony's primary arbiters of divine authority. Obviously, such opinions had to be curtailed and condemned, but action required proof. Magistrates had heard some Hutchinsonians on this subject; Stephen

Greensmyth, for example, had been fined £40 for asserting that all but three ministers taught a covenant of works.[11] And the ministers had undoubtedly told Winthrop something of the conferences with Hutchinson. Nevertheless, the magistrates had apparently never heard Hutchinson so speak, for they did not testify against her. Instead, Dudley and Winthrop accused Hutchinson of making statements which she then denied. Finally, Hugh Peters, followed by other clergy, attempted to rescue the situation by formally reporting what Hutchinson had said at the December conference.

Peters, who hoped that he and his fellow clerics "may not be thought to come as informers against the gentlewoman," proceeded to inform against her. He claimed that Hutchinson had described wide differences between most of the clergy and Cotton, that Cotton "preaches the covenant of grace and you the covenant of works." Hutchinson had discounted their piety, arguing that such preaching signified an absence of the spirit. Cleric after cleric rose and spoke to his own memory of her statements, and, while some were relatively mild and hopeful and others almost vindictive, their testimonies overlapped in impressive corroboration. Hutchinson challenged these accounts, at one point asking Wilson for his notes of the conference.[12]

The following morning Hutchinson brilliantly redirected and enlivened the Court by demanding that those testifying against her swear an oath. Already this evidence did not sit easily, for the conference had been private, and in testifying against her the clergy were betraying a confidence. Now claiming that the ministers were both accusers and witnesses, she invoked standard legal procedure. She had refreshed her memory with Wilson's notes and would call witnesses to support her recollections, but first the original testimony must be taken under oath. The obvious affront had its predictable effect, and Winthrop and Dudley ardently defended the ministers' integrity. Yet amidst the furor were sown seeds of doubt. The conference had occurred almost a year before, and, as Simon Bradstreet argued, "Mrs. Hutchinson, these are but circumstances and adjuncts to the cause, admit they should mistake you in your speeches you would make them to sin if you urge them to swear." Although Bradstreet implied that his concern grew out of the possibility of minor errors concerning peripheral matters, the specter of major errors appeared. Moreover, the clergy proved reluctant to swear, lending credence to Hutchinson.[13]

Of three witnesses called in her behalf, two were frightened into silence, but the third delivered his troublesome testimony in full. John Cotton had not wanted to testify, but his memory of the conference agreed with Hutchinson's. He regretted that he and his colleagues were compared, but he did recall mild disagreements concerning the covenant of grace and the seal of the spirit, and, he gently reminded them, he had supported Hutchinson's position. Finally, he declared that she did not say they were under a covenant of works, nor that they did preach a covenant of works. Despite further challenges, questions, and objections, Cotton never did countermand his testimony.[14]

Hutchinson chose this moment to proclaim her vision. Turning to her own spiritual conversion, Hutchinson recounted early doubts, her ultimate dependence upon God, and God's response to her pleas. She had become "more choice" in selecting a minister, for God led her to distinguish the voices of truth. When asked how she knew that it was the spirit speaking to her, she claimed that it came through "an immediate revelation....By the voice of his own spirit to my soul." Comparing herself to the prophet Daniel, she declared that, as God had delivered Daniel from the lion's den, so had God promised that he would protect and deliver her from her adversaries. Her accusers pounced upon this testimony. They believed that any claim to a miraculous deliverance was blasphemy, for the age of miracles had long passed. By the end of the proceedings, the overwhelming majority of the court would agree with Winthrop's disingenuous conclusion to "Pass by all that hath been said formerly and her own speeches have been ground enough for us to proceed upon."[15]

Yet, if she really had condemned herself, why did the examination continue? After she had proclaimed her revelations, new indictments began, and witnesses testified to previous prophetic declarations. However, the weight and character of these testimonies precipitated not immediate censure but a prolonged debate upon the nature of revelation itself. When asked to denounce Hutchinson, Cotton refused, presenting, instead, an abstract discourse upon the two sorts of revelation, aggravating and confusing his hearers as he refused to render a judgment. Finally, Winthrop closed the debate, "Mr. Cotton is not called to answer to any thing," yet he could not silence everyone. As William Coddington said, "the spirit of God witnesses with our spirits, and there is no truth in scripture but God bears witness to it by his spirit..." Court delegates returned to the earlier charges and the lack of substantial evidence. In the end, three clergymen testified, under oath; she was then convicted and banished.[16]

While most have judged her declarations as weakness, one might as easily see this as a moment of strength. Hutchinson seemed to revel in her prophetic moment as the Court stood riveted upon her words. The magistrates and the clergy wanted, needed, these revelations to be discounted, but I suspect that, rather than provide the evidence against her, the power gathered in her speech frightened Winthrop, warning him of just how necessary it was to remove her. He revealed this anxiety in his own account:

> Mistris *Hutchison* having thus freely and fully discovered her selfe, the Court...did observe a speciall providence of God, that...her

owne mouth should deliver her into the power of the Court, as
guilty of that which all suspected her for, but were not furnished
with proofe sufficient to proceed against her, for here she hath manifested, that her opinions and practise have been the cause of al our
disturbances, & that she walked by such a rule as cannot stand with
the peace of any State...[17]

Long suspected of spiritual charisma grounded in her prophetic revelations, Hutchinson had undermined the authority of secular and sacred
officers. At last she had openly asserted that power, for which her opponents were profoundly grateful, but they remained unable to convince
Cotton or all Court members that her claims were blasphemous.
Winthrop and the clergy returned to charges of sedition, winning her
banishment with the acquiescence of all but three representatives.

Because she was sentenced at the beginning of winter, the Court
extended a questionable mercy in permitting Hutchinson to remain in
the colony until spring, but demanded that she reside in the home of an
unsympathetic cleric, where she became the unhappy focus of extensive
clerical counsel. Supposedly interested in her repentance and ultimate
salvation, the clergy began an emotional and intellectual barrage that
explored a range of theological questions that had been raised in neither
of the 1636 conferences nor in her November trial. All of this material
was brought forward to her final examinations before the Church.

On 15 March 1638, the Church of Boston, depleted by the emigration,
voluntary and otherwise, of many Hutchinsonians, heard charges. Their
investigation focused upon her beliefs concerning the immortality of the
soul, the resurrection of the body, and the union of the individual spirit
to Christ. None of these questions had been raised before, as Hutchinson
insistently noted. In the records, Hutchinson seems a neophyte, working
out her beliefs with pastors, but in a public forum determined to
condemn her. The preliminary church trial ended predictably with an
admonition.[18] Interestingly, the elders requested that Cotton deliver the
verbal chastisement as the pastor who commanded Hutchinson's highest
regard and might therefore have the greatest impact. Unspoken, but of
greater import, would be the effect of fixing Cotton's alignment with the
majority position.

Throughout the church trial, the sexualized language of the accusers
reflected a central subtext. In his own account, Winthrop argued that, as
a midwife and healer, Hutchinson took advantage of women during
childbirth or illness and "insinuated" herself into their hearts; these
seduced women would in turn ensnare their own husbands.[19] During
the church trial itself, one man asked whether she held "that foule, groce,
filthye and abhominable opinion held by Familists, *of the Communitie of
Weomen.*" Cotton assured her that from just one of her opinions – her
denial of the resurrection of the body (a new accusation raised at the

church trial) – "all promiscuus and filthie cominge togeather of men and Woemen without Distinction or Relation of Marriage, will necessarily follow…more dayngerous Evells and filthie Unclenes…than you doe not Imagine or conceave." He even questioned her marital life: "And though I have not herd, nayther do I thinke, you have bine unfaythfull to your Husband…*yet that will follow upon it…*." [20]

The following week, Hutchinson acknowledged her errors, admitting that she had uttered dangerous words and extravagant phrases open to the misconstruction. However, she said, she had never believed such heresies; her errors were in her expressions, not her Judgment, but she accepted responsibility for her errors and admitted that she had slighted the ministers. Despite this promising start, the caliber and sincerity of her repentance was challenged. Dudley noted that she repented only those errors discovered after November and left untouched those raised at her state trial (although no one else mentioned them, either); moreover, he saw no repentance in her countenance. The theological issues were murky, her continued adherence to her revelations was troubling, but, happily, Hutchinson's insincerity made her a liar. Because she had troubled the church with her errors, upheld her revelations, and had "made a Lye," she was excommunicated. [21] As she left the church, she was accompanied by friend and disciple Mary Dyer.

In their response to Hutchinson, the sacred and civil authority utilized state and church courts to rid the colony of her person and to discredit her intellect, integrity, and spirituality. With excommunication the leadership removed all legitimacy from her religious authority. Criticisms of her private meetings, of women teaching men, of a "haughty" carriage, indicate the centrality of gender. Winthrop was forced to engage a woman who refused to accept a subordinate status, refused to respect the boundaries of housewife, and refused to remain silent. In proclaiming her right to teach others, to speak, Hutchinson challenged the assumptions of the social order; in gaining an audience, she represented a real threat. Women and men had sought her out, week after week. Her followers challenged many clerics at key points, and in acting upon their new lessons the Hutchinsonians increased her influence in the colony, undermined the ministry, and threatened the stability of the government.

Twice in 1636, the clergy held a conference to reach some accord about problematic beliefs and preaching, and, while these conferences were ostensibly called to establish some clerical consensus, Anne Hutchinson sat as a primary participant at both, indicating that the real purpose was less clerical accord than the unofficial examination of, and negotiation with, an influential lay religious leader. Hutchinson, with her extraordinary spiritual charisma, represented a *female* power, thus threatening to overturn the most basic inequality structuring the social order. For Winthrop, the extraordinary means he used to defeat Hutchinson were justified. Her violent death, in 1743, during an uprising of Native

Americans on Long Island, was a sign that could be (and was) read by Winthrop and his cohort as divine vindication, a reaffirmation of the patriarchal order as divinely countenanced.

Banished and excommunicated, Hutchinson joined her family in Rhode Island, where she experienced a freedom of religion unknown in Massachusetts, and lived amidst a religious diversity that included not only many of her own followers, but also separatists and Baptists. She found a more inclusive religious climate, one that recognized the importance of women and encouraged women's spiritual growth:

> Mr. Williams and the rest did make an order, that no man should be molested for his conscience, now men's wives, and children, and servants, claimed liberty hereby to go to all religious meetings, though never so often, or though private, upon week days...

Joshua Verens, for example, was censured because he "refused to let his wife go to Mr. Williams so oft as she was called for...." And while some in the assembly said that they never meant that such an order should extend "to the breach of any ordinance of God, such as the subjection of wives to their husbands," others obviously acknowledged the religious freedom of women as well. As one member explained, "if they should restrain their wives, etc., all the women in the country would cry out on them, etc."[22]

As the religious turmoil in England increased in the 1640s and 1650s, many of the sectaries, including the millennialist Fifth Monarchists, the levelling Ranters, and a band of male and female Seekers who sought guidance in the voice of the Holy Spirit, the Quakers, would all have representatives in Rhode Island. The significant number of sectaries in Rhode Island, particularly the growing number of Quakers, also reflected a cultural climate that encouraged women spiritually. In England, many complained that the sectaries were far too open to women in terms of numbers and leadership; one government official commented that all Quakers were women.[23] The Quakers attracted many women once connected with Hutchinson, including Katherine Marbury, Hutchinson's sister, and Mary Dyer. This is not surprising, since many of the characteristics of this mystical movement were likely to appeal to a Hutchinsonian: their openness to the Holy Spirit, or the inner light; their rejection of education, birth, or wealth as the basis of personal authority; the sharing of power among all members of the movement, male and female, particularly the power of public speech. Under the leadership of George Fox, a number of small societies of "Friends" appeared and established connections through correspondence and the travel of gifted itinerant preachers. The organization attracted large numbers of the disfranchised, including women, and a vast network of house-communities was established and stabilized as Quakers developed strategies for building congregations, resisting persecution, and maintaining communal integrity. Within ten years of the restoration of Charles II to the throne, this society proved one of the few sectaries that survived intact.

Almost from the beginning, Quakers were found not only in Rhode Island, but in Massachusetts as well. This nascent, resident enclave of Puritan dissenters was founded, nourished, and fostered by itinerant preachers from England. Yet, while welcomed by those Puritans vaguely dissatisfied with the religious institutions in Massachusetts, to the Puritan leadership the Quaker itinerants brought an appalling vision, a central challenge to colonial order. Magistrates saw themselves as guardians of pure doctrine and practice, and they initially responded as if the Quaker crime were blasphemy. Later, leaders argued that Quaker practices were by nature anarchic and would undermine the moral fabric of their nation. From the outset, Puritan magistrates were so anxious that, upon their arrival in 1656, Anne Austin and Mary Fisher, the first Quakers to land in Massachusetts, were imprisoned. The following year a Quaker widow coming to collect debts owed her dead husband was led to prison, her dower rights denied, while Dyer, landing in Boston on her way to Rhode Island, was also imprisoned. Their self-identification as Quaker so threatened the colony that their very presence, even for reasons of business, could not be tolerated. More Quakers came; the colony intensified their efforts. Countless Quakers were beaten and imprisoned, a few maimed, and several escorted to the border whipped at the cart's tail. During the height of the persecutions in 1659 and 1660 four Quakers were hanged. Among the four, and the only woman to be executed, was Mary Dyer.

The Quakers did pose something of a threat to the colonial order. Politically, Quakers denied the right of government to interfere with religion or worship, supporting separation of Church and State. In England, they refused to pay tithes and resisted government efforts to enforce church attendance. Socially, Quakers rejected hierarchy in all forms, affirming that the equality of souls before God countermanded artificial hierarchies of wealth and birth. Theologically, Quakers carried this equality into spirituality. They believed that divine revelation beyond the Scriptures continued down to the present day, argued that all believers had access to that revelation, and therefore rejected any elevated role for an educated, ordained clergy. Their belief in the inner light, inner to each person, countered any efforts on the part of Church or State to discipline individuals' religiosity. Still, one is left to marvel at the harshness of the magistrates' treatment, the most severe that the Quakers met in the British empire.

Between 1656 and 1666, several dozen Quakers came to Massachusetts, initially seeking converts. Although the magistrates moved with extraordinary speed to apprehend Anne Austin and Mary Fisher and to confiscate and destroy their books, they knew that they were acting upon the presumption of disorderly intent rather than upon any violation of the law. Thus, in the wake of the Quakers' appearance, with fears that more might follow, the General Court, in October 1656, passed a series of laws designed to eliminate the Quaker threat and then published these laws in broadside form. Ship captains who knowingly brought Quakers were fined £100 and required to return them to the port of embarkation. Those possessing Quaker books or writings would be fined £5 per item. Moreover, any Quaker arriving from outside the colony was to be "committed to the house of correction and at their entrance to be severely whipped, and by the master thereof be kept constantly to work, and none suffered to converse or speak with them during the time of their imprisonment...." Anyone defending Quaker opinions was fined 40s, if they persisted £4, and still continuing, he or she would be imprisoned until they could be banished.[24] The apparent ineffectiveness of the law led the magistrates, the following year, to raise the stakes. Every male Quaker who (once banished) returned would have one ear cut off; for the second offense, his other ear. Every female Quaker who returned after banishment would be severely whipped. Both would be imprisoned until they could be sent out, and, if they returned, their tongue would be bored with a hot iron. Only one step remained, and, in the face of a continued Quaker presence, that was taken the following October. If convicted of returning yet a fourth time, he or she would be executed.[25]

Amidst the rising intensity of Quaker witness and magisterial severity, Mary Dyer joined William Robinson and Marmaduke Stephenson in challenging the capital law. In September 1659 all three had been banished. Dyer returned home, while Robinson and Stephenson traveled north to cultivate the embryo communities in Salem, New Hampshire, and Maine. When the two men returned south, they decided to test the law and so returned to Boston with a group of local Quakers, who publicly proclaimed their support by accompanying the banished. Stephenson, Robinson, and their companions were all imprisoned by the authorities; the prisoners were soon joined by Dyer, who felt called to unite herself to this cause. All three were tried and sentenced to death. At the last moment, following the execution of Stephenson and Robinson, with the rope around her neck, Dyer was reprieved. Despite her protest she was forcibly removed from the scaffold and carried out of the colony.[26]

Quaker hagiographer George Bishop would describe Dyer as "a Comely Grave woman, and of a goodly Personage, and one of a good Report, having an Husband of an Estate, fearing the Lord, and a Mother of Children." The Massachusetts magisterium never, in the 1630s or 1650s, found her grave, or comely, or good. She not only returned, again, but she publicly denounced their brutality and injustice. When she entered Boston, she was set upon a horse and cried out "Woe be unto you for Humphrey Norton's sake! Woe be unto you, because of the Cruelty done to him!"[27] (Norton had had one ear cropped.) When reprieved the first time, both Quaker and Puritan accounts agree that she refused to descend the ladder and had to be physically removed. The following May, she "rebelliously, after the sentence of death [was] past against her, returned into this jurisdiction."[28] When questioned, she proclaimed herself a witness against their laws.

> I came in Obedience to the Will of God the last General Court, desiring you to Repeal your unrighteous Laws of Banishment upon pain of Death; and that same is my work now, and earnest Request, because ye refused before to grant my Request, although I told you, That if ye refused to Repeal them, the Lord will send others of his Servants to Witness against them.

When asked if she were a prophet, she said "She spake the words that the Lord spake in her; and now the thing is come to pass."[29] The Court sentenced her to be hanged on 1 June.

Escorted to the place of execution by a band of soldiers, her speech overwhelmed by beating drums, Dyer maintained her stance until the end. On the scaffold one leader proclaimed that she had brought the punishment upon herself: she reaffirmed her call to testify against unrighteousness. Some promised her life if she would return to Rhode Island; she said that she must follow the will of God, even unto death. When Pastor Wilson urged her to repent "and be not so deluded and carried away by the deceit of the Devil," she denied any need for repentance. At last, some asked her if she had said that "she had been in Paradise. And she answered, Yea, I have been in Paradise several days....And so sweetly and cheerfully in the Lord she finished her Testimony, and dyed a faithful Martyr of Jesus Christ."[30]

Although Dyer is rarely heard in the records, during her trials and execution her voice loudly condemns the colony's attempts to silence, through intimidation and violence, the word of God's spirit revealed in the voices of Quakers. When first sentenced to death in October 1659, Dyer wrote to the General Court on behalf of

> that holy people and seed which the lord hath blessed forever, called by the children of darkness (cursed Quakers) for whose cause the lord is rising to plead with all such as shall touch his anointed or do his prophets any harm.

Like all Quaker itinerants, Dyer demanded the repeal of unjust laws and expressed her certainty that if the magistrates would only listen to the voice of the spirit within, they would be so moved:

Take you counsel, search with the light of Christ in you, and it will
shew you of answers as it hath done me and many more who hath
been disobedient and deceived as you now are ... you will not repent
that you were kept from Shedding blood though it were by a
woman.[31]

For Dyer, her returns to the Bay colony in October 1659 and May 1660
were expressive testimonies against the injustice of Massachusetts law,
mandated by the holy spirit's voice within her.

Soon after Dyer's execution Quakers in England managed to bring the
Massachusetts persecutions to the attention of the newly restored king,
Charles II. Although no friend of Friends, Charles had no intention of
letting colonists assume such authority, and in 1662 he called for an end
to executions and maiming. Massachusetts continued to imprison
Quakers, and whip them at the cart's tail, for a few years more, but by
the end of the decade the severity decreased as the futility of the persecution became apparent. Moreover, while the resident Quaker communities
grew, they grew more quietly, and a new generation of magistrates
turned to more pressing matters: a pan-Indian uprising, English imperial
policies, and colonial wars.

Mary Dyer represents an intriguing, illuminating example of New
England's female Quakers. She was initially arrested during the first
moments of the persecutions, after the magistrates had nominated
Quakers as serious disturbers of the peace. The government constructed
restrictions and procedures that it believed, wrongly, would restore social
order by silencing or excising the Quakers. Dyer stood among the many
English and New England Quakers who could be neither silenced nor
removed, who deliberately returned to Massachusetts to challenge the
law and, by extension, the social order itself. Like others who suffered
anti-Quaker brutality, Dyer was initially imprisoned and banished; when
she returned, she was whipped and imprisoned again. Her confrontations reached their climax amidst the height of anti-Quaker fervor; she
was neither the first nor the last to be executed.

In the October 1658 session, an exasperated General Court justified
harsh laws as necessary to control a tumultuous people who displayed
no respect for government and law. The magistrates' tone swung
between confusion, frustration, and outrage. The problem was partly the
Quakers: Puritan leaders could not understand and, therefore, could not
successfully address a people whose extreme disrespect, or delusion, led
them to risk torture and death:

Notwithstanding all former laws made (upon experience of their
arrogant, bold obtrusions to disseminate their principles amongst us)
prohibiting their coming into this jurisdiction, they have not been

deterred from their impetuous attempts to undermine our peace and hasten our ruin."[32]

However, the roots of the crisis also lay in the magistrates. Their rigid, unwavering commitment to a political hierarchy ruled by themselves, accompanied by an intense fear of any who failed to value order or reverence their status, rendered them unable to tolerate any Quaker presence in public, private, or even printed space. The execution of four Quakers, including one woman, and the criticism this generated, revealed the limitations of the magistrates' vision and the ultimate failure of their policy.

When considering the limited vision displayed by the magistrates, it is impossible to understand the Quaker debacle apart from the female Puritan community of the early seventeenth century. Mary Dyer was one of several women of extraordinary personal authority, her strength lodged in private spirituality but expressed and demonstrated upon the public stage. Such women, and the men who supported them, threatened the base of the patriarchal social order because they were women acting out their power in the public world of religion and the State. She had been a disciple of Anne Hutchinson, a woman who preached and proclaimed her right to a public voice out of the inspiration and authority of the Holy Spirit: a woman who was silenced, excommunicated, and banished because she threatened the patriarchal order. Unlike Hutchinson, who left Massachusetts to pursue her vision alone and in peace, the Quakers pursued their vision through confrontation empowered by the Spirit.

Among Quakers, women had power that was supposed to be held by men only. Many Quaker women were preachers. Most of the visible, public Quakers were women, not because women outnumbered men, although women might have during the foundational years, but because preaching women attracted more attention than preaching men, even the "mechanick" preachers of the lower classes. Such women, and the fact that they were permitted, even encouraged, to leave husbands and children behind to missionize, demonstrated to the average Puritan that Quakers were set upon destroying family and society as established in the sacred texts and English tradition. As with Anne Hutchinson, who was warned by John Cotton that it would be only a matter of time before she committed adultery, Puritans argued that Quaker beliefs and practices would naturally lead to sexual licentiousness. The witnessing of Quaker women, who walked naked through towns in witness against Puritans' hypocrisy, was proof of this conclusion.[33]

Women, empowered by the spirit, behaving like male ministers was bad enough, but Quaker men refused to stop or discipline or even speak out against those women – Quaker men supported women's activism. These men also rejected the necessity or even desirability of learning as a

mode of understanding God and instead turned to the passive acceptance of the inner light. In other words, men were acting like women.
That this reception of the spirit empowered these men as well did not
alter this gendered dynamic because the men relinquished all power
until they were moved by God's spirit. And, just as disturbing, Quaker
men refused to participate in the aggressively masculine culture. In an
assertively patriarchal society, two things are necessary for patriarchy to
be maintained. Yes, women must be subordinated, but men must agree
to dominate. Not only were Quaker women spiritually and socially independent, activist participants, but Quaker men refused to hold their own.
They not only refused to dominate women, but they espoused a spirituality that threatened masculine identity.

Quaker spirituality was, in the end, a female spirituality, female
according to the terms that gender was constructed in the seventeenth
century. I do not mean by this that this religiosity had great appeal for
women, although it did; such appeal could be explained just as easily by
the fact that Quakers opened power channels to women. But beyond this
simple identification of women with Quakerism, Quakers' mysticism,
like the spirituality of Anne Hutchinson, demanded qualities that were
considered female: submission, passivity, openness, and passion. This
religiosity also moved toward a personal, intimate relationship between
the believer and God, which became gendered because the dominant
metaphor for intimacy was sexuality – the male God embraced the
believer who must, by definition, be female, since the only legitimate
sexual paradigm was heterosexual. By their acceptance of the inner light
and their willingness to participate in the Quaker meeting, Quaker men
proclaimed themselves spiritually feminine. They recognized the potential spiritual power of women, refused to fill their own necessary role in
the power dynamics of patriarchy, and established a separate, integrated
authority through a mystical experience.

Whether fighting a psychological battle for their own sense of self or a
political battle to enjoy the power that patriarchy gave, Puritan leaders
needed to silence those feminine voices. Theologians began to speak of
God as father, not lover, and of saints as sons or daughters, not wives.
Out of this construction men were able to identify with the masculinity
of God; they became closer to the divinity than women. Another part of
this process was rhetoric and practice that emphasized preparation,
education, and sanctification, and de-emphasized the conversion experience. Now, the devout Puritan had to develop his mind and educate
himself in the deliberately obscure, complicated, technical language used
by God. He also had to prepare himself so that he could open his heart
and suppress his passions when grace came.[34] Rationality and reason
were at a premium, and men reaped the benefits of their superior intellectual abilities and strength of will.

However, what moved these ideological changes forward in the seventeenth century were the battles fought against identifiable, personal, female foes. Anne Hutchinson was such an enemy, strong in her challenge, dangerous in the appeal she had for others, men and women. For the second generation, the Quakers provided a similar challenge. They denied the legitimacy of state power over religion, rejected clerical authority over the soul, and suggested that simply opening one's soul to God would bring peace, satisfaction, and authority. The women were strong; the men had relinquished power; they were the world turned upside down. Puritan magistrates did everything in their power, and beyond it, to stop this spiritual force. Yet neither whips and scaffolds nor fines and ridicule could effectively silence the challengers. All that the magistrates and clerics could achieve was a firm, recognized separation between Quakers and New England Congregationalists and the growing alienation of Puritans from the mystical spirituality of the founding generation.

# 4   The devil's minions

As Puritan magistrates and ministers moved to exercise and maintain full control over the colonial community they governed, they sometimes found themselves obliged to take drastic, severe action to enclose and disarm threats to their holy experiment. They dealt with common sins through the common law, and proved especially expeditious in managing heretics, reflecting a judgment that spiritual dangers were extremely difficult to discover and had the greatest potential for instigating sin and destruction. Yet to attend only to crimes committed, without some care to deflect if not forestall future challenges, was to court disaster. Maintaining order required a clear vision and constant vigilance: those whose very presence threatened disruption had to be controlled. In other words, magistrates needed to silence women and, in fact, the lower classes, since the only way the patriarchal hierarchy would work was if the disfranchised classes remained so. The Puritans' social order was predicated upon a small, powerful governing community at the top ruling subservient, and happy to be so, masses beneath. They might have invited the middling sort of man to share with them the authority that came with minor, frequently onerous local offices, but from women and the poor, all they asked, and what they demanded was respectful obeisance, or at least silent acquiescence.

In working to silence female voices, magistrates were assisted by two ideological constructions that dominated contemporary perceptions of women and gender. Of primary importance was their concept of feminine godliness and piety, drawn by theologians from those biblical figures whose virtue epitomized acceptance of higher authorities. The chastity of Susannah, the patience of Sarah and Hannah, and the nurturance of Rachel and Mary were all celebrated within a framework of passive subservience to divine will and male dominion. Even the valorous Esther, for all her glory, claimed victory (and honor) through obedience to her uncle and subservience to her husband. The worthy matron of Proverbs 31, active enough in her housework, played a supporting, rather than leading, role in the governance and service of her family, not unlike Dorothy Dudley who, for all her alms to the poor, mastery of servants, and instruction of family, was first "A Worthy matron of unspotted life, A loving mother and obedient wife ...."[1] While a man might be praised for decisive action and strong leadership, subjection, obedience, and especially passivity became ensconced as traditional female virtues.

Still, a gendered construction of virtue was not the sole, or even the strongest, weapon in Puritans' cultural arsenal. In their cosmology, evil was inexorably linked to the feminine. Such a commonplace explained, in a sense, why virtuous women necessarily followed strong and good (and male) leadership. The evil latent in women justified coercive efforts to deny any autonomy, much less authority, to women. The evil proclivity of women rendered female activity in and of itself suspect and, thus, reinforced the installment of passivity as a virtue in women. In other words, a gendered conception of virtue combined with a gendered conception of evil to provide a simple rationalization for enclosing and disempowering women who claimed any sort of power, since such a claim by definition demonstrated that that particular woman was falling short of virtue and living up to her evil potential. Many accusers identified Anne Hutchinson's essential sinfulness in her assertive, "masculine" activity. She conducted private religious meetings, challenged ministers, argued points of doctrine, and failed to subordinate herself to her husband who was, in any case, criticized for his passivity: "a man of very mild temper and weak parts, and wholly guided by his wife."[2]

When Puritans discussed the virtuous women of the Bible, they rarely included Jael and Judith, who killed enemy generals, or Deborah, the one female judge of Israel.[3] Jael and Judith may have, like Esther, used the feminine wiles of beauty, hospitality, and sex to trap their prey, but neither needed, solicited, nor used male assistance. So, too, while Deborah's military campaigns were led by a man, she alone was prophet and judge. The bravery and wisdom of these women undoubtedly compromised the notion that female virtue must be passive, but even more, their independence and self-sufficiency looked disturbingly like the dangerous strength of the Bible's evil women. The temptation posed by Eve, Bathsheba, and Delilah served as warnings to men; the lust of Potiphar's wife, who tried to seduce Joseph, and Lot's daughters, who did engage in sexual relations with their father, was despicable. Equally wicked were the disrespectful Michal, who scolded her husband David, and Job's wife, who berated her husband for his acceptance of fate. Surely Esther's compliance was better appreciated when set against Vashti's obstinate refusal to obey her husband's command. Of course, the arch-villainess of the Bible was the proud Jezebel, idol worshipper and unrepentant queen. She seduced her husband into her idolatry, took the prerogatives of his rule upon herself, and brought mayhem into the kingdom, and death and destruction onto herself. Just before her end, she had painted her face and dressed her hair and was therefore marked by her own hauteur and arrogance as she fell to her death.[4]

Woman's evil provided much more material for discussion than had her goodness. The female mouth was corrupt: nagging and gossiping were particularly feminine sins, for "scolding is the manner of Shrewes," and "their tongues vindicate themselves and scold, abuse, and disparage others; their lips utter lies & deceits."[5] Historian Carol Karlsen has noted that "scold" became a label for angry women, developing a particularly negative connotation, at points synonymous with "witch." (There was no comparable accusatory label for angry men.)[6] Women showed themselves to be fickle, inconstant, and sly. They manipulated and nagged because they were frivolous, greedy, and selfish. They exploited, sometimes robbed, their husbands in order to satisfy vanity with rich foods, elaborate clothes, and fine jewels. Such vanity signaled the deep pride at the heart of every woman's being, a pride reflected in a wife's resistance to her husband's guidance, in fact to all male authorities.[7]

Ever since Eve had lured Adam into sin, women had displayed a "naturall perswasivenesse of such incensing to evill forcibly." As John Brinsley had noted, Satan singled out women not only because of their weakness, but also because of their power:

> As fit to *work upon*, so to *work by*; A fitting *Instrument*, being her self deceived, to deceive her Husband, by conveying the same suggestions unto him, who would the lesse suspect what came through her hands, of those cordiall and entire affection he was so fully perswaded.

Seduction followed seduction naturally, reproducing wickedness and error across the landscape. "And silly women being thus seduced, seduce their husbands, as *Eve* did *Adam*...dangerous champions in a schism, and there be no such ensnaring attractives to errors & factions, as women are." This was the picture of a creature both in need of protection and in need of restriction, a creature at once threatened and threatening. "For when women beare rule over men, having catched and bewitched them in their subtill snares, what is it that they will not do for them?"[8]

While the beauty of Esther, the chastity of Susannah, and even the housewifery of Bathsheba may have inspired hopes and praises of women's potential, the wretchedness of Michal, Delilah, and Jezebel fascinated and horrified Puritan preachers. Eve may have been the mother of the human race, but it was as the tempted and tempting pawn of Satan that she was most frequently memorialized. Yes, woman was inclined toward frivolity, vanity, extravagance, sloth, scolding, scandalmongering, pettiness, envy, stinginess, and pride. However, such small vices represented but the outer edge of a vast pit of corruption.

> And if we but seriously consider the nature and qualities of the generality of that sex, even in all ages from the fall of man unto this present, we may well perceive that they have not been onely extreamly evil in themselves; but have also been the main instruments and immediate causes of Murther, Idolatry, and a multitude of other hainous sins, in many high and eminent men.[9]

Evil flowed deeply in woman's body, and her essentially evil nature bore frightening fruit. The predilection of women toward error, heresy, and blasphemy was matched biologically by the occasional production of monsters. Tales of "monstrous births" were a common (and popular) form of sensationalist literature during the sixteenth and seventeenth centuries.[10] From the extraordinarily graphic descriptions that constituted a significant segment of these stories, twentieth-century medical analysts have recognized a range of mild to severe birth defects as well as the expulsion of blood and tissues from the body. However, early modern physicians and philosophers were just beginning to understand such tragedies as natural, and they sought the causes in nature. Nicholas Culpeper, as the author of a popular, "scientific" directory on midwifery that demonstrated his ignorance of contemporary medical developments, provided an excellent example of this transition from miraculous to natural explanation. While he had looked toward menstrual fluid for the cause of slight deformities, he believed that a monster could develop from the meeting of "humane seed, and the seed of a beast." He did believe, however, that this was far less likely than that a woman's imagination had been damaged, for women looking at men in vizards had been known to bring forth monsters with cloven feet, horns, and beaks.[11] With Culpeper, the scientific common man, looking toward the imagination, it is not surprising that many Puritans looked toward such events as providential communications from God, sometimes warnings, sometimes punishments, and sometimes the predictable fruit of the sins of a woman.

In her *Cheap Print and Popular Piety,* Tessa Watt notes the prominence of this subject in the popular religious press. She found that such publications, whether broadsides or penny godlies, generally included a picture and always a vivid, detailed description.[12] *Strange Newes from Scotland* was typical of such tales. The pamphlet included a picture of the monster as well as a detailed description, but the primary text quoted the dying speech of the mother, who claimed that this birth was the judgment due her sinful convictions. She had been a sectarian and had desired the ruin of the church and state government as well as the destruction of the established ministry. The monster, of course, represented the outward manifestation of her horrid opinions.[13]

Predictably, when Mary Dyer and Anne Hutchinson both suffered childbirth tragedies, New England leaders had no difficulty interpreting such special providences as reflections upon their wickedness, although individual interpreters differed as to the final import of the message.[14] When called for advice following the stillbirth of Dyer's horrifyingly deformed child, Cotton counseled that it be buried and the details concealed, because "God might intend only the instruction of the parents, and such other to whom it was known, etc.," and providence had managed to remove most of the witnesses before the birth. But what Cotton saw as a private rebuke Winthrop proclaimed as public evidence against both parents and midwife: "The Father and Mother were of the highest form of our refined Familists....The Midwife, One *Hawkins* wife of St. *Ives*, was notorious for familiarity with the devill, and now a prime Familist."[15]

Similarly, after her banishment to Rhode Island, Hutchinson was said to have given birth to some thirty monsters.

> Then God himselfe was pleased to step in which his casting voice, and bring in his owne vote and suffrage from heaven, by testifying his displeasure against their opinions and practises, as clearly as if he had pointed with his finger, in causing the two fomenting women in the time of the height of the Opinions to produce out of their wombs, as before they had out of their braines, such monstrous births as no Chronicle (I thinke) hardly ever recorded the like...

Both Dyer's and Hutchinson's births were seen as judgments, clear, harsh expressions of divine displeasure. They were also punishments tied to, or perhaps one should say growing out of, their femaleness, illus-trating the perceived connection between mind and body.

> And see how the wisdome of God fitted this judgement to her sinne every way, for looke as she had vented mishapen opinions, so she must bring forth deformed monsters; and as those were publike, and not in a corner mentioned, so this is now come to be knowne and famous over all these Churches, and a great part of the world.[16]

Woman may have been created in the image of God, similar to men in terms of her mind and soul: "she had perspicuity of understanding, she had purity of will, she had correspondency of holy and chaste affections, both to God and her husband."[17] And surely women, with flexible wits capable of both good and evil, were equal with men in the chief aspect of their identities, "that gracious and free benefit wherby they have ever-lasting life given them." Otherwise, women were unequal, for "all the parts of Gods image were more cleare in Adam then in Eve; and the woman was then the weaker vessel, as the Serpent knew."[18] Essentially, women were weak – morally, intellectually, and emotionally weak. Of course, while such weaknesses rendered women more susceptible to ordinary temptations, they also opened the door to diabolical invasions by Satan himself.

Possession remained a fearsome threat throughout seventeenth-century New England, for Puritans knew that the devil walked the earth, eagerly capturing souls and bodies as he could. Many cases of possession were eventually traced to witchcraft. Thirteen-year-old Martha Goodwin and her younger brother John, for example, were suddenly taken with fits that were successfully attributed to Goodwife Glover, a Roman Catholic Irish woman who had already been accused of witchcraft by her husband on his deathbed. In one of the rare cases of confession, Glover was convicted and hanged, but not before she threatened the Goodwin children with further trouble from other witches. In fact, the fits did continue until a second suspected woman died, at which point the children gradually recovered. In his account, Cotton Mather emphasizes the violence of the fits, the blamelessness of the children, the orthodoxy of their father (who had refused to use magic to contravene the witchery), and the malevolence of the witch. The story as told is straightforward and uncomplicated. Glover's low status as a laundress, her ethnicity, and her religion worked to make her an outsider, reinforcing his conviction of a guilt identified by her husband and, thus, the community long before the parents name her. She gratifyingly confessed, eradicating all doubt, and the fits ended fairly quickly after her execution and the death of a second suspect.[19]

The simplicity of the Goodwin case, especially in terms of the innocence of the children, stands in stark contrast to most cases of demonic possession. Most possessed persons were described as in some way complicit, if not entirely responsible, so that accounts of such possessions provided both a précis of Satan's methods with individuals and a map charting the insinuation of evil into the society. Although men could, theoretically, have experienced possession, the ranks of the afflicted were dominated by women, particularly those women whose weaknesses of nature were further exacerbated by their youth. In key ways, Puritans read possession as a concrete realization of diabolical temptation. Susceptible young women were offered beauty, finery, success in courtship, and freedom from labor if only they would join with the devil's work. That girls could be tempted by such superficial rewards cleared pathways for Satan's exercise of power. While the possessed were tormented because they refused to capitulate to Satan's demands, namely that they sign away their souls, ultimately their bodily contortions and uncontrolled behavior revealed an inability to defuse the devil's power. Their eleventh-hour defiance merely deflected that power from enslaving their souls to enslaving their bodies. Stories of possessed individuals thus became a popular sort of cautionary tale. They provided sensational entertainment in their graphic retelling of the incredible behavior of the victims framed as terrifying warnings of demonic power and the final end of moral laxity.[20]

In such discussions of the possessed, ministers implied that the devil invaded when resistance to evil was low: this, combined with traditional understandings of femininity and youth, satisfactorily explained to Puritans the primary appearance of possession among the young and female. Those who were in the midst of doubts, who were prey to resentments of their earthly estate, and who seemed confused over their spiritual estates, were most easily attacked. As the investigating minister uncovered the history of sin for the days, if not months, that preceded attacks, possessions could often be seen as predictable consequences, if not earned punishments. Yet an essential part of the definition of possession was that the victim was forced to act against her will, so all hesitated to condemn the outrageous speech and behavior that characterized the possessed. Within this framework, the victim retained the sympathy and tenderness of her parents, guardians, and master even as she verbally abused parental and spiritual authority, refused to work, destroyed property, and even physically attacked her elders. Such a person could not be held personally responsible for the actions of Satan (or a witch), even though such sins were committed through her body. Her guilt lay in an initial evil inclination that opened the door. The goal of the pastor was to stop the behavior and speech, either by exorcising the devil or disempowering the witch, and return her to her "normal" faculties – that is, to submission and obedience to older, male parental and clerical authority.

The case of Elizabeth Knapp, recorded in 1672, provides a rare, detailed glimpse of the social and ideological forces working to construct and interpret such experience in the mind of religious leaders like Samuel Willard.[21] Here Satan himself inflicted the evil, although she, lacking moral strength and piety, opened the door to his success. The record begins on 30 October 1671, when Knapp cried out about her legs and her breast, then complained of being strangled. The following day peculiar behavior continued: she reported seeing "persons" in the cellar and fell into violent fits. From that point until the end of the narrative, 15 January, the violent behavior continued. For those three months physical antics, uncontrolled fits, self-injuries, delusional visions, and verbal and physical attacks on observers and care-givers alternated with periods of lucidity. She gave contradictory accounts of the source and nature of her torment, acknowledging and denying her own dealings with the devil. At times, she expressed repentance and concern about her spiritual estate; at others she denied any understanding of the devil's activities. At different points she named two different witches, but both accusations were quickly dismissed and the accused vindicated. When Willard concluded his account, Knapp was still possessed, and Willard had no reason to expect the devil to cease his efforts.

Reflecting the uncertain nature of this inquiry, Willard ended his account with a series of unanswered questions, to which he proposed answers. The first three address the reality of the possession. Willard argues that the distempers were real, not "counterfeit," for in her fits Knapp experienced strength far beyond her ordinary capabilities. He also found much evidence indicating that the source was diabolical rather than natural, and that Satan actually spoke through her, for he observed no use of mouth or throat when such utterances were heard. Apparently, the answers to these three questions, though not firmly decided in the eyes of the entire community, were clear enough to him. The real key lay in the fourth question, and circled the reader back into the narrative itself. In asking "Whether she have covenanted with the Devil or no," Willard had come to the core around which the story is woven.[22] Here, signing the covenant became emblematic for the entire question of personal responsibility of the possessed. This inquiry Willard failed to close, yet his extraordinary efforts to clarify this to his own satisfaction reveal a fascinating, multilayered picture of women's proclivity to evil.

According to Knapp, Satan began his attack in a standard fashion, offering her "such things as suited her youthful fancy, [like] money, silks, fine clothes, ease from labor, to show her the whole world." Although Willard had noticed some change in her two weeks before the first attack, Knapp claimed that Satan had first appeared to her three years before, an "appearance, occasioned by her discontent...."[23] The theme of discontent – with her status, the burdens of her labor, her residence – reverberates throughout the text, as Knapp frequently returns to this as the cause of her condition. She also confessed to such ordinary sins as profaning the Sabbath, disobeying her parents, and neglecting religious ordinances, and extraordinary ones such as attempted murder and suicide. Such repentance remained a hopeful sign for the young minister, yet he remained troubled at her failure to address her "sin of renouncing the government of God and giving herself up to the Devil."[24]

Willard's comment regarding submission to God's government came in the wake of one of her particularly convoluted stories, in which she had actually signed something proffered by Satan, although she claimed she did not know what it was. The signatory action was actually presented within a framework that belied any obvious conclusion that Knapp had covenanted with the devil. She said that, because she later had second thoughts, Satan urged her to sign again, implying that she had not consented to any covenant. She would later deny that she had ever entered into any sort of agreement. Such vacillation continued, bringing many to believe her lost, and yet the resurgence of tears and confessions, and the moments of despair, worked to convince Willard otherwise. The frequent contradictions in her tales, her failure to sometimes reach true repentance, and her refusal to deal fairly with those attempting to help her, marked her as either a great sinner or a tragic victim. That Willard spent so much time attempting (and failing) to decide reveals his own confusion. In the end, even if she did covenant with the devil, Willard recommended charity and compassion and identified her as an object of pity, thus framing Knapp as victim rather than agent. Still, if she was to be pitied, she should also alarm the reader as "a monument of divine severity."[25] The flaws in her character opened the way to a work of Satan, work whose end was far beyond sight.

Key to interpreting the web of evil that Willard saw spun around the possessed were three interrelated problems. The first was disorderly speech as reflective of the possessed state. A range of speech transgressions and dysfunctions characterize the afflicted. Elizabeth Knapp in her own voice attacked the reputations of women, whom she accused as witches, as well as the authority of her superiors. At certain points she was rendered "speechless." Toward the end of the ordeal satanic speech emanated from her body without her physical effort, speech characterized by gruff, masculine intonation and insulting comments directed at the minister. A second feature of possession was the false aura that surrounded the individual and rendered her difficult to trust. As "King of Lies," Satan inflicted his deceit into the mind and heart of his victim. Not only was the victim cajoled and tricked by the devil's lies, but she became a teller of lies herself. Thus, when examining Knapp's repentance, Willard was left wondering whether the contradictions reflected Knapp's falseness or Satan's insinuation of falsehood into her mind.

This raises the third crucial question, the assumption of loss of control. I believe that, with the odd exception, such as the Goodwin children, it would be wrong to argue that Puritans saw the possessed as entirely passive. Much in their pre-possession behavior indicated a dangerous inclination toward sin, and this inclination had to be acknowledged and mourned before spiritual health could be restored. In this flirting with temptation, this willingness to entertain some sort of communication with Satan, the possessed resembled their counterparts – witches. In the end, however, the possessed were judged unwilling victims, perhaps unwilling at the last moment, but unwilling. The witch, however, was a willing, consenting participant in the evil and thus, in all likelihood, lost. Hence the intensity with which Samuel Willard pursued the ultimate, true intentions of Elizabeth Knapp. In his mind, even the signing of some sort of covenant was not adequate evidence if she truly repented her actions.

The clearest evidence of the intrinsic evil of women was found in the predominance of women among Satan's human servants: witches. Wherever witches were hunted – the European continent, Scotland, England, or New England – communities, churches, and the courts found that most witches were women. In Germany, France, and Scotland, where witch fever ran high, women represented about 80 percent of the accused, while in English counties, where far fewer witches had been sought and discovered, women constituted between 90 and 100 percent of accused witches. Such statistics reflected contemporary beliefs that most practitioners of witchery were female; King James I had estimated that the proportion of female to male witches was 20:1. Even men who were accused of witchcraft were frequently connected, by marriage or kinship, to a female witch.[26]

During the first century of New England settlement, 1620–1725, 344 persons were accused of witchcraft; 78 percent (or 267) were women. Of the 103 accused witches brought to trial, 89 (or 86 percent) were female. Moreover, of the 75 men accused, about half were connected by blood relation, marriage, or as a supporter of a woman accused of witchcraft.[27] Like the history of witch trials on the European continent and in Great Britain, accusations were not raised at constant, regular intervals. Instead, flurries of accusations would be followed by periods of tranquility, with two major outbreaks accounting for three-fifths of all accusations, and almost two-thirds of all trials, convictions, and executions.

While gossip and rumors were whispered during the early decades of settlement, in 1647 Alice Young of Windsor, Connecticut became the first person to be hanged for witchcraft in New England. The following year Massachusetts Bay executed Margaret Jones. Accusations and trials continued intermittently for the next fifteen years, climaxing in the Hartford scare of 1662–1663, when nine women and four men were accused of witchcraft, five were tried (four women and one man), and four (three women and a man) convicted and executed. Following the Hartford outbreak, witchcraft prosecutions declined, perhaps a reaction against the previous panic. Between 1663 and 1687 only twelve (nine women, three men) of seventy-five reputed witches came to trial; three, all women, were convicted but no one was executed.[28]

In 1688 Massachusetts again saw fit to hang a witch, the widow Glover, and four years later Salem seemed seized by a diabolical conspiracy. The initial signs of witchery were the possessions of the daughter and niece of Samuel Parris, the village pastor. As more young women were swept into the ranks of the afflicted, increasing numbers of women and men were accused, tried, convicted, and hanged. Unlike the case of the Goodwin children, the deaths of the supposed witches brought no relief, so that, as spring progressed to summer, accusations went beyond Salem, beyond outcast women to identify some of the most respectable, irreproachable women and men of the colony as witches. At one point the names of Samuel Willard, Margaret Thatcher (mother-in-law of magistrate Jonathan Corwin), and Lady Mary Phips (wife of the new governor) were suggested, and at that point the governor temporarily halted, and later suspended, all proceedings. Before that day, 185 persons had been accused of witchcraft, 27 had been convicted, and 19 executed.[29] These would be the last persons executed for witchcraft in

New England, although there would be one last trial in 1697. When, in 1724, Sarah Spencer sued Elizabeth Ackley and her husband for defamation because they had accused her of witchcraft, the magistrates questioned the sanity of the Ackleys.[30]

Many historians have argued that the Salem outbreak represented a different case from other moments of accusations and trials, but as Carol Karlsen has demonstrated, the accused witches of 1692 Salem shared many of the characteristics of those accused at other times and places in New England.[31] Women accounted for three-fourths of those accused in 1692, and nearly half the men were related to accused women. More than four-fifths of those tried and convicted (22 of 27) were women. All convicted were sentenced to death, but the executions of eight of the women were delayed: two because of pregnancy, and six because the convicted were turning state's evidence. The difference of Salem had to do with the numbers and scope of the accusations, the spread of possessions and accusations to other towns, and the ease with which the accused were convicted. The ideology informing ministers and magistrates evaluating possessed girls and searching for witches, and the language they used to address the problem remained the same.

The conviction that most witches were female grew out of a complicated network of ideas. The nature of witchcraft as understood during this era played upon contemporary knowledge of women's work, women's character, and the nature of evil. Witches were not merely wicked; their sins were the sins of women writ larger, baser, more destructive. Elite theological and popular beliefs constructed a circle of meanings where the definition of witch matched the definition of woman in so many particulars that no one could be surprised that most witches were women or that so many women were inclined toward witchcraft.

Throughout the late sixteenth and seventeenth centuries, there flourished two distinct definitions of witchcraft.[32] On one side was a definition shared by the common people and reflected in court proceedings. Most English men and women, and their New England counterparts, identified witches by their maleficium, harm that witches inflicted through magic. Methods included charms, potions, curses, and wax dolls, essentially the magical manipulation of matter and speech. Through such magic a witch brought illness or death to her neighbors, disease to their cattle, destruction to their crops, or simply the mischief of cream that would not churn into butter or beer that would not brew. Generally, an individual would be accused of witchcraft because some extraordinary distress that afflicted a person, family, or neighborhood could be connected to the actions, speech, attitude, or mere presence of a suspected witch. Trials of witches always presented evidence of maleficium, including testimony to the initial provocation of the witch, the magical means used by the witch, and the result of her efforts. In England and the colonies, almost all trials of witches were responses to popular accusations of maleficium, and it is unclear whether the populace ever accepted any definition of witchcraft that did not incorporate maleficium.[33]

By the beginning of the seventeenth century, however, English theologians had begun to move beyond this definition toward an understanding of the witch as one who had negotiated a contract with the devil. This point of view was partially enacted into law in the English witchcraft statute of 1604, an act that directly tied some forms of witchcraft to diabolical compacts, a crime punishable by death. Nevertheless, the law continued to provide lesser penalties for lesser degrees of magic, reflecting the popular belief that not all witchcraft was tied to the devil.[34] Theologians became convinced that sorcery existed only in league with the devil. While the church and the state had once condemned only "black" magic, the new definition served to condemn all sorcery. No longer was magic judged by the effected goal of its practitioner, or even by the methods used; now, by its nature, magic was evil. The witch was a blasphemer, in league with Satan.

This was a position that Puritan theologians found reasonable and especially powerful. They adhered to a scientific perception of a natural world ordered by divine law and rejected the possibility of altering nature without supernatural assistance. While one could pray to God for beneficence or vengeance, human prayers could not bind an omnipotent God in the way that charms and incantations unfailingly manipulated nature. That such spells and potions worked demonstrated the involvement of another supernatural force working in opposition to God. Puritans knew that Satan walked the earth, seeking individual souls as he worked to destroy God's kingdom. He might promise riches, health, status, or power, but one of his primary lures was the power to work magic. Spells and potions were tools of the devil, dependent upon the devil, and they might be given to anyone who signed a contract with him.[35] When individuals were tried for witchcraft under Puritan governments, courts found it essential to prove this diabolical contract. Juries might convict on maleficium alone, but New England's judges sought proof of a devil's pact before condemning a witch.

These two perceptions of witchcraft flourished side by side, coming together in accusations pointed at the same individuals. Each described a malevolent figure to be feared, an individual more likely to be female. Women tilled the gardens where powerful herbs and roots could be cultivated; they had charge of the hearth and of cookery, where those herbs and roots could be brewed into potions and secreted in charms. Healing and medicine were also within women's domain, and the individual who could heal could also bring disease. Specialists in healing were especially vulnerable. For example, Margaret Jones of Charlestown, convicted and executed for witchcraft in 1648, was known to practice physic, "and her medicines being such things as (by her own confession) were harm-

less, as aniseed, liquors, etc., yet had extraordinary violent effects..."
Moreover, despite her claims to be a healer, she actually brought on
illness: "she was found to have such a malignant touch, as many
persons, (men, women, and children,) whom she stroked or touched
with any affection or displeasure, or etc., were taken with deafness, or
vomiting, or other violent pains or sickness."[36]

Added to this special knowledge was woman's weakness of character.
She was petty, jealous, impulsive; she boasted a short temper, held deep
grudges, and nursed "a *secret dislike of, and discontentedness with her
present condition*, the condition wherein God himself had set her."[37]
Jones's behavior at her trial was "very intemperate, lying notoriously,
and railing upon the jury and witnesses, etc."[38] A woman was the sort of
envious, vindictive person easily tempted to use magic against her
neighbor, and as a good housewife she had the skills to do so.

Those intellectuals who defined a witch as one who had signed a
compact with the devil certainly appreciated the corroboratory evidence
of maleficium, since anyone engaged in sorcery must have been in
league with Satan. Additionally, their writings reinforced popular
opinion regarding women and witchcraft, since theologians had already
concluded independently that Satan would have better success in entrap-
ping women. Women were gullible, unsophisticated, easily controlled,
and manipulated by the unscrupulous. A woman's envy, pettiness, and
discontent "letteth in a *Sea of Temptations* upon her, so making way for
her seduction."[39]

Here, again, the sexual language of seduction pointed up the femaleness of witches. Medieval perceptions of witches – gathered together,
organized, and published in 1486 in the authoritative *Malleus Maleficarum*
(The Hammer of Witches) – placed illicit sexuality at the center of the
contract with the devil. Engravings and woodcuts often portrayed
women copulating with the devil (or with demons) as part of witches'
rituals. Witches were known to have familiars, either sexual partners or
the products of sexual relations with demons, and the presence of such
an animal was important evidence against an accused witch. So too,
accused women were subjected to invasive body searches as court representatives sought out witches' teats. These teats were sucked by demons
or familiars, and they were variously understood as sources of nourish-
ment for foul offspring or a center of sexual pleasure. Predictably, these
excrescences were often found near the breasts and genitals.[40] Margaret
Jones was discovered to have a "teat in her secret parts as fresh as if it
had been newly sucked," and after it had been noticed another search
revealed that it had withered, and "another began on the opposite side."
Further, while she was in prison, she had been seen sitting on the floor,
"her clothes up", and a small child, undoubted her familiar was seen to
run from her to another room and where it vanished.[41] The sexual understanding of witchcraft was revealed not only in New England writings

about witches but in the character of the accused witches themselves, for many had been previously convicted of sexual crimes.[42] Women were more likely to become witches not only because they were simple-minded, vindictive, and greedy, but because they were sexually depraved.

In her exploration of witch trials in New England, Carol Karlsen found that many of the women accused of witchcraft shared more commonalities than gender or sexual deviance. A significant number of these women were reputedly skilled in healing or midwifery; many were related by blood to others who were suspected of witchcraft. But the most startling particularity was the fact that they were property owners in their own right. Many of the accused were women who, through lack of a male heir, inherited property from husbands or fathers. Far from the "powerless, poor" stereotype that has often been ascribed to accused witches, many, Karlsen argues, were individuals of some authority whose ownership of property challenged patriarchal structures by not passing inheritances on to men. The value of the property need not be large; it was the fact of ownership and control that appeared to rankle. From this perspective, an important defining characteristic of witches takes on a new image. Many historians have noted that women likely to be accused were cantankerous, obstreperous. Karlsen found that this was often the case, except that the "crankiness" often represented a woman's complaints about her inability to maintain her property against the incursions of neighbors or competing heirs, added to complaints about the town's unwillingness to act in her behalf. From this perspective, envy and pettiness come to mean a woman's frustration and anger in response to the town's denial of her rights.

Consider, for example, the case of Ann Hibbens, wife of a first-genera-tion magistrate who managed to distress her husband, irritate her neighbors, infuriate Boston's carpenters, aggravate the ministers and elders, and alienate the colony's governors. She was heartily disliked and judged culpable of every conceivable female sin, including witchcraft.[43] Hibbens first appeared in the public eye in 1640, when the church admonished and later excommunicated her. Hibbens had embroiled herself in a dispute with a carpenter hired to refurbish her house. She claimed he had agreed to do the work for £2; the joiner claimed the work was worth £13. Each went to others for support, and the case was arbi-trated in favor of the joiner. Hibbens remained unsatisfied. According to her accusers, she continued to rail against the carpenter, the town's workmen, and the arbitrators. She involved the pastor and then refused his judgment. She believed she had been cheated by a "confederacy" of the town's carpenters, then tried to get justice, and was condemned for her efforts. The church admonished her for destroying reputations, sowing discord, and refusing proper respect to her superiors. When

Hibbens added a complaint against the church itself, she was excommunicated.

Hibbens' insistent defense that she *had* been in the right became the primary evidence of her hardness of heart. "Her carriage hath been so proud and contemptuous and irreverent"; she exhibited "contempt and pride of spirit"; "an incorrigible spirit"; "without any sign of sorrow and brokenness of spirit."[44] In addition to her pride and contemptuous spirit, other standard female sins were raised, including slander, covetousness, gossip, and scolding. At one hearing, as she discussed the facts of the dispute, a congregant complained, without preamble, that she had usurped her husband's authority. In delivering the sentence of excommunication, John Wilson gave special attention to her want of subjection to her husband.[45] In his account, John Winthrop came close to accusing her of seduction in the way she drew individuals, including himself, to her opinion. Having found himself in the embarrassing position of initially agreeing with her, Winthrop could only lay the blame upon her.[46] Fourteen years later, the year following her husband's death, she was tried as a witch. The jury found her guilty, the magistrates overturned the decision for lack of evidence (and, perhaps, because of Hibbens' high rank). The General Court reviewed the case and convicted her. In 1656, she was hanged for witchcraft, or, as one disapproving minister claimed, for "having more wit than her neighbors."[47] Cantankerous to the end, Hibbens' attitude and behavior perfectly matched the character of a witch.

Of course, the best-known witch trials occurred in Salem Village in 1692. When Parris's daughter and niece began to display irrational, uncontrolled, and downright bizarre behaviors, physicians and consulted clergymen were fairly quick to diagnose the "illness" as diabolical possession. Rather than attributing this possession to the unmediated efforts of Satan, the community concluded that witches actually inflicted the pain and suffering onto the girls. When the girls could not name their afflicters, names were suggested by the investigating adults, and Sarah Good, Sarah Osborne, and Tituba, Parris's slave, were identified. Not only did the possession not cease, but more and more young women were added to the ranks of the possessed. The net was cast wider, both geographically and socially, until almost two hundred persons were accused, and nineteen executed. Early accusations identified witches who fit the type, like angry, downwardly mobile Sarah Good, or the previously accused, sexually suspect Bridget Bishop; but later complaints were raised against saintly women like Rebecca Nurse, initially acquitted by the jury who, at the instruction of the judge, changed its verdict. At the end of the spiral, accusations reached such high social ranks that the ruling elite could no longer tolerate the trials, and they were first suspended, then halted. Within ten years the Massachusetts government would formally repent its role in these perse-

cutions, formally acquit all persons, and as far as possible provide resti-
tution.

A nagging historical question addresses the possessed: not the
behavior of the possessed, which can be interpreted within a wide range
of analytical paradigms from the religious to the psychological to the
biological, but the response of the adult observers. Not surprisingly,
fakery and fraud were dismissed rather quickly, as knowledgeable
witnesses judged that such suffering could not possibly be pretended (a
needle sticking in a body, bruises and cuts) or self-induced. Moreover,
when the occasional individual did suggest that the girls feigned possession, he or she usually fielded an accusation of witchcraft in return.
However, it is astonishing that the girls were almost immediately judged
as innocents, in no way responsible for their predicament. While the
afflicted group did include Betty Parris, Abigail Williams, Parris's niece,
and Ann Putnam, daughter of one of the leading families of the town,
many of these young women were servants who, by their status, might
be expected to lack credibility, especially when accusing their masters.
Also, some of the young women were hallucinating and dreaming of
being attacked by diabolical beings such as wolves; when Osborne told
of such a dream, it became evidence against her. Finally, it was known
that this group of girls had been experimenting with magic, attempting
to see their future sweethearts in the white of an egg. (It would later be
said that they saw a coffin.) Such behavior was well understood to
involve dangerous incursions into the satanic world, and yet the
possessed were never held accountable for their actions.

Two important factors explain the quickness with which the non-
possessed moved toward accusations of witchery and away from any
skepticism of the possessed. Paul Boyer and Stephen Nissenbaum have
disentangled the overwhelming social conflicts that underlay the actions
of the adults who accused and defended the accused.[48] The social
tensions of Salem Village during the decades before the outbreak, exacerbated by increasing economic dislocations and inequalities, had inspired
envy, distrust, anxiety, and bitterness. Because of their close proximity to
Salem Town, the needs of the waning agricultural community were
eclipsed by the demands and rewards of a growing urban society.
Resentful Puritan farmers tried to explain their declining fortunes, and
they found it easy to blame affluent and wealthy neighbors who had,
historically, opposed the efforts of the farmers to become independent
from the town and now refused to support the new minister. Was it so
hard for them to believe that such ungodly opponents were using the
tools of Satan to destroy the community?

Of equal cultural, if not social, importance to the adults who sympa-
thized with the possessed was the presence of a true outsider. When
Samuel Parris assumed the pastorate of Salem Village, he brought a
household that included not only his wife, children, and niece, but also

two slaves, Tituba and John Indian, whom Parris had purchased while living in Barbados.[49] Tituba seems to have worked primarily as a household servant, and the records indicate that she was deeply involved with the care of the children. Before 1692, historical records reflect Tituba's unexceptionable behavior and character; there is no evidence that she was involved in the egg-white incident. Even when on trial, no one brought any accusations of maleficium against her. Her first (and only) known tampering with magic was baking the witch cake. The request came from Mary Sibley, an upstanding neighbor woman and Parris supporter, and a cake of rye meal and the girls' urine was baked in ashes and fed to a dog, with the result that the fits became worse. With this action, Tituba identified herself with magic, albeit "good" magic, setting the stage for further accusation. She easily became one of the first three women accused of witchcraft.

Having learned of her role in baking the witch cake, Parris beat her and, following the accusations of the possessed, pressured her to confess her complete knowledge and total involvement in the witchery. For reasons that cannot be known, Tituba finally acceded to Parris's demand and agreed to confess everything. With the help of leading questions and other hints from her examiners, Tituba created a testimonial that involved Sarah Good, Sarah Osborne, and the possessed girls in tales of night rides, witches' sabbaths, and satanic pacts. After she, Good, and Osborne had been arrested, and the afflictions did not cease, she suggested that the examiners look among the town's elite.

Despite the demonstration of Boyer and Nissenbaum, as well as other historians, that Salem was already steeped in contention and bitterness, Elaine Breslaw argues forcefully that it was Tituba's confession that created the atmosphere of a massive diabolical conspiracy involving women and men, of all ranks and occupations, including a minister.[50] Her confession certainly provided the first outline, with details, of a large-scale bewitching. Breslaw further suggests that in constructing her confession Tituba took control of her own fate. True, she was convicted and condemned to die. However, since her testimony remained essential to the trials of other accused witches, the magistrates postponed her execution until all information had been gathered. She, and five other confessed witches, escaped hanging because the proceedings were suspended before they had "finished" testifying. Moreover, her acknowledgment of her sin, her willingness to report her colleagues, and, especially, her display of true repentance placed her at center stage of a complex cosmological drama that Puritans understood. In repenting, Tituba became an object of compassion, not unlike the possessed women who confessed that they were paying the heavy price for their foolishness.

Many factors, including her position in the Parris household, made Tituba a logical person for Sibley to approach about a witch cake. Yet other peculiarities were likely at work. Tituba was Indian, not English;

she came from another part of the world, the Caribbean; her background, before she was purchased by Parris, was questionable because unknown. There may have been no known incident of Tituba's bewitching or harassing or provoking any person, but her race and status made it extraordinarily easy to imagine.

Native Americans had long played central roles, real and metaphorical, in New England's Puritan destiny.[51] Within seven years of their arrive in Boston, Puritans battled the Pequots over land usage and encroachments. The Pequots were described by the English as an unprincipled, vicious people, and the strength and power of the Pequots prior to English colonization made several native communities willing to join in alliance with the Puritans. Such righteous convictions justified the primary atrocity of the brief war: the destruction of a Pequot village and the massacre of its female, elderly, and child residents – a massacre that appalled the Puritans' native allies. While the Pequots were destroyed, skirmishes with other communities continued through the 1640s, after which an uncomfortable peace held for a generation. In 1675 and 1676, Indian leaders organized an extraordinary alliance that seriously threatened the very existence of Massachusetts. Indians destroyed towns, killed soldiers, and captured women and children before they were finally defeated. In 1692, western Massachusetts was embroiled in the first of four wars against France and its native allies.

Metaphorically, Indians came to be understood as actors in a biblically based drama, in which the Puritans represented the chosen people, the Israelites, while the various native tribes represented pagans – Canaanites, Assyrians, Babylonians.[52] Puritan historians referred to Indians as dogs and wolves; and their villages as kennels. They were described both as tools used by God for punishing an unfaithful people and as agents of Satan sowing his discord. Since most Puritans reduced Amerindian religiosity to magic and devil worship, it would not have surprised them to see the devil insinuate one of his own into a Puritan cleric's household and a village for the purpose of mischief and destruction.

Important as well was Tituba's Caribbean background. Parris had purchased her while he lived in Barbados and, upon his return to Boston, became one of the few slaveholders in the colony. Most New Englanders had very little immediate knowledge of the Caribbean, yet they knew of its difference from their own colony. The Caribbean climate was tropical, almost unbearable for residents of England and New England alike, filled with trees and fruits unknown elsewhere. Barbados itself was a plantation society, where sugar was grown for high profit with slave laborers imported from Africa, itself a mysterious continent thought to be populated by uncivilized peoples practicing pagan rites. While Tituba herself was Indian, and known to be so, people may have assumed that she had known Africans in Barbados. For Tituba, her cultural role as an

Indian outside of, or antithetical to, Puritan destiny was overladen by the exotic atmospheres of Africa and the Caribbean.[53]

In her race and her gender, then, Tituba represented the ultimate evil potential. As a woman and a slave, that is, a person powerlessness among men, she would be perceived to be discontented and therefore vulnerable to temptation. As an emigrant from the Caribbean, she would be suspected of hidden talents and unknown experiences in witchery. As an Indian, she seemed already marked as the devil's own. In other words, the relative darkness of her skin, her hazy background, and her exoticism rendered her suspect, a conveniently safe suspect. Her ethnicity would overlay and reemphasize the failings that characterized her as a woman, so that it became eminently suitable for Satan to choose her as his assistant in his efforts to bring his kingdom to New England. She was also a safe scapegoat in that her race and her foreignness, combined with her gender and status, set her truly outside the boundaries of the Puritan landscape. Samuel Parris may have brought danger to the village in her person, but Salemites could have found comfort in the conviction that Satan's doorway into the community was not one of themselves. Like the Irish Roman Catholic Glover, Tituba was an exotic outsider – the paradigmatic witch.

The gendering of witchcraft stands as the best evidence of the gendering of good and evil. Puritan men's philosophy and experience bred bright hopes and deep suspicions that men moved more easily toward holiness and women toward sin. The human soul was gendered; biology was destiny, spiritually as well as socially. The spiritual essence of woman differed significantly from the spiritual life of the normative believer (that is, man), and, while the holy man was a spiritually active individual, the holy woman passively submitted her spirit to male guides. Activist women were likely to find themselves in moral and theological difficulties. Women were intellectual inferiors unable to fathom the profound and complex knowledge necessary to approach the Bible, much less the providences and creative actions of God. When women did attempt to interpret the Scriptures, chaos reigned, as the case of Hutchinson so regrettably demonstrated. Added to their mental incapacity, women's weak character – their pettiness, vanity, and excessive sexuality – required not only guidance but restraint if they were to have any hopes of attaining salvation. Unfortunately, many women were too willful and obstinate to recognize these facts about themselves and keep silence. Instead they courted the attentions and promises of Satan. Although never formally accused, Anne Hutchinson, Mary Dyer, and early female Quakers were all suspected of witchcraft. For some leaders, the very existence of female power, even charismatic power, implied the presence of Satan since God, a God of order, would never empower a woman to this extent. This, of course, directly confronted Puritan religiosity itself, a mystical spirituality that affirmed the ability of all women as well as men to experience conversion and touch God.

With the 1701 decision of the Massachusetts colony to overturn all Salem witchcraft convictions, the transformation of New England's religious culture moved quickly forward. The eighteenth century – braced with Newtonian physics and increasingly sophisticated, courtly manners – would lead political and social leaders and intellectuals, if not common believers, toward a more scientific view of the natural world. This turn toward rationalism and away from witchery accompanied an increasingly strong challenge to the intense, Spirit-based religiosity of the Puritans. Education and godly behavior, always important, became preeminent while the mysticism of the conversion experience disappeared for most Puritans. This, in turn, threatened the primary road to spiritual power for the disfranchised, including women.

Threatened, but it did not destroy. This century of the Enlightenment would also bring renewed interest in the human connection with the Spirit. New immigrants, with a vital religious culture, would come to the colonies, and the enthusiastic promise of New England religion would reappear, almost in sympathy, but certainly in concert, as New England made important connections outside the boundaries of its own little world. While many theologians would be shocked and embarrassed by this new appearance of the Spirit, charisma and the basic human attraction to charisma remained. In the midst of it all, women would again find deep, personal, spiritual satisfaction and were soon to be found in the forefront of an experiential religious movement.

# Part II

# The rise of evangelical religion

# 5    Witnesses to the New Light

During the decades of Puritan settlement and growth in New England, English colonists had found their ways to other sites along the Atlantic coast. In the region surrounding the Chesapeake Bay, settlers supported a culture founded not around religious idealism or even family safety, but upon the possibilities of windfall profits. Established in 1607, Virginia's first two rocky decades were characterized by starvation, disease, and disorder. The English further added to their instability and mortality by provoking violent confrontations with the native residents upon whom, incidentally, the English were completely dependent for food. However, in the 1610s, John Rolfe had begun experimenting with tobacco seeds, and within ten years Virginia had settled down to growing tobacco on a grand scale and enjoying an enormous economic boom. Maryland, founded in the 1630s, immediately followed suit, and while the exorbitant profits had already proved ephemeral, tobacco remained a strong enterprise.

Chesapeake society was fairly unstable through much of the seventeenth century: mortality was exceedingly high, and men vastly outnumbered women as planters worked to recruit top labor for their fields. Most immigrants, from the most dependent indentured servants[1] to the wealthiest "younger sons" of English gentlemen, planned to make tobacco fortunes and return to England; few lived long enough, and many left orphans in need of protection, but widowed women and men often found in marriage a pathway to upward mobility. In both Virginia and Maryland, economics, politics, society, and culture all revolved around and were constructed by the needs of tobacco cultivation, including use of unfree labor. By 1700, a stable plantation society had been established throughout the Chesapeake region. Health had improved, and a native-born Anglo-American society had emerged. The plantation economy, so unbalanced by the increasing demand for a decreasing supply of servants, had been restabilized with the importation of African slaves. The number of African arrivals between 1690 and 1740 was so large that, by 1750, the Chesapeake region prospered through the exploitation of a stable community of chattel slaves.[2]

Further south, English planters from Barbados organized a colony in Carolina in the 1660s. Carolina's planters were well-versed in the practice and value of slave labor, and they brought their African slaves with them. By 1710 South Carolina had turned to rice production on a plantation scale, and the proportion of colonizers had tipped toward an African majority. Government and social custom were increasingly organized around the necessity and problems of controlling slave labor. The Stono Rebellion of 1739, an uprising in South Carolina that came to involve more than a hundred Africans, added to white fears and provided the rationalization European colonists used to justify an increasingly harsh slave code.

It would be wrong to say that there was no religion in the southern colonies, or even that religion was of no importance. Although Puritan investors were involved in planting Virginia, the churches established there and in Carolina were Anglican. Few, widely spaced, and 3,000 miles from the oversight of the Bishop of London, the churches functioned within a "congregational" model. By the end of the seventeenth century, a significant number of churches and ministers served the burgeoning planter culture, generally organized under the control of Virginia's elite. Maryland, though founded by a Roman Catholic proprietor as a haven for English Catholics, actually numbered very few Catholics among its residents. During the seventeenth century, the majority of Marylanders may well have been Anglican, but they generally enjoyed the absence of any established institutional church. However, following the Protestant uprising in 1689, when the non-Catholic residents ousted the colony's leadership from government, the populace began to organize Anglican congregations. By 1740, the Church of England had established its dominance throughout the southern colonies. To be sure, a fair number of dissenters had moved into these colonies, including Lutherans, German and French Calvinists, a few Baptists, Congregationalists, Presbyterians, even some Quakers. Nevertheless, the Church of England remained the established church in the Chesapeake, the Carolinas, and the new colony of Georgia, and Anglicans represented the majority of the churched population in Virginia and Maryland.[3]

Although hopeful English religionists had founded the Society for the Propagation of the Gospel in Foreign Parts (SPG) to fund clerical leadership and missionary work in the New World, English Protestants made singularly little progress beyond the boundaries of Euro-American settlements. Only a handful of New England Puritans across a century of settlement made any efforts to convert native Americans, and in the southern region even less was accomplished. So, too, English Protestants experienced small, erratic success in converting African slaves. Since one of the rationalizations for the enslavement of Africans was their "heathenism," masters' fears that they would be required to free

Christianized slaves may have discouraged initial efforts. (Caribbean Quaker planters who opened their religious meetings to their slaves were severely criticized and sometimes prosecuted.) That fear was quickly assuaged by legislation that established slave status by race rather than religion, yet few missionaries exerted significant efforts among Africans and even fewer experienced success. More seems to have been accomplished by religious planters than by clergy. In fact, the Anglican church, and the SPG, had more than they could manage trying to provide ministers to the Europeans.[4]

Among settlers needing ministers were those settled in the mid-Atlantic colonies. Originally established in 1624 by the Dutch West Indies Company, New Netherlands encouraged the settlement of a wide range of colonizers: men and women from old and especially New England; French Huguenots; a small African community of ex-slaves who had purchased their freedom; an even smaller community of Jews from Recife, Brazil. In 1664, Britain captured New Netherlands without a battle and supported the development of this most diverse of colonies, separating East and West Jersey from the newly reorganized New York. The predominant religions were Dutch Reformed, Anglican, and the English Calvinism brought by New Englanders.

New York's early history was characterized by conflicts between Dutch and English overladen by class strife, with the churches sitting squarely in the middle. The Dutch Reformed Church had negotiated with the Anglican establishment a shared institutional status and financial support. Although Dutch ministers and congregations still placed themselves under the authority of the Classis at Amsterdam, the Classis was less and less able to support them with either money or clergy. As the influence and dominance of the English grew, and "Dutch" New York became anglicized, more Dutch congregants required English-speaking pastors. Outside New York City lived Dutch congregants alienated from a church they believed had sold out to the English. By 1720, the countryside was filled with disaffected Dutch congregants alongside old New Englanders who also dominated Long Island. Together these two communities would stand against the central authority exercised (or pretended) by the Anglican and Dutch Reformed alliance, and, as in the southern colonies, a congregational polity would effectively override the institutions' efforts to maintain hierarchical control.[5]

The final gap in the British colonial coastline was filled in 1682 with the establishment of Pennsylvania under the proprietorship of Quaker William Penn. From the outset, Pennsylvania followed a policy of religious toleration that neither persecuted nor privileged any religious institution or its members. This, combined with the economic opportunities inherent in lush farmland, an excellent climate, and a well-situated port, created a prosperous refuge not only for Quakers, but for persecuted religious minorities and mainstream majorities alike. Although

English Quakers would monopolize the political leadership for at least seventy years, they quickly became a numerical minority in the colony. Within thirty years, Welsh Quakers, Anglicans, New Englanders, and German Mennonites had joined the "Holy Experiment"; in 1701, Philadelphia alone had five different churches or meeting houses – Quaker, Anglican, Baptist, Congregationalist, and Presbyterian. Beginning in the 1720s and continuing until the onset of the Revolutionary War, waves of Scots-Irish Presbyterians and German Calvinists, Lutherans, and Moravians swept into the colony. Additionally, English Catholic, Jewish, and African communities arose during the eighteenth century. Here, each religious community organized its own congregation according to its own theological guidelines, financing it without the interference or the assistance of the government. This diversity, shared with New York and New Jersey, gave the mid-Atlantic colonies a unique regional identity and rendered them particularly susceptible to religious activism.

Despite the varieties of climates, economic systems, and social structures found in the British colonies of the eighteenth century, women's lives were surprisingly similar. With the exception of the extremely wealthy, and these were few indeed, women were continuously occupied by the demands of the household economy and the bearing and rearing of children. As in seventeenth-century New England, the limitations of the English common law and the concept of coverture significantly circumscribed women's abilities to act independently of husbands. Not only could wives not own property, they had no legal authority in directing the rearing of their children despite their social role as primary caretaker. Some women were quite active in the management of household affairs: they were considered by family and community members as essential participants and took over the management of husband's affairs in their widowhoods. However, beyond a few anecdotes of powerful widows and husbands sharing responsibilities, the evidence indicates that most women knew little about their husband's/family's economic affairs and were unable to manage independently. Most women, when left without husbands through death or desertion, turned to fathers, brothers, or adult sons for protection and guidance.[6]

At the beginning of the eighteenth century, the ministry and the lay leadership in Anglican and Calvinist congregations continued to be open to men only. Nevertheless, as in seventeenth-century New England, many eighteenth-century congregations provided women with some wisps of authority through their church memberships. While men were praised for civic virtue, for learning, and for economic productivity, women were honored for their piety and devotion to family. In the late seventeenth century, throughout New England women, not men, filled the churches. Devout mothers were the hope of the next generation as ministers such as Cotton Mather praised the loyalty of his female adherents even as he lamented their numerical domination and hoped in some way to attract more male followers.[7] In the eighteenth century, as other denominations established themselves with a stable institutional base, they too found their congregational rolls dominated by women, and housewives and mothers were urged to take a leading role in the religious education of their children, servants, and slaves.

Some historians have explained this dynamic as the result of secularization: an ideological transformation from a dependence upon theology and divine providence to a reliance upon science and natural law as the language and theoretical framework for explaining the universe. To this framework some historians have added the nascent capitalist economy that would eventually take men and their work out of the home. Men, better educated and economically rational, grew dissatisfied with the limitations of religious explanations and institutions, and as the church became irrelevant to cosmology and material production, men left its membership rolls to women. Together secularization and the rise of capitalism increased the male public–female private sphere polarity, with the church understood as part of the private sphere. This is a compelling portrait of change, supported somewhat by the evidence, but there are problems. The modernization described does not truly take root until the end of the eighteenth or even the beginning of the nineteenth century; yet some congregations were numerically dominated by women a hundred years earlier. Furthermore, as religious activism waxed and waned, the proportion of male to female members radically changed up and down depending upon the time, the region, and the particular denomination.

Historian Patricia Bonomi has offered an alternative explanation, one supported by the history of evangelicalism in the eighteenth and early nineteenth centuries. She argues that this feminization of the churches resulted from the strengthening of the institutional structure of the churches themselves. Newly formed religious networks engaged the commitment and real work of significant numbers of laymen and laywomen and consequently endowed them with real power. While women often reaped a surprising spiritual authority, the congregations were built through the struggles of laymen who led prayer groups, organized disciplinary committees, raised money, and built buildings. As the institutional structure of a church network stabilized, the demands on lay leadership lessened and, therefore, involved fewer persons. Moreover, as authority over spiritual affairs was extended to a professional ministry, the actual power of laymen in congregational business declined. In search of real political and social power, laymen left the church to women under the care of a male pastor.[8]

This explanation is further corroborated by the demographic history of the Anglican Church in the Chesapeake. Through the 1760s, churches were controlled not by pastors appointed by a bishop, but by lay vestries who sat on disciplinary issues, managed finances, and retained the authority to hire and fire their ministers. In fact, vestries provided another venue, along with the county courts, through which the elite could reinforce their power. No decline in male membership afflicted the Anglican Church in the Chesapeake until after the American Revolution, when the church, reorganized independently from the Church of England, established its own bishops and a system of hierarchical controls.

Finally, the perspicuity of Bonomi's paradigm is confirmed by the particular history of the Quakers, or Society of Friends. Born of Puritan heritage during the religious and cultural tumult of the 1640s and 1650s, these disciples of George Fox emphasized the workings of the Spirit in the believer's soul above all other sources of sacred authority. They did not deny the inspiration of the Holy Scriptures; rather, they endorsed the primacy of divine revelation: an inner light within all persons without respect to sex, birth, wealth, or education. All women and men inspired by the light were commanded by God to preach the Gospel to others, regardless of worldly status. As Margaret Fell proclaimed,

> God hath said that his *Daughters* should Prophesie as well as his *Sons*. And where he hath poured forth his Spirit upon them, they must prophesie, though blind Priests say to the contrary, and will not permit holy women to speak.[9]

Like other sectaries, Quakers were gifted with an overwhelming missionary zeal, and Quaker women as well as men toured the British Isles, the British colonies, and the European continent bringing the good news of the inner light to others. These efforts won many converts and earned severe persecutions, especially in New England.

With the restoration of Charles II to the English throne in 1660, Quakers suffered increasingly harsh penalties. Their Spirit-oriented religiosity engendered an unswerving skepticism (and hostility) towards institutional religious authority in any form, and they were imprisoned and fined for refusing to attend Sunday services or pay tithes. Quakers also acted out their rejection of an educated, paid ministry by publicly denouncing the clergy and the church for their hypocrisy. Whether in pamphlets, oral declamations during services, or public performances, such as testifying, naked, against the physical abuse of Quakers, the Friends did threaten an English social order dependent upon deference and institutional authority. However, as the persecutions continued, Quakers began to conserve their energies and turn inward, away from evangelical efforts to convert others and transform society to the task of maintaining their families, community, and their own cultural integrity. Toward this end, William Penn successfully solicited a colonial charter from the king.

Penn's "Holy Experiment" experienced significant birthing pains. Accompanying their utopian visions of peace and perfection were serious disagreements about the structure of the religion itself. Like the New England immigrants of 1630, Pennsylvania's anti-institutional Quakers found themselves building an institution of weekly, monthly, quarterly, and yearly "Meetings" (with each level incorporating a larger geographic and demographic segment). During the first decade, the primary "division" recognized among Quakers was that between "Public Friends" and others. Although neither ordained nor paid, these Friends were essentially preachers granted sacred and secular authority because of the spiritual gifts so clearly manifested in meetings. Of course, spiritual inspiration did represent a legitimate (and the only) rationale for status; still, such inequality was resented within a community that theoretically prized equality. In 1690, George Keith spoke for many when he challenged this spiritual aristocracy. He proposed the construction of a creed as a touchstone that could open the way for all who subscribed to participate in decision-making. This effort was successfully derailed by Quaker leaders, who argued that the price of such institutionalization would be the inner light, but the community also expanded its leadership fairly quickly. While some religious meetings were centered upon a preacher, other "silent" meetings were held in the expectation that the quiet would make space for the light to move within the ordinary believer. Additionally, Quaker men of worldly prominence joined those of the Spirit in determining the secular affairs of the community, and women's leadership was refocused upon spiritual matters and explicitly female affairs.[10]

Among things that did not change was the Quaker emphasis upon the family. In his *Quakers and the American Family*, Barry Levy has outlined the importance of family organization in maintaining the society and fostering the spiritual growth of children. As early as the 1650s, George Fox had advocated a reconceptualization of the family that incorporated a spiritual marriage and a "redefinition and intensification of child-rearing." He argued that women were essential to the promotion of the Spirit within the community, and he called upon householders to share authority with wives, who should be rational and self-disciplined as well as pious. Women should be involved at all levels in making decisions regarding matters that explicitly touched upon areas of women's particular expertise: sex, childbirth, and child-rearing.[11] By 1700, separate women's business meetings had developed in both England and North America, generally with the responsibility of reviewing marriage applications, distributing charity, and "maintaining spiritual and moral discipline among women in all their spiritual-physical intimacies with children and men."[12]

While the "holy conversation" of wives and mothers raised children of Quaker virtue and loyalty, Quaker men, unlike their Puritan colleagues, did not restrict women's converse to the hearth. Preaching women were highly valued in the mid-Atlantic Quaker community, and many continued, along with preaching men, to travel the circuit, speaking at local and regional meetings of worship. In his examination of female ministers in two Pennsylvania Quaker communities, Levy found that not only were the families of such women noted for their "holy conversation," but their households enjoyed an affluence that could support the upbringing of the children as well as promote their preaching vocations. What was most interesting, however, was not that female preachers came largely from the ranks of the wealthy, because not all of them did, but that the women's spirituality served as a pathway for social mobility. Three notable ministers, Jane Fenn, Susanna Hudson, and Elizabeth Sampson, were originally servants whose gifts eventually led them into marriages with worthy (and wealthy) Quaker men seeking spiritual companions in marriage.[13]

Among the most famous was Elizabeth Sampson Sullivan Ashbridge, born in Cheshire, England, in 1713.[14] Having eloped from her home at the age of 14 and left penniless when her stocking-weaver husband died five months later, Sampson, cast off by her father, went to live with her mother's relations in Ireland. There she first encountered the Quaker community. Strict discipline was maintained in the household and Sampson, a young woman of "vivacity" who loved to sing and dance, found her situation disagreeable. She got herself on board a ship to North America, ended up indentured, and was sold to a harsh master who sexually assaulted her. After three years of servitude, Sampson bought out the last year of her indenture and plied her needle to earn her keep. She continued to take delight in good company, and she married a schoolteacher named Sullivan who was attracted by that very vivacity. Her autobiography narrates a singular account of her search for God's truth and her discovery of the Spirit among the Quakers, as well as her realization of her own spiritual gifts, accompanied by a counterpoint of her husband's resistance to her religious explorations. At the last, Sullivan himself became interested in Quakerism. Yet, before this change bore any fruit, he enlisted in the army while drunk, as a pacifist Quaker refused to fight, and was beaten so severely that he died within nine months in 1741. Five years later, having paid all of Sullivan's debts, Elizabeth Sullivan married prominent Quaker Aaron Ashbridge, among the wealthiest men in Chester County, Pennsylvania. The two maintained their homestead until Elizabeth felt called to preach in Britain. She traveled to England in 1753 and died, in Ireland, two years later.

Elizabeth Ashbridge's personal narrative echoes other examples of the genre.[15] She would reap the whirlwind of her personal failures three times. First, at a young age she went against the wishes of a virtuous mother and respectable father and ended up penniless. So too, she fled the safety of a righteous Quaker household in self-indulgence and, once again, found herself an indentured servant abused by a lecherous master. Yet a third time she indulged her passion for dancing and married a man whom she neither loved nor valued. Within the circle of her sorrow, Ashbridge found the Spirit she sought; although, repelled by their unconventionality, especially their preaching women, she had resisted the pull of the Quaker community as long as possible. However, at last finding herself swept up by the Spirit, she read books, attended meetings, and realized that she must join. As she tried to foster her spiritual growth, her unsympathetic husband, preferring her lighthearted and jolly, threw many obstacles in her path. Throughout, Ashbridge credits the religious opportunities available throughout her life – a godly mother, Quaker relations in Ireland – even as she failed to take advantage of them. Only after she had been mortified by sorrows and humiliation was she able to embrace the light within her and take up the strict discipline. Once chastened, she understood that God had thrown the guidance in her path in sending her to a Quaker meeting in Rhode Island, reconnecting her with Quaker relations in Pennsylvania, and selectively placing Quaker writings in her path. Although she wrote of moments of connection with the divine, in fact she chronicles a slow process from lighthearted girl to sorrowful wife, exploring believer, committed Quaker, and dedicated "Public Friend."

Elizabeth's marriage to Aaron Ashbridge stands as the final reflection of the power of spiritual goodness within the Quaker community. At Sullivan's death, the widow is again left penniless, and only through her own labor as schoolmistress and needlewoman was she able to maintain herself as she paid off her husband's debts. Yet her character and spirituality alone attracted the attentions of one of the leading Friends of the country. Aaron wrote that he found her companionship "mutual, dear & agreeable," and he described her as "Lovely Creature; possessed of a more lovely mind; adorn'd with Grace and truth; exalted on the wings of ever Lasting Love...."[16] Despite his great love, when Elizabeth felt herself called to return to England and Ireland, he honored her light and watched her go. Quakers remained dedicated to the family, convinced that family fostered the spiritual growth of the husband and wife and that the children were dependent upon the spiritual gifts of both parents. This commitment mandated equal spiritual education for girls and boys, opening the way for women's spiritual development. Against this overwhelming commitment to family, Quakers honored the voice of the Spirit as it inspired and directed each individual soul. This ungendered spiritual equality, tempered by communal requirements, frequently pulled Quaker men and women in two directions. Quaker men may have preferred intact households to traveling, preaching wives. However, unlike their Puritan forebears, they were unwilling to sacrifice the inner light for communal stability, choosing instead to build community through the embrace of, and adaptation to, the light.

In many ways, the Quaker communities of the eighteenth century were an anomaly. With the absence of a professional clergy, the meetings retained their institutional dependence upon male Quakers, and so the men remained actively involved throughout the century. Also, as the network stabilized, the Spirit became somewhat less important than structures and precedents in directing the business through the Men's Meetings. Nevertheless, as family remained a central aspect of cultural continuity, and women were recognized as "experts" in family matters, women retained their voice in some of the central business of the community, with the Women's Meeting taking on marriage inspections and charity disbursements. Over all this, the religious meetings remained important, and the Spirit continued to be heard through the voices of women as well as men, undermining the smooth operation of the paternalistic family. And, while the Quakers became increasingly male-dominated throughout the eighteenth century, their refusal to deny the Spirit enabled Quaker women to develop their skills as pastors, administrators, and, especially, preachers.

While the Quakers were happily building their experimental colony, fostering their own spiritual growth within a religiously pluralistic society created by their own policy of toleration, other colonies were experiencing the pangs of cultural transformation. According to many clergymen, the turn of the century was not an auspicious time for religion; yet, it was not so terribly bad. In 1718, Solomon Stoddard had celebrated his fifth "harvest of souls" in Northampton, western Massachusetts. Most of the young people experienced grace in their souls and witnessed their conversions before the rest of the congregation. In the mid-Atlantic region, several Calvinist congregations were forming themselves into a presbyterial organization that would enable them to build new congregations and sponsor preaching in areas not being served by a regular pastor. Also, religious revitalization in the Palatine and the Methodist movement in England were just getting underway, and, beginning in the 1720s, significant numbers of immigrants were bringing their own peculiar brand of communal piety into the colonies. Both European movements and the extensive immigration would have an enormous impact upon the colonies, nourishing a spiritual revitalization movement that has come to be known as the Great Awakening.

The Great Awakening swept the colonies from the 1720s to the 1760s. The first stirrings of revivalism appeared in the middle colonies with the new immigrants and itinerant preachers; the spiritual vitality spread north and south, continuing until the political upheavals of the American Revolution shut down, at least temporarily, the religious enthusiasm. Participants recognized the movement as an international one, which, in their world, meant that similar revivals were occurring throughout the colonies and in the British Isles.

The Awakening began and ended (where it *did* actually end) at different times, affected different communities, and had varying histories in each region; but the many commonalities overrode these differences. The communal rituals of intense, emotional revivalism, with their animated, frightening preachers and shrieking, weeping, fainting participants, appeared everywhere. Throughout the colonies clergymen took sides for or against the Awakening. Supporters of the Awakening, New Lights, saw the essence of true faith as holy love – religion of the heart; they believed the revivals to be the work of the Holy Spirit and understood the extreme physical manifestations as natural outcomes of an enlightened soul responding to the real threat of damnation. They described their opponents as legalists who mistook correct behavior for conversion, thinking for faith, and eloquence for inspiration. These opponents, Old Lights, found the essence of true faith in right reason – religion of the mind; they considered the revivals delusions of an ignorant, vulgar populace fed by irresponsible, priestly demagogues. In all regions, congregations identified themselves as Old or New Light, and clerics and communities on each side made connections across denominational boundaries with those who shared their views of the revivals. In other words, even as they experienced divisions and schisms within their own denominations, congregations were uniting with other churches to promote the work of the Spirit.

The earliest signs of this revival arose within congregations of recent Scots-Irish immigrants, descendants of the Scots who had colonized the northern Irish province of Ulster.[17] Amidst the harsh (and reportedly irreligious) conditions of the Irish colonial frontier, a few Scottish Presbyterian ministers, beginning in 1625, had led a series of religious revivals. The revivals, which blossomed into communion services, were characterized by large-scale popular participation and enthusiastic community response as the congregation (and visitors) were led through a recognizable conversion experience. As these settlers had come from western Scotland and continued to visit "home," this revivalistic culture soon flourished there as well. For the next century, experiential religion flourished on both sides of the Irish Sea. In the second and third decades of the eighteenth century, the Scots-Irish, mostly in response to economic pressures and several cycles of famine conditions, began to emigrate in large numbers.[18] When they came, they brought their religiosity with them, and experiential spirituality flourished on both sides of the Atlantic.

The earliest recorded outbreak of revivalism among these Presbyterians occurred in Freehold, New Jersey, in 1729. There an entire congregation felt a strong sense of its sinfulness, realized the punishment that deservedly awaited, turned to Jesus in hope, and felt the joy of the Spirit's grace in their hearts. A group of clergymen led by William Tennent (who established a school – the "Log College" – to train ministers) and his sons advocated for experiential piety, removing erudition from the center of their vocation and replacing it with the personal experience of grace. In their judgment, a minister who had not felt the Spirit had not experienced conversion and was not fit to preach. A battle over ministerial qualifications plagued the Presbyterian community for twenty years, inspiring epithets and disrespect among clerics and from their congregants and dividing the church into Old and New Light synods in 1741. However, the revivalist religiosity and ideology attracted such large numbers of congregants and clerics that by 1758 the two synods reunited into a single church that largely favored the New Lights.

While many of these New Light ministers and congregants came from Ireland, they, alone, cannot account for the outpouring of the Spirit in this region. Theodorus Jacobus Frelinghuysen, the Dutch pastor of Raritan, New Jersey, who embraced an experiential spirituality, publicly reproached congregants and ministers who did not agree with his position. While he alienated some Reformed pastors and laypersons, he gathered and constantly increased a community of supporters whose influence extended beyond congregational and, later, ethnic boundaries.[19]

Of greater importance, a significant portion of the Presbyterians were descendants of New England Puritans, primed for such a movement by their own spiritual history. The Scots-Irish had brought exciting, communal revivalistic rituals, while the English contributed an ideology that pulled out of these community enterprises a focus upon the individual. Even without the clear example of the Scots-Irish or the Dutch, religionists in New England were discovering this new communal religiosity. Solomon Stoddard was, upon his death in 1729, succeeded at Northampton by his grandson, Jonathan Edwards.[20] A gifted intellect, theologian, and philosopher, Edwards was also a highly sophisticated spiritual leader. He followed Stoddard's lead in preaching the awaiting terrors of hell and the glorious promises of salvation, hoping to lead his congregation out of their spiritual malaise and toward the awareness of sin and damnation necessary to experiencing the comfort and assurance of divine grace. The region experienced a few, scattered revivals, and in 1734, a two-year revival of religion exploded in Northampton. The revival so overwhelmed Edwards with its power that he published his *Faithful Narrative of the Surprising Work of God*, where he claimed to have brought at least three hundred persons to Christ, having his greatest success among the young. These were true conversions, he assured his readers, marked by changes in morals and behavior as well as sentiments. And, while he may have been discouraged by the ending of the revival, and by the evidence of the devil's handiwork in the suicide of his uncle, Joseph Hawley, he continued to feel hope in the conversions of such individuals as the young maiden Abigail Hutchinson and the 4-year-old Phebe Bartlet.[21]

The culture of the Great Awakening represents the first appearance of the evangelicalism that would come to shape religion in the United States. This culture has its roots in the Puritan emphasis upon the spiritual journey of the individual and the deeply emotional, sometimes passionate, always personal, connection with God. At the same time, however, there was added a new layer of communal rituals and understandings and language that facilitated the individual's spiritual journey. It was as if the intensity of the believer's personal relationship with God was acted out at a group level so that all could witness and appreciate (or decry) the excessive tribulation and joy experienced by the truly saved.

In other words, while Awakening converts progressed through spiritual stages not unlike those of their Puritan forebears, the entire experience was quickened and intensified, climaxing with a powerful "moment" of connection. In recounting their experiences of grace, converts told of an awakening to a sense of their own sin, a conviction of their personal evil and the eternal punishment waiting, and their inspired efforts at reform to escape sin and death. Such superficial reformation of behavior was, of course, worthless, and many revival preachers worked to push hearers beyond this reformation to a point of true despair in their spiritual condition. Only then was the path opened for the grace of God. The Holy Spirit arrived in power and freed the human soul from its enslavement to sin.

During the Great Awakening, the earlier stages of conversion might well last weeks or even years. Nathan Cole, for example, was in misery for two years on his spiritual journey, while Deborah Prince languished amidst insecurity and doubts for almost five years.[22] Often, personal affliction first awakened the individual to her sins. Deborah Prince "narrowly escaped being drowned," while Jemima Harding and Hannah Heaton both recorded the fears and experience of childbirth as pushing them forward spiritually. Illness, too, played an important role, and the conversion processes of both Prince and Abigail Hutchinson were accompanied by illnesses that, after their conversions, finally took their lives. Mercy Wheeler spent five years abed, unable to walk or speak, until her conversion effected a cure, while Phillis Wheatley "languishe[d] under weakness and pa[in]...the inward [was] refresh'd and strengthen'd more abundantly by him who declar'd from heaven that his strength was made perfect in weakness!"[23] While an immediate fear of death (and, by implication, damnation) jarred believers out of their complacency, long-term suffering chastised and disciplined the sufferer. Heaton, for example, wrote not only of her physical sufferings but of the mental anguish endured at the hands of a husband who did not support her religious choice, children who were irreligious and disrespectful, and a town that brought her to trial for attending the religious services of the revivalists rather than the town church.

In addition to their afflictions, many converts wrote of the importance of hearing itinerants. Prince's story is almost formulaic: hearing George Whitefield renewed her dedication to her pious labors; attendance upon Gilbert Tennent's preaching disturbed her and raised new doubts. Heaton traced her own spiritual history back to her father's solicitousness in taking her to hear these two great itinerants, while Hannah Harkum Hodge spoke of the preaching of John Rowland, Samuel Finley (two Log College men), and Gilbert Tennent as essential to her spiritual growth. She too, however, gave preeminence in her history to Whitefield. Invoking the image of the Samaritan women whom Jesus converted, in part by telling her of her past, Hodge declared that Whitefield

> had so exactly described all the secret working of her heart, her views, her wishes, her thoughts, her imaginations, and her exercises, that she really believed he was either more than mortal, or else that he was supernaturally assisted to know her heart."[24]

George Whitefield, scarcely 25 years old, was a disciple of John Wesley and an active proponent of his reform efforts in the Church of England. Like many reformers of the previous century, Wesley had become convinced that the Anglican Church was more concerned with form than substance, and that bishops and priests actively sought places among gentlemen rather than their duties among the dispossessed. He called the church to address the needs of workers, of the uneducated, and he questioned the sincerity of religionists who privileged reason over faith, status over morality, and eloquence over clarity and truth. He and Whitefield added to this commitment a zeal for conversions and a gift for preaching. For almost a year, beginning in autumn 1739, Whitefield traveled up the North American coast, and back down again, attracting multitudes of hearers. Because he heartily criticized clerics who rejected his methods and message, he was denied regular pulpits. Whitefield easily turned to the open air, and, frankly, he'd soon have been preaching out of doors anyway, since the numbers of persons attracted to his sermons could never have fit into a building.

In many ways Whitefield symbolized the Great Awakening. He preached outside (his Philadelphia devotees built an especial outdoor platform for him), and he preached not at regular hours, but whenever he arrived. Extemporaneous sermons berated huge audiences with catalogs of sins, threats of punishment, and calls to repentance. Unquestionably, many hearers were deeply affected by him, testifying with swoons and screams. But Whitefield was an itinerant, not a pastor, and he rarely stayed in one place long enough to nurse individuals through the entire conversion process. Essentially, Whitefield's intensity, disregard for time and place, and disregard for established church hierarchies and professional courtesies, characterized much that set the Great Awakening apart. What seems most important, though, is the impression of immediacy, a concern about the here and now and a conviction that change can happen without delay.

To a certain point, stories of converts read like accounts written by seventeenth-century saints. The fears of hell, the self-disgust, and the despair at his or her depraved state were told by Puritan church members and evangelical converts. So, too, evangelicals used intimate, often erotic language to describe their relationship with God. Irene Shaw reported that she "felt ravished with the Love of God," while Heaton saw a "man with his arms open ready to receive me his face was full of smiles he loockt white and ruddy and was just such a saviour as my soul wanted." Sarah Osborn "could utter no other language but, 'Come in, Lord Jesus, take full possession; I will come to thee, thou art mine, and I am thine,'....surely my heart reached forth in burning desires after the blessed Jesus. O, how was I ravished with his love!"[25]

Men as well as women so responded to the Spirit's work. Benjamin Lyon recorded his deep longings and joy:

> to feel Ardent Desire After nearness, After Conformity to my heavenly Father, O to have love Inflamed towards him...O to be Encirkled in those Blessed Arms of Everlasting love... I do here, upon the bended knees of my soul...Joyn my Self in Marriage Covenant to him...I do here with all my powers Accept thee, I Do take thee for my head & husband for all times & Conditions, to love, to honour, & to Obey thee before all Others.[26]

It was as if evangelicals had rediscovered a relationship that had been lost. The divine relationship that had thrilled their forebears was offered again, and women and men again accepted God and experienced the ecstatic joy he brought.

Key differences between the seventeenth and eighteenth centuries remained, however, reflecting the accelerated pace and the more intense, assertive presence of the Spirit. Converts wrote of *immediate* transformations. Nathan Cole heard God's voice call him, twice, and before he could "stir my tongue or lips," his "heart answered O yes, yes, yes...When God appeared to me every thing vanished and was gone in the twinkling of an Eye, as quick as A flash of lightning." Hutchinson endured an extraordinarily tortuous week until her anxieties fell away, and she felt all day "a constant sweetness in her soul," while Prince languished and struggled for five years until, on her deathbed, she suddenly spoke a "new Language." Hannah Heaton, while attending a meeting, went from despair to tranquility as she recalled "Seek and you shall find come to me all you that are weary and heaviladen and i will give you rest."[27]

Adding to this sense of immediacy was the visual nature of the connection with God. In the seventeenth century, believers felt the presence of the Spirit, were awash in God's grace, or heard the voice of God in their hearts. In the eighteenth, they saw visions. On the morning after her conversion, Hutchinson told her brother "that she had seen...Christ the last night..." Narrator Edwards clarified this vision, "i.e., in realizing views by faith," impressing upon his readers a metaphorical use of language and, thus, preventing a charge of overblown enthusiasm. Whether or not Hutchinson was speaking literally or metaphorically is unknown.[28] To Elizabeth Mixer were revealed visions of heaven and Christ: "CHRIST Smileth! I behold Heavens Gate Open; the Angels with golden Cups in their Hands! I See sparkling Crowns and Diamonds, and Saints singing Hallelujahs, Praising GOD." This interpretive account, featuring quotations from Revelation and the Epistles, confronted the power of death and called all individuals to see Christ and lose all fear of death. "If People did see the Loveliness of CHRIST, they would not Sin as they do."[29] About eighteen months before she died, Elizabeth Lee noted that God "wonderfully appeared for her and gave her such glimpse of glory that her soaring spirit could hardly be contained within the claiy tenement." Heaton saw an open-armed Jesus who "was just such a saviour as my soul wanted."[30] Mary Reed's extraordinary visions gave her an authority over her minister. Nathaniel Gilman consulted her for spiritual direction and guidance in preaching, sometimes reading her visions aloud to his congregation.[31]

Even when converts wrote of backsliding, the personalized supernatural played a large role. Cole and Heaton both felt a personal devil actively struggling against them. During the years surrounding her conversion, Osborn recorded constant battle with Satan, the great liar, who tempted her to despair many times. Soon after her conversion,

> Satan assaulted me in as furious a manner, seemingly, as though he had appeared in bodily shape, though with my bodily eyes I saw nothing. I believe the combat lasted, at least, two hours, as fierce as though I had talked with him face to face.[32]

One of the most striking accounts came from the diary of convert Susanna Anthony. She attributed various evil inclinations alternatively to her own weaknesses and to the devil. She also reported that Satan physically assaulted her. "I seemed as one really possessed of the devil....satan seemed to have had full power of me." At other moments, Anthony said she had

> "twisted every bone out of its place: and have often since wondered that I never disjointed a bone when, through a violence of my distress, I wrung my hands, twisted every joint, and strained every nerve; biting my flesh; gnashing my teeth; throwing myself on the floor."[33]

With the zeal and drama associated with both individual and community spiritual histories, the escalation of religious excitement had, by 1741, brought the colonies to crisis. Following Whitefield's first tour, the Awakening was revived in New England, sweeping beyond the environs of the Connecticut Valley and moving east as far as Boston. Congregations and clergymen began to take sides, questioning the nature of faith and destroying the last traces of religious consensus. Some New England congregations fell into each camp; some congregants, dissatisfied with their current ministers, separated off into a competing congregation. Heaton, as has been mentioned, stopped attending the local pastor and instead followed after the New Light "Separates." Further south, the Presbyterian Synod in the mid-Atlantic colonies divided. In Philadelphia, for example, Hannah Harkum Hodge left the ministry of her Old Light pastor Jedidiah Andrews and sought spiritual guidance among the Log College men. Yet, as old networks were destroyed, new ones were created. Thomas Prince was publishing accounts of revivals from New England, the mid-Atlantic colonies, and Scotland; correspondences were initiated among colonial clergy, John Wesley, and revival supporters in Scotland; Jonathan Edwards became a significant theologian throughout the colonies and Great Britain.[34] On both sides of the Atlantic, participants rejoiced in the Spirit.

While some communities, notably the Congregationalists and the Presbyterians, were divided and re-formed, others were left intact. The colonial Anglican Church remained united against, but not unaffected by, the revivals. Listeners attracted by the threats and promises of revivalist preachers simply left their congregations to join New Light churches. So, too, in the regional strongholds of Calvinism, many Congregationalists or Presbyterians, uncomfortable with the New Light direction of their own ministers, might have joined the Anglican communion.

This era also observed the arrival or rebirth of churches unanimously pro-revival. Among German immigrants, for example, a new community of religious enthusiasts arrived in the 1740s and began actively recruiting members and disrupting the German Reformed and Lutheran communities from their settlement in Bethlehem, Pennsylvania.[35] Tracing their origin back to the preaching of John Hus, the new Moravian congregation had come to depend upon an intensely personal relationship with Jesus at the center of their spirituality as a sign of their own salvation. Initially, the Moravians actively proselytized among other German immigrants, rupturing congregations as they attracted adherents. In one case their influence extended much further: an extremely pious woman of New London, Connecticut, was so moved by New Light preaching that she formed her own sect that called for the practice of celibacy. Her community would later join the Moravians.[36]

Moravians' utopian design originally included communal ownership of property, shared labor, and religious "choirs" that were segregated by age, gender, and marital status. These provided structures through which individuals could progress through stages of spiritual development with others at similar stages. Although the ultimate leadership of the community was restricted to men, women worked as spiritual guides and leaders for other women. The placement of children in a nursery at eighteen months of age enabled married women to be full participants in community life, and the establishment of the choir of single sisters called many women to full community membership without requiring marriage as a rite of passage to adulthood. This idealism would crumble within twenty years as economic pressures, along with changes in European leadership, moved the community toward the more ordinary structures of individual family housing and private property.

Of even greater impact was the rise of a revitalized Baptist Church in New England. English Baptists trace their history back to the early seventeenth century as one of the many communities of dissenters under the Puritan umbrella. Characterized most clearly by a rejection of infant baptism or, alternatively, by the espousal of believer's baptism, some Baptists followed a Calvinist theology and others were rather Arminian. They appeared in New England in the 1630s, and in Rhode Island's tolerant climate Baptists established a headquarters from which they could proselytize throughout the region. Because the Baptists attracted some important figures, they posed problems for Massachusetts. While Lady Deborah Moody, for example, had the grace to leave the colony voluntarily, other converts and itinerants remained outspoken advocates and received the predictable punishment of heretics: whippings, fines, and prison terms.[37] By the beginning of the next century, the political and social climates had changed sufficiently to ease such persecutions, particularly of reformed Protestants. About twenty small, focused communities prospered in New England, especially Rhode Island, and the mid-Atlantic region.

Baptists had never given up their concentration upon the gifts of grace and the importance of the conversion experience, and they were overwhelmed by the Spirit during the Awakening. Under the leadership of charismatic itinerants such as Isaac Backus, the Baptist movement grew tremendously and divided into "Regular Baptists" and the more enthusiastic "Separate Baptists." Moreover, Baptists at this point enjoyed a comparatively egalitarian religiosity and granted extraordinary spiritual authority to laypersons, a practice characteristic of sectarian communities not yet institutionalized. Like their Puritan forebears, in their struggle against a structured, hierarchical, and patriarchal establishment, Baptists found the Holy Spirit's clear gifts to individuals empowering for the community as a whole. During the excitement of the 1740s, extant congregations attracted new members, new congregations were formed throughout the northeast, and the Baptist movement began to move south. By 1790, about 750 Baptist churches crossed the nation, extending south to Georgia and west to the frontier.

The Baptists were not the first to bring evangelicalism into the Chesapeake region. Following Whitefield's brief performances, several graduates of Tennent's Log College preached, in turns, in Hanover County, western Virginia, with Samuel Davies establishing himself in 1749 as the permanent pastor of several small congregations. By the late 1750s, the Baptists had moved in, and if the Anglican majority found the Presbyterians troublesome (and they seemed to; Samuel Davies worked hard to gain official permission to preach as a dissenter), the Baptists were downright peculiar. With a membership initially recruited among the lower and middling classes, the Baptists made a virtue out of necessity in their rejection of the ostentatious displays and entertainments of gentry culture that represented and reinforced the social hierarchy. Instead, Baptists embraced an egalitarian anthropology and expressed their politics in pietistic rituals, replacing balls, races, and extravagant hospitality with communions, baptisms, and foot-washings. Extemporaneous prayers were appreciated, read liturgies decried, and inspired lay witnesses were valued above learned clergy. Out of an intense religiosity, Baptists had developed a clear sense of who they were and why they mattered, and these rituals, combined with a special language of fervent piety, a strict moral code, and a workable system of enforcing discipline, bound community members together as dedicated souls seeking God.[38]

Besides a few conversions produced through the efforts of plantation masters and SPG ministers, the first serious work toward the Christianization of African Americans came during the later years of the Great Awakening. Whitefield reported numbers of Africans, slave and free, in his audiences. Davies claimed that more than a thousand Africans frequented the various places at which he preached, and he rejoiced in their sincerity and praised their poetic and musical gifts. However, the greatest successes during this era were experienced by the Baptists.

Why should evangelicals, particularly Baptists and, at the end of the century, the equally fervent Methodists, succeed where others met so many obstacles?[39] First, Euro-American evangelicals exerted extensive, long-term efforts in proselytizing among Africans. During the eighteenth century, the evangelical communities were the only ones ideologically prepared and equipped to pursue serious commitments towards drawing in the unchurched and calling out to society's dispossessed. All souls were of equal importance to God, and evangelical itinerants worked ceaselessly among settlers on the edge of survival: struggling frontier farmers and urban laborers, those deprived of the world's favors and excluded from the concern of most. Of particular import was their devaluation (if not rejection) of the benefit of learning and erudition.

Evangelical converts were not required to understand complicated cate-
chisms or recite creeds; they were not even required to read, although
many preachers thought that eventually all Christians should learn to
read for the sake of the Bible. What was necessary was a true sense of
one's own sins, a sincere repentance, and an acceptance of the atoning
work of Jesus Christ. No long, tedious preludes of lessons in reading and
theology delayed conversion for the illiterate. Instead, the Spirit,
working through divinely inspired preachers, gathered the newly saved
home.

This conviction that salvation was equally available to all was
reflected in a somewhat egalitarian polity that did, in fact, regard both
black and white hopefuls as souls in direct relation with God. There was
not complete racial equality: at a congregational service, for example,
Africans could be expected to stand, or even move outside, if there was
not enough space for all white participants. However, religious communities were not segregated, the preaching office was occasionally taken
up by Africans and the black preacher acknowledged by the white
congregants, and the disciplinary processes did involve black as well as
white congregants. And, while none of the churches ever, finally,
condemned slavery and slave ownership, Baptists did hold masters
accountable for conduct toward their slaves, disciplining excessive
brutality and insisting upon a respect for the marriage ties of African
couples.[40]

In addition to the activism of evangelicals and their egalitarian
ideology and practice, several historians have explored the sympathetic
parallels between evangelical religiosity and Africans' spirituality.[41] The
relative unimportance of written language always mattered when evan-
gelizing in non-literate communities, but, through the storytelling of
preachers, biblical lessons were passed along and retained as the stories
themselves were incorporated into the ancestry and folklore of the
people. The value placed upon extemporaneous prayer, preaching, and
testimony opened the door to personal performances by individuals who
found themselves moved by the Spirit. The emotional, experiential
nature of the revival services echoed other communal ceremonies.
Baptist John Leland had found that black Baptists were "more noisy, in
time of preaching, than the whites, and…more subject to bodily exercise,
and if they meet with any encouragement in these things, they often
grow extravagant."[42] In particular was Africans' love and ability for
music, an inclination that might find no fulfillment in the word-based
Protestantism of the seventeenth century or the classical music traditions
of the eighteenth, but one that could flourish in the evangelical world.
Samuel Davies recorded that several Africans "have lodged all night in
my kitchen, and, sometimes, when I have awakened about two or three
a-clock in the morning, a torrent of sacred harmony poured into my
chamber, and carried my mind away to Heaven."[43]

Ideologically, the immediate call of God resonated well within a community where visions were a recognizable aspect of the spiritual journey and religious leaders were identified by their connection with the divine. Mechal Sobel has argued that the metaphor of rebirth in the Spirit reverberated well since traditional African spirituality tied death and rebirth to the call of the gods.[44] So, too, Christine Heyrman believes that African-American evangelical converts were sometimes expressing African beliefs in evangelical "cadences," with the eventual product a "distinctive Afro-Christianity, a religious mosaic that melded discrete survivals from disparate West African beliefs and practices with elements of evangelical Protestantism."[45] At one Methodist gathering in North Carolina, Joseph Travis witnessed a slave woman who "with many extravagant gestures, cried out that she was 'young King Jesus.' " She had proclaimed that she was filled with the Spirit of Jesus Christ, but her expressions reflected a traditional African context in which the individual spoke with the voice of the Spirit as one possessed. Travis judged this statement a blasphemous trespass across the boundaries of acceptable Christian belief, and he excommunicated her, "stating that we would not have such wild fanatics among us...." Travis later reported the woman's submission, as she became a "rational and consistent" church member.[46]

Although begun in the 1750s, the potential of the Awakening's call to the black community was not realized until after the turn of the century. As late as 1800, no more than 5 percent of all African-American adults in the southern states had joined one of the evangelical churches, mostly Baptist and Methodist.[47] However, in a region stridently stratified by race, the presence of any significant numbers of African Americans pushed churches to move beyond abstract promises to concrete demonstrations of their egalitarian theological principles. Questions were raised concerning slavery, and many congregations advocated an end to the institution and the excommunication of any who refused to free his or her slaves. Although this proposal proved too extreme for the southern colonists, that it was discussed at all (and seriously discussed) points up the latent radicalism of this era's evangelicalism. Additionally, many congregations worked to ensure black congregants as much spiritual authority as their callings allowed. Black men of high spiritual attainments were placed upon disciplinary committees investigating black and white members, occasional black men were recognized as preachers, and white congregants were sometimes called to account for sinful dealings with their slaves or free black men and women. Moreover, in their acceptance, even encouragement, of African-American preachers, the evangelical churches were implicitly (if not explicitly) encouraging the formation of smaller prayer and study groups among and sometimes led by African Americans. By the nineteenth century, these separate networks and communions, led by community members, would serve as a source of personal strength and spiritual and political power for African-American Christians.

Similarly, women's communities remained an empowering source of nurturance for their members. Poet Phillis Wheatley, for example, found spiritual support in a correspondence with friend Arbour Tanner, confiding her religious hopes, worries, and pleasures. "Happy were it for us if we could arrive to that evangelical Repentance, and the true holiness of heart which you mention. Inexpressibly happy should we be could we have a true sense of the beauties and excellence of the crucified Saviour." Esther Edwards Burr and Sarah Prince kept up a three-year correspondence through which they admonished and encouraged one another. Sarah Osborn found a true spiritual companion in Susan Anthony, while Deborah Prince had joined a female society "for the most indearing Exercise of social Piety." In Philadelphia, it was reported that, after Whitefield had first preached in Philadelphia, "four or five godly women in the city, were the principal counsellors to whom awakened and inquiring sinners used to resort, or could resort, for advice and direction." Of course, not all women were equally nurtured by women. Hannah Heaton recorded many conversations with other female believers, and while most exchanges involved discord or disappointment, a gloomy spirit was occasionally refreshed by riding home with a woman with whom she could talk about "God's dealings with her soul."[48]

The strength discovered in female evangelical networks sometimes empowered women to claim and exercise spiritual authority within their larger church communities. As with crossing racial boundaries, individuals frequently did not recognize equality across gender lines; in fact, many evangelicals avidly opposed any acknowledgment of women's authority. Nevertheless, the circumstances of the eighteenth century combined with a Baptist theology that pushed against artificial hierarchies like class and education to open spiritual opportunities to women and justify their presence in the public forum of the church. In her *Disorderly Women*, Susan Juster cites several examples of both men and women voting in church affairs. While such notations are scarce, Juster persuasively argues that the absence of gender-specific language in church records, the explicit use of gendered language in the early nineteenth century, and these few references, suggests that church governance was a responsibility often shared by all church members, male and female.[49]

Women also raised major questions about speaking publicly: witnessing, voicing their concerns and criticisms, preaching, and joining the ranks of leaders. Throughout the era, women refused to attend churches, railed against churches, and called them to account. And, while evangelical leaders may have felt gratified when a Hannah Heaton criticized standing ministers, they were less pleased when they found themselves the subject under discussion. Isaac Backus was quite distressed to find himself chided by Ann Dellis for his condescending attitude. "I look upont that I have a right and may see duty to go into the meeting-house when you preach there to Stand as a witness for god how his work is handled and his Spirit treated by you," she wrote. Lois Adams was censured by the Canterbury Separate Church for "usurp[ing] authority over the Chh in that she Did in a Chh meeting autharitivey teach and admonish the house Church which is contrary to the word of God."[50]

Few challenged the ability of godly women to arouse spiritual instincts and lead their female friends, children, servants, and even husbands and other men to God. Devereux Jarratt, while a young school-master, was introduced to experiential religion through the quiet efforts of Mrs. Cannon, mistress of the house in which he boarded. Nightly she requested his presence as she read sermons to her family, and Jarratt attended at first only to "gain a favourable opinion," hard work since "Flavel's sermons are too experimental and evangelical for one, so igno-rant of divine things, as I was, to comprehend." Following several weeks of this effort, Jarratt reported that he was awakened to the fact that "I was a stranger to that spiritual illumination and its consequent discov-eries, and, of course, was yet in a dark and dangerous state." Although he had barely begun the real journey, the change in his conduct, as a result of his new awareness, "soon became visible to my benefactress, which was matter of great joy."[51]

The controversy surrounded not women's guidance over private lives, effected in private homes, but their addressing larger audiences in the public space of the church. The question brought tension into congrega-tions, and, if the leadership tried to pacify conservative elements by denying women's Spirit-given authority, they might find themselves missing several key female members. In Lyme, for example, seven women were cited for "usurping the authority over the church and for neglecting the public worship of God in this place and church meetings and for building up a meeting hild by our admonished members." Two years later, two more women joined them.[52] In other words, evangeli-calism often gave women a voice, but when they exercised that voice many were judged the founders of scandal and divisions.

Evangelical churches opened the doors to women's exhortation; that is, to women testifying to their spiritual experiences and witnessing to the power of the Spirit. Some women, inevitably, were led in directions that directly challenged their communities. David Hall wrote in his diary about a "troublesome" woman who insisted upon singing while others prayed and who disrupted his sermon with "panting fits." Isaac Backus described one Mrs. Chase who spoke so loudly that various congregants moved outside to escape her. She merely followed them outside and continued to expound. In their radical acknowledgment of the power of the Spirit, the Separate Congregationalist and Separate Baptist churches were far more open to women moving beyond the occasional outburst to taking on a role as an exhorter, or even preacher. In Virginia, Martha Stearns Marshall and Hannah Meuse Clay developed strong reputations as lay exhorters. Marshal was said to be a woman of "good sense, singular piety, and surprising elocution" who could melt "a whole concourse into tears by her prayers and exhortations." An outstanding exhorter, who appears to have delivered formal sermons on texts, was Sarah Wright Townsend. She preached at regular Sunday meetings of the Separate Baptist community on Long Island from 1759 until at least 1773. At one point a more conservative segment of the congregation proposed uniting with the Regular Baptists, a move that would have restricted Townsend's opportunities to preach. She and her followers left the church yelling "Babylon! Babylon! Babylon!" Her faction must have held the power balance in the congregation, however, because while the community did, eventually, join with the Regular Baptists, it was not until 1789, seven years after her death.[53]

Within this evangelical community, women's discovery of power inevitably led to contention with those who supported, even in the most limited fashion, respect for the patriarchal boundaries encircling women. Hannah Heaton's complex relationship with her nonsupportive husband spoke directly to her own conflicted views about the ultimate authority women reaped from their relationship with the divine, and her journal revealed her ambivalence about female authority. She wrote with both admiration and reserve about a female "Separate" who had assembled a group of followers. "She was a cunning creature & had great knowledge in the scriptures she was much for talking and in all her discourse with us she would pretend to know and see something clear away beyond us." Yet while granting that "she was a person of good behaviour," the troubled Heaton further noted that the neighbor was "fild with pride she caused devisions among us and was a means to break up our meetings…."[54]

Among the most extraordinary female leaders, and one who main- tained her respect for the authority of the male ministry, was Sarah Osborn. Born in 1714, she emigrated with her mother from London to Boston at the age of 8, with the family moving to Newport when she was 15. At 18, she married Samuel Wheaton, at 19 she was widowed with an infant son to support, which she accomplished by taking over a school. Eight years later she married Henry Osborn, a pious but sickly widower with three sons, no money, and unable to work. She returned to school teaching, and her school grew very large – reportedly seventy or more students at times. Among these students were the daughters of Joseph Fish, pastor in North Stonington, Connecticut. A correspondence begun while the girls were under her care continued to flourish after they had completed their education. These letters, along with excerpts from her diary, provide an illuminative window into Osborn's religious leadership and the spiritual experiences of women during this era.[55]

In the 1740s, Osborn joined with several young women in a prayer society.

> I earnestly pleaded with God that he would not suffer me to live any longer an unprofitable servant; but would point out some way, in which I might be useful. And that I might now be as exemplary for piety, as I had been for folly. And it pleased God so to order it, that I had room to hope my petitions were both heard and in a measure answered. For soon after this a number of young women, who were awakened to a concern for their souls, came to me, and desired my advice and assistance, and proposed to join in a society, provided I would take the care of them.[56]

She quickly assumed the leadership of the women's group, and, although frequently asserting that she had no desire to force her own opinions on the group, the majority usually took the pathway that she had chosen. The group met continuously for more than fifty years, including at its height about sixty members. The women established a set of rituals for themselves, rules for spiritual proceedings (including an agreement to maintain confidence among themselves), and guidelines for welcoming new members and excluding unruly ones.

When the Awakening returned to Newport in the 1760s, Osborn was at the forefront; undoubtedly her position as head of a large school and her experience as a teacher provided both the reputation and the verbal and interpersonal skills needed to establish and maintain such a position. The women's group continued to meet in her home, and in 1760, she modestly wrote to Fish: "We do at Least at some times know what it is to have Christs sencible gracious Presence with us refreshing seasons these we begun to meet last January...."[57] At this point, many more women affiliated with a range of groups expressed a desire to join the group, but she hesitated about those whom she judged would be divisive – Separates, a Baptist, and a follower of New Light preachers (an interesting list from an evangelical). However, within seven years several new groups were formed, and all these women participated in at least one group meeting at her home.

The year 1767 probably represents the high point of Osborn's evangelical leadership. At that point the Osborns hosted private religious groups every evening of the week. On Thursdays and Saturdays, Osborn hosted and catechized the children of her school, joined by many more in the town – sixty-four girls and nineteen boys respectively. On Monday evenings, between forty and fifty young women, between 9 and 20 years old, met at her home for prayer and instruction; on Tuesdays, a number of boys did the same. In addition to the children and her women's society (Wednesdays), there were Sunday gatherings of African-American Christians, a society of young white men who met in a different room, and a Friday evening meeting of a number of heads of families who gathered for private devotions and "religious conversation."[58] The formation of private prayer groups was not an innovation. Puritan dissenters had a long history seeking spiritual succor in private groups: some because they found nothing edifying in their congregational pastors; others craving more than regular meetings and preachings provided. As Barbara Lacey has suggested in her study of women and the Great Awakening, this development of religious societies gathered according to gender, race, and age reflects the upswing in religiosity in the city and indicates that many believers were not fully satisfied by the established church.[59] Like Anne Hutchinson before her, Sarah Osborn found herself the leader of more than a women's group, and, like Hutchinson, she came under ministerial criticism. Yet, while Hutchinson ended up excommunicated and driven out of her community, Osborn and her women's group worked and canvassed until they had effected the call of Samuel Hopkins to the congregation in Newport.[60]

Fish had long approved of the women's group and Osborn's role in it. He was "much pleasd & edifyd with your acct of the Female Religious Society...I saw nothing Savouring of Vain Ostentation in anything you Said of...the Society."[61] However, after she had told him of the proliferation of her religious activities, he must have responded critically, for her letter was followed eight months later by a second one defending her meetings and her leadership. Osborn's self-defense moved in several separate directions, providing a broad introduction to her religious activities and mind-set. In response to one set of criticisms, she quickly retreated from any implication that she was teaching men: "I have no thing to do with them, only Have the pleasure of Seting my candlestick and Stool. This convenient retire Habitation God gave me in answer to prayer,...and I cant Help rejoicing in opportunity to improve it." Satisfied merely to sit among them and listen, Osborn expressed pleasure that the men never invited "ministers disapprovd of." In this realm, as well, she noted that those who met at her home on Friday evenings directed their own gathering. "I by no means Set up for their instructor. They come indeed for Mutual Edification and Sometimes condescend to direct part of conversation to me and so far I bear a part as to answer etc., but no otherway."[62]

A second justification was that no one but herself would take on the responsibility. In regards to the meeting for African Americans, she assured him that "My Revd Pastor and Brethren are my wittnesses that I Have earnestly Sought, yea in bitterness of Soul, for their assistance and protection." She expressed concern that she was moving outside of her sphere: "To avoid Moving beyond my Line, while I was anxiously desirous the poor creatures should be favrd with some sutable one to pray with them, I was Greatly distresst; but as I could not obtain [help] I Have Given it up...." However, since no pastor would become involved, she took the duty upon herself, reassuring Fish that her role lay within acceptable boundaries. "I only read to them talk to them and sing a Psalm or Hymn with them....They call it School and I Had rather it should be calld almost any thing that is good than Meeting, I reluct so much at being that Head of anything that bears that Name...." Further, she delighted in the apparent devotion of the participants. The African Americans "cling and beg for the Priviledge and no weathers this winter stops them from Enjoying it." She was especially pleased at the change in behavior and sexual morals that she noted within the community.[63]

What is interesting is that Osborn appeared much less defensive, much more confident in her response to what seems to modern ears a far more insulting challenge. Eight months before, she had written to Fish in the joy of her success, eager to tell him of God's workings through her home. In his response, Fish apparently asked "Have you Strength ability and Time consistent with other Duties to fill a Larger sphere by attending the various Exercises of other Meetings, in close succession too." Osborn's response revealed the power that an evangelical woman could reap from her relationship with God. "As to Strength Sir it is Evident I gain by Spending; God will in no wise suffer me to be a Looser by His Service...I always feel stronger when my companies break up then when they come in...." She found that her health actually improved through a winter of almost constant meetings of religious societies. The question of ability struck her as a false one, since no person had any ability to lead souls to God except through divine grace. "I trust christs Strength is Made perfect in my weakness, and at sometimes am Made open to Glory Even in my infirmities, that the Power of christ May rest upon me and rejoice that I am nothing and can do nothing without Him." As to house-hold duties, she noted that she was assisted by the parents of many children of her school. She clearly scorned the place of a woman with "a full purse and Nothing to do but Look after" her family. If God had called her and was using her to his glory (and from her perspective the proof lay in the flourishing results), then she had no right to flee that responsibility or turn away from such leadership.[64]

Explorations of Great Awakening always return to questions of power, the power that lodged in the Holy Spirit. The Awakening's proponents, like seventeenth-century Puritans, privileged the work of the Spirit; but, unlike Puritans, evangelicals had lost the balancing emphasis upon learning. Those who did emphasize erudition had left this fold entirely, and while individual ministers like Jonathan Edwards or Gilbert Tennent were certainly highly educated clerics, their original discussions of spiritual progress focused almost entirely upon the actions of grace within the heart. The futility of intellectual study as a spiritual method led New Light preachers to highlight the simple yet intense piety of a child as a model for faith. In the gendered and racialized thinking of this new Enlightenment era, the attainments of the adult mind were associated with European men, and women and African Americans were judged to be simpler. In their childlikeness, both women and African Americans came to represent the quintessential spiritual convert. In Edwards' *Faithful Narrative*, his two examples of Awakening converts were the young, unmarried women, Abigail Hutchinson and Phebe Bartlet, a 4-year-old girl who spent most of her time praying, instructing other children, and listening to ministers.[65]

In privileging heart over mind and love over reason, the evangelicals opened the doors of authority to a whole new community of the dispossessed. Education was generally a marker of class and a guarantor of status, but the emphasis upon spiritual achievements allowed members of the lower and middling classes to become preachers or lay leaders. Racial boundaries were sometimes crossed, and the talents of a spiritually gifted slave might well be recognized by the evangelical community. The third difficult boundary was, of course, the gender boundary, yet even here within evangelical communities women organized their own spiritual networks and provided guidance to others. In some congregations, women were involved in administrative and disciplinary decisions, and a few singular women found within the power of the Spirit a voice and authority all to themselves. As Sarah Osborn (with the confident humility of the gracious convert) described herself and her call to leadership, she was

> a Servant that Has a Great work assignd Him and However unworthy and unequal he may think Himself, and others may think Him, and However ardently He may wish it was in Superior Hands or that His Master would at Least Help Him, yet if He declines He dares not tell Him, well if you dont do it your self it shall go undone....Dont think me obstinate then Sir if I dont know How to Let Go these shoals of fish (to which my dear Susa compares them) that we Hope God as Gatherd ready to be caught in the Gospel Net when Ever it shall please Him to shew His dear Ministers on which side the ship to Let it down for advanight – the Harvest truely appears to be Plenteous but the Labourers are few.[66]

Toward the later years of the Awakening era, New Light ministers became disenchanted. Like their Puritan forebears, they sought the empowering authority of the Holy Spirit when it reinforced their own pastoral leadership and gave them an edge over other power holders (that is, clerical rivals). They applauded the laity's support of their ministry and encouraged congregants to forsake any pastor who failed to evidence a true experience of the Spirit. Also like their Puritan forebears, they stopped short when they realized that such authority could also be used against them. Gilbert Tennent, who himself had supported, even encouraged, dissatisfied laypersons to change pastors, came to attack the Moravians for "dividing" congregations. White southerners grew uneasy with granting spiritual authority to African-American preachers, while northern white evangelicals would soon stop short of acknowledging the full ability of the black Christian community to govern itself. And many clergymen and laymen would become unhappy about the religious authority that women had assumed. Initially, Sarah Osborn had received extensive support from Newport's ministers in her efforts to serve the religious community. By 1766, however, their assistance was withdrawn as clergy came to realize that she attracted larger audiences than they did.[67] By the beginning of the nineteenth century, the authority extended to women would begin to be rescinded, but these few decades in the middle of the eighteenth century stood as a brief time when women again felt, not only the thrill, but the rewards of grace.

# 6 Gender, revolution, and the Methodists

At the close of the eighteenth century, the landscape of the British colonies had changed dramatically. Politically, these were no longer separate colonies but states united in a national republic whose constitution had been ratified twelve years before. The disparate colonies had banded together in 1776 to declare themselves independent of British colonial authority, and after eight years of warfare that independence had been recognized by Great Britain. Economically, the nation of agriculture and commerce began to explore the promising possibilities of industrial production. Geographically, the settlement frontier continued to move west at an extraordinary pace, opening opportunities for settlers and igniting more conflicts with native Americans. By 1800, the nation of thirteen states had become sixteen, including not only another New England state, Vermont, but the western states Kentucky and Tennessee. By 1820, the nation had twenty-four states, industrialization had taken hold, the frontier approached the Mississippi River, and, within the decade, native Americans east of the Mississippi faced removal from their homelands. As the nation expanded, the intoxicating independence, moving frontier, and republican politics combined to transform society, culture, and religion.

In the summer of 1801, Cane Ridge, Kentucky rocked with the excitement of an immense revival. Growing out of a season of massive Presbyterian communion services, the Cane Ridge Revival was attended by 10,000 to 20,000 settlers. Although scheduled as a communion service, pastor Barton Warren Stone invited Methodist and Baptist pastors and preachers, as well as other Presbyterians, to preach. For six or seven days and nights, men, women, and children listened to preachers, read the Bible, prayed to God, and testified to each other. One observer described

> assembled in the woods, ministers preaching day and night; the camp illuminated with candles, on trees, at wagons, and at the tent; persons falling down, and carried out of the crowd....If they speak, what they say is attended to, being very solemn and affecting – many are struck under such exhortations. But if they do not recover

soon, praying and singing is kept up, alternatively, and sometimes a minister exhorts over them – for generally a large group of people collect, and stand around, paying attention to prayer and joining in singing. Now suppose 10 of these groups around, a minister engaged in preaching to a large congregation, in the middle, some mourning, some rejoicing, and great solemnity on every countenance, and you will form some imperfect idea of the extraordinary work![1]

They also undoubtedly enjoyed the confluence of people and the chance to see family, renew acquaintances, make friends, and perhaps even find spouses. The magic of this moment was immeasurable, and the impact was awesome. As Stone reported, "The numbers converted will be known only in eternity. Many things transpired there, which were so much like miracles, that if they were not, they had the same effects as miracles on infidels and unbelievers; for many of them by these were convinced that Jesus was the Christ, and bowed in submission to him."[2]

Barton Stone had been inspired by the successes of his older colleague, James McGready. On the sparsely populated frontier, both served several small congregations because none was large enough or wealthy enough to pay or occupy the time of a minister. Central meetings developed as a means of concentrating the pastor's energy and pulling his flock together. McGready had seen the social and geographic isolation of the frontier homestead as both a problem and an opportunity, and he responded with the "camp meeting": a religious gathering of several days for people that were obliged to find shelter and food at the meeting itself because they were so far from home. Wisps of enthusiasm were scented in 1800, but the Cane Ridge Revival really swept the imagination of evangelical empire builders who immediately picked up the camp meeting as a way to bring westerners to the Gospel and conversion and, eventually, into the church. Camp meetings, with their clerical cooperation and popularity among the people, became a primary method of evangelical expansion.

In her memoirs, Zilpha Elaw provided a detailed portrait of the place and progress of such meetings where "the hardest hearts are melted into tenderness; the driest eyes overflow with tears, and the loftiest spirits bow down: the Creator's works are gazed upon, and His near presence felt around." Learning of the place and time from extensive advertisement, "each family takes its own tent, and all things necessary for lodgings, with seats, provisions, and servants; and with waggons and other vehicles repair to the destined spot, which is generally some wildly rural and wooded retreat..." From all over, "hundreds of families, thousands of persons" arrived for a week's prayer and worship. Tents were pitched around a circular enclosure, with the center space saved for the congregation. The minister's platform, of boards and fence rails, was placed on rising ground. At night the place was lighted by bonfires, candles, and lanterns. For six days public preaching, exhortation, testifying, and prayer alternated with smaller, more private meetings:

> at the close of the prayer meeting the grove is teeming with life and activity; the numberless private conferences, the salutations of old friends again meeting in the flesh, the earnest inquiries of sinners, the pressing exhortations of anxious saints, the concourse of pedestrians, the arrival of horses and carriages of all descriptions render the scene portentously interesting and intensely surprising.

On the last day, following a "solemn love feast," everyone packed to leave. To conclude the meeting, a procession led by the preachers marched around the camp, a farewell hymn was sung, and the people, in procession, shook hands with the preachers. "Hundreds of Christians, dear to each other and beloved in the Spirit, embrace each other for the last time and part to meet no more, until the morning of the resurrection."[3]

As in the Great Awakening movement, the effects of the Spirit manifested themselves physically. Like Whitefield's hearers, revival participants screamed, wept, swooned, and heard the voice of God, but this new generation also experienced grace and exhibited its impact in a far more dramatic fashion. Elaw claimed that she sank onto the ground and lay there unmoving, whether "in the body or…out of the body" she did not know. While there her spirit "seemed to ascend up into the clear circle of the sun's disc; and, surrounded and engulphed in the glorious effulgence of his rays," she heard a voice promising to lead her. "I saw no personal appearance while in this stupendous elevation, but I discerned bodies of resplendent light; nor did I appear to be in this world at all, but immensely far above those spreading trees, beneath whose shady and verdant bowers I was then reclined." Awaking from her trance, she found herself surrounded by hundreds of weeping persons, and she knew that "God was so powerfully near to me."[4] At a meeting in 1812, Eliza Hankins fell into a trance, insensible and unmoving for thirty-two hours, and then "jumped up singing and shouting…lighted up with an unearthly radiance." The impact upon the community was enormous. "[T]he whole congregation was overwhelmed, and we felt ourselves in the presence of a superior being, rather than that of an artless, unsophisticated country girl."[5] Stone acknowledged that the behaviors he observed at revivals were often excessive and eccentric, "much have I since seen, that I considered to be fanaticism," but he never doubted the sincerity of his converts or the divine grace precipitating their actions. He remained convinced that the Spirit of God was moving the congregations, and in his memoirs he devoted an entire chapter to recording and interpreting those actions.[6]

Stone reported that all sorts of saints and sinners might be expected to fall senseless, generally following a piercing scream:

At a meeting, two gay young ladies, sisters, were standing together attending to the exercises and preaching at the same time. Instantly they both fell, with a shriek of distress, and lay for more than an hour apparently in a lifeless state.

The young women came to, cried, and then collapsed again, until each began to smile and speak of the glory of the Gospel. Stone also described the jerks (or convulsions), often accompanied with noises like barks:

I have seen the person stand in one place, and jerk backward and forward in quick succession, their head nearly touching the floor behind and before...I do not remember that any one of the thousands I have seen ever sustained an injury in body.

Some bodily exercises were peculiar to saints. The newly converted might dance as the "smile of heaven shone on the countenance...While thus exercised, I have heard their solemn praises and prayers ascending to God." They also laughed while remaining "rapturously solemn," and sang not from the mouth or nose, but entirely from the breast. Not surprisingly,

such music silenced everything, and attracted the attention of all. It was most heavenly...Doctor J.P. Campbell and myself were together at a meeting, and were attending to a pious lady thus exercised, and concluded it to be something surpassing anything we had known in nature."[7]

John Lyle reported that at Cane Ridge at least two-thirds of those affected were women and children, although historian Paul Conkin found that the physical exercises were not restricted to any particular race or class. Even a few ministers and professional men were overwhelmed by the actions of the Spirit.[8]

In some ways the camp meeting seems a slightly modified version of a Great Awakening revival; at other points the religiosity of the early nineteenth century resembles an unwieldy, unruly offspring determined to establish its distinction from the past. In both eras, clerical leaders were particularly gifted preachers who first called all their listeners to repentance and later explored the promise and glory of Jesus' atonement and God's saving grace. The impact of sermons upon the listeners was often immediate and tangible, setting off emotional responses sometimes reflected in bodily afflictions, although these seem to be more extreme in the later period. There remained an emphasis upon the spiritual journey of the individual believer, along with the conviction that this journey could be effectively promoted within a community of revival participants. However, in the eighteenth century the community process generally involved a home congregation; even an itinerant preacher depended upon the home church to continue the work of individual conversion. Later, the community was the camp meeting itself, and the complete transformation often occurred during the week of the revival. This may well have been an accommodation to the realities of the geography. Where believers scattered about a vast frontier could only be served by traveling pastors, where there were no permanent spiritual resources, the camp meeting had to provide not only the sinners' alarm, but the entire environmental support for conversion. A process that had taken many years in the seventeenth century had been significantly reduced to one or two years of preparation and an immediate moment of enlightenment in the eighteenth. Now, the entire experience was collapsed into a seven-day event. Perhaps this need to compact a transformative spiritual experience into a few days increased the intensity of the experience and the violence of the physical manifestations.

In addition to these differences in degrees of enthusiasm and speed of conversion, a few more substantive changes appeared. The organization of the revivals became amazingly careful and complicated, and it was done exceedingly well. Denominations coordinated revival schedules, preaching invitations, and camp services, and they advertised meetings across a region. Preachers began to grant explicitly that these were social occasions, almost as if they were planning to take advantage of a festival for proselytizing. The nineteenth-century revival leader was also a more sophisticated student of human psychology. George Whitefield judged every aspect of his career and his success as a reflection of the presence of the Spirit. Providence had led him to North America to preach among people hungry for the word of God. Nineteenth-century revivalists certainly believed in the outpourings of the Spirit, but ministers saw not the overarching hand of providence as much as humanly organized opportunities for individuals, who made choices, to find God. The hand of human organization could be seen in the formal layout of the grounds, the provision of food, water, and fodder, as well as in the organization of the meeting's activities. The seating was segregated by sex and race, with women on one side, men on the other, white people in front and black hearers in the back. The preaching leadership was largely white and male, with black male exhorters often brought to preach specifically to the black audience. African-American and Euro-American women did participate vocally, but in lesser roles, such as counseling individuals who had been convinced. Where they were most likely to be seen was in the arena still controlled by the Spirit: some individuals felt called to testify to their own experiences; others, among the convicted, rose to the leadership within the small groups of awakened sinners as leaders in prayer, singing, or exhortation.[9]

By 1800, the common-man ministry had arrived. Education was nothing, spiritual inspiration was everything, and any man who felt the call could be examined and then ordained to preach or lead a congregation. Thus, fairly early, Presbyterians found themselves outside the evangelical network. The excesses of revival participants was difficult enough, but the national denomination, unstintingly committed to an educated clergy and knowledgeable laity, had deep troubles with the rising anti-intellectualism. Even worse, a rising Arminian theological trajectory countermanded the basic doctrines of the established Calvinist churches.

Eighteenth-century evangelicals had remained dedicated to the predestinarian Calvinism of the seventeenth century; the Tennents had even convinced George Whitefield of the truth of Calvinist theology. By 1820, evangelicals had almost completely turned away from patient passivity to calling for an active seeking after God. As providence had given way to human planning in the matter of camp meetings, so the salvation of sinners was now connected to their own efforts. Those dedicated to predestination and tied to the hope of God's irresistible grace, now heard about the potential (and need) for self-intervention in their own salvation. No more were the elect a small, exclusive enclave closed to all except by God's arbitrary and predetermined will. Now, any person with the will to turn to God could do so and be saved. For settlers whose lives demonstrated daily their capacities to control their environments and build families, farms, and towns in the wilderness, a theology offering some human control was extremely attractive and, in the end, reasonable.

Preachers and congregants on the frontier resisted not only the limitations of Calvinist theology but also those of the church organization itself. Barton Stone rejected the entire Presbyterian hierarchical structure as well as its doctrine and grew interested in the rising "Christian Connection," a movement of men and women who found all denominational strictures false and divisive. In their rejection of church traditions, they pushed their egalitarian potential even further. The absence of ordination procedures and examination committees opened the way for several women preachers.

Nancy Mulkey, the daughter and sister of popular Christian preachers, became widely known for brief exhortations:

> She would arise with zeal on her countenance and fire in her eyes, and with a pathos that showed the depth of her soul, and would pour forth an exhortation lasting from five to fifteen minutes, which neither father nor brother could *equal*, and which brought tears from every feeling eye.[10]

Another fairly young woman, Nancy Gove Cram, enjoyed four years of preaching in fields and barns on the New York frontier and published her own collection of hymns and poems before she died in 1815. Amidst her great success she drew the wrath of several Presbyterians for both her revivalist cant and her gender.

> She is remarkable, neither for the delicacy of mind, which is the ornament of her sex, nor for that information and good sense, by which so many of them are characterized. She is abundantly gifted with that spirit of her head, which opposes literature, order, and whatever christians usually have considered, as of vital importance to the interests of religion…[S]he never studies, and *compliments* her Maker with being the author of crude invectives.

One leader of the Christian church claimed that at least seven active ministers were converted under her influence. One of her converts, Abigail Roberts, was instrumental in the founding of four churches.[11] A third Nancy, Nancy Towle, dreamed that she was called to preach, and, although she received no support, she embarked upon an itinerant ministry that would take her over 15,000 miles through the northeast, the south, Canada, Ireland, and England. She described encounters with women preachers among Christians, Freewill Baptists, Universalists, and Methodists, and called for more women to join the preaching work.[12]

Among the Christians and Freewill Baptists, Catherine Brekus has counted at least forty-one women preachers. These women were not ordained or even licensed, but they became known through letters of commendation, among the Baptists, and the publication of their names in the Minutes of the Christian Conferences in denominational newspapers. In addition to preachers, literally hundreds of women could be found as exhorters throughout these networks, speaking at camp meetings as well as regular parish gatherings. Moreover, they were encouraged and praised by many non-Calvinist clergymen for their "melting exhortations," "ardent prayers," and "powerful testimonies." Although women exhorters could be heard through the nation, women preachers were found primarily in the New England, mid-Atlantic, and midwestern states. In the south Barton Stone and his colleagues established the Disciples of Christ, very like the Christian Conference except in two things. They closed the pulpit to women and permitted no challenge to clerical authority from women, slaves, or even free laymen.[13]

While evangelical Presbyterians grew increasingly uncomfortable with their unsympathetic, inflexible hierarchical structure, an alternative denominational network, almost synonymous with inflexible hierarchical structure arose to propound Arminian evangelicalism: the highly organized (and amazingly successful) Methodist Church. The first systematic Methodist preaching began in the mid-Atlantic colonies in the 1760s. They were rather successful fairly quickly, and in 1771 John Wesley appointed Francis Asbury as the "Superintendent of the American Colonies." A brilliant organizer and indefatigable worker,

Asbury developed a structure, recruited preachers, and inspired their labors. Finding fewer than 1,000 members in 1771, Asbury and his staff more than doubled the membership in only two years. Conversions continued during the Revolutionary War itself, and, by 1781, the Methodists counted 10,000 followers. After the war's end and the final separation from England, an independent Methodist Church in 1784 gathered the growing constituency of 15,000 into a single church network.

Methodist preaching followed the evangelical style of the Baptists, and they appealed with equal success across regional and racial lines. In addition to the Euro-American urban dwellers and farmers, in both the coastal east and expanding frontier Methodists recruited a considerable number of African Americans, both free and slave, into their churches. While Baptists allowed congregations to organize themselves wherever the opportunity and the Spirit appeared, Methodists imposed the complex, hierarchical, and highly successful system of circuits and conferences pioneered by Asbury. Preachers were assigned to serve one circuit of stations serving small groups, or classes. The system was well suited to the dispersed population of the new nation, particularly the west, and it published the Gospel message fairly quickly. This extraordinary organization, its rhetorically skillful preachers, a fiery message of threatened damnation and promised salvation, and a commitment to individual spiritual authority and ability, provided the basis for amazing growth. By 1800, the denomination had almost 65,000 members; twenty years later, nearly 250,000; and, by 1830, more than 500,000. In 1850, with more than 1,000,000 members, the Methodist churches (for there were now several) reflected the largest evangelical network in the United States. They numerically dominated the west, represented the majority of southern churchgoers, and in New England, that bastion of Calvinism, were the second largest church.[14]

Like most reformed churches in North America, Methodism arose and migrated from England. John Wesley, the fifteenth child of an Anglican clergyman, Samuel, and his extremely pious wife, Susannah, planned to follow his father as a respectable Anglican priest; but he soon found himself following his mother's intensely pietistic lead. With his younger brother Charles he gathered his "Holy Club," or "Methodists," while a fellow at Oxford. His interest in the British colonies led him, in 1735, to missionize for the Society for the Propagation of the Gospel in Georgia, where he proceeded to alienate the colonists with his anti-slavery stance. Upon his return to England, he began to hear his own call to evangelical leadership. Although ordained in the Anglican Church, he did not accept a pastorate; rather he, like Whitefield, envisioned himself as an itinerant gathering souls to God. He traveled thousands of miles on horseback every year, covered the entirety of the British Isles in his "circuit", and preached in fields and foundries to farmers, miners, workers, and their wives and children.

Wesleyan theology was distinctly Arminian, and, while Wesley never denied the need and efficacy of grace, he left significant responsibility on the shoulders of the believer. The structure and language of his sermons and letters incorporated powerful evangelical models, appealing to the senses and emotions to affect his most hardhearted listeners. He admired Jonathan Edwards as a spiritual leader, despite their theological differences, and he worked to make Edwards' writing on experimental religion available in England. Like the Great Awakening preachers in the colonies, Wesley struggled not to educate but to guide, encourage, or force his listeners to the brink of despair and beyond to the joy growing out of the assurances of faith. Critical of the Anglican Church for its self-absorption and spiritual aridity, he denied the need for extended theological education and challenged the efficacy of sermons designed merely to impress the hearer with stylistic elegance. Wesley advocated a plain style, like the Puritans, and believed the Gospel message was available to all who opened their hearts. He followed a call to the poor and middling classes, among whom he enjoyed great popularity. Fairly early Wesley established a support system that could continue the work of conversion as he moved on to preach elsewhere. Early in the movement's history, he recognized spiritual gifts among laypersons and opened the way for lay leaders to teach, minister, even preach, in his absence. In 1744 he held a conference of lay preachers that later became an annual meeting and would, eventually, form the foundation of the separate Methodist Church.

From the beginning women played an important role in the Wesleyan movement, though it was with ambivalence that Wesley and many of his female disciples faced this question. Against his conviction that women had no appropriate public role in the church, Wesley had the example of his mother Susannah. The wife of a priest and the mother of many children, she was also known throughout her neighborhood for piety and wisdom. Stories indicate that she held herself in subjection to her husband, yet her husband was away from home a great deal, and on those occasions she held family prayers and directed scriptural study. In those seasons her audience could grow quite large, though in humble fashion she explained that the increase was accidental, implying, of course, that it was the work of the Holy Spirit. She often proclaimed the domesticity of her work, arguing that her efforts fell within the private world of women, even though many who were not family attended. In the winter of 1711, with her husband gone and the parish under the care of a weak curate, she led a Sunday-evening society that reputedly had 200 people attending. According to accounts, the curate complained to Samuel, he challenged his wife, and she agreed to obey his decision. However, she warned,

If you do, after all, think fit to dissolve this assembly, do not tell me that you desire me to do it, for that will not satisfy my conscience: but send me your *positive command*, in such full and express terms as may absolve me from all guilt and punishment for neglecting this opportunity of doing good when you and I shall appear before the great and awful tribunal of our Lord Jesus Christ.[15]

Granting her husband's authority as well as the dictum that women should not have a public ministry, Susannah Wesley nonetheless took upon herself a neighborhood leadership in witnessing and pastoral care under the protective umbrella of domesticity.

Through his mother's example, Wesley had an original sense of the power of women's spiritual leadership. As his movement grew and evolved, he became increasingly aware of women's potential. Moreover, several factors made it easier for him to accept women's preaching with the same grace that his father had acknowledged Susannah. Methodism was a movement within an established church. All leaders of the movement, unless ordained in the Anglican Church, were lay preachers, so there was never any question of an ordained women's ministry. Also, the movement was growing at a remarkable pace, with classes rising up throughout the country. Leaders of both genders and all classes were needed. Women were regularly found among the most important patrons of the new movement, with many providing meeting houses, paying itinerant's expenses, or holding services in their homes. Alice Cross, for example, organized a small local society and had a pulpit erected in her largest room, to be used as a place of worship, while Selina Hastings, Countess of Huntingdon, provided so much support to Whitefield and his work that she was essentially able to control his network.[16]

Most important, however, was Wesley's own understanding of the call religious leaders heard. As he wrote to one of his strongest preachers, Mary Bosanquet, "I think the strength of the cause rests there: on your having an extraordinary call. So, I am persuaded, has every one of our lay preachers, otherwise, I could not countenance his preaching at all." Like Gilbert Tennent, Jonathan Edwards, and George Whitefield, Wesley saw the movement as the work of the Spirit, "an extraordinary dispensation of His providence. Therefore I do not wonder if several things occur therein which do not fall under ordinary rules of discipline."[17] Thus the way was opened for women like Frances Mortimer, Mary Bosanquet, and Sarah Crosby, whose "words she spoke were clothed with power..."[18] These women, and many others, recorded internal struggles as they answered first the call to conversion and then the call to preach. They grounded their being in the personal experience of God, and, like their sisters across the Atlantic, were swept into the arms of Jesus. Hester Ann Roe Rogers proclaimed the joy she felt:

> I was instantly filled with such humbling depths of love to God, and union with Him, with such discoveries of my own nothingness, as wholly swallowed up my soul in gratitude and praise…This is what I wanted: I am emptied of self and filled with God.[19]

From this promising beginning, Rogers became one of the most important leaders in Macclesfield, a center of the Methodist movement.

The Methodist Connection that Asbury established in the United States was far less open to women's leadership. Women were certainly important in the building of the early Methodist community. Barbara Ruckle Heck has been called the "Mother of American Methodism," having, in 1760, in New York, pressured Philip Embury to form the first Methodist class. She and her husband then continued in their work, organizing a string of Methodist groups in the northern region of the state and, after 1778, in the St. Lawrence River Valley. Prudence Gough, wife of wealthy Marylander Henry Gough, has been immortalized as the quintessence of the godly mistress serving her domestic congregation, leading her husband to conversion, and providing extraordinary hospitality to Asbury and many of his circuit riders.[20]

There was also the pastor's wife, in the person of Catharine Livingston. A wealthy, well-connected woman, she married itinerant Freeborn Garrettson and then served in a fashion similar to Gough, and, through her influence, expanded the movement further. That she experienced the Spirit deeply and found spiritual authority there is unquestionable. She once wrote to a friend of two dreams. In the first, she was to be crucified, while in the second, she "saw my own corps and was greatly shocked at the solemn spectacle. I thought I had another body and was soliciting the servants to remove the old one." The union of the soul to Christ is unmistakable in the images of both the suffering and the resurrection, yet she explained the dreams "by the love of God being so shed abroad in my soul that I could rejoice in God with joy unspeakable and a belief that I was cleansed from all sin."[21] Fanny Newell was the wife of a circuit rider in Maine. She traveled with him and became known for her public prayers. Newell said she had felt a call to preach, but had shrunk back because of female weakness; she referred to her duty to follow this call to preach as her "cross." Despite her own belief that she lacked gifts of eloquence (a perception apparently not shared by her hearers), she finally began exhorting congregations after her husband had finished his sermon. She justified herself through her call: "Whatever may be said against a female speaking, or praying in public, I care not; for when I feel confident that the Lord calls me to speak, I dare not refuse." Her husband accepted her efforts, comparing himself and his wife to Moses and Miriam.[22]

The spiritual authority of these women and their personal power to act for the good of the Methodist Church was impressive. In his laudatory biographical dictionary *The Women of Methodism*, Abel Stevens identified fifteen women deeply involved in the movement. They hosted preachers, organized classes in their homes or neighborhoods, and accompanied Asbury on his journeys. Yet, in titling his chapter "Asbury and his Female Friends," Stevens has revealed much about the limitations of such women's authority.[23] Asbury had once commended a "Sister Jones" for her words in exhortation and prayer along with several "holy women" who spoke at a meeting.[24] But these women were not Nancy Towle. Their activism was restricted to the domestic, private realm, and, while their influence may have spread far, they rarely enjoyed a public voice beyond the local class meeting.

Why did white Methodist women in the United States rarely find the opportunities for preaching or leadership enjoyed by their English foremothers? First, Wesley's approval of women in such roles was always tentative and conditional, never uncomplicated or wholehearted. In extending his approbation he certainly went beyond the tolerance of many of his English colleagues. After his death in 1791, space for strong, public women began to disappear in the English community; it is not surprising that it never took hold in the distant United States. Second, as the Methodist movement separated from the Anglican Church and began to ordain its own ministers, lay preachers became subservient to ordained leaders. While women might have served as lay preachers in either nation, and in fact did serve in England under their extraordinary calls, there was never a suggestion that women could be ordained. Finally, even after separating from the Church of England, English Methodism remained a dissenting church, in opposition to the establishment. Methodist leadership, not recognized by political or religious institutions, was grounded in the authority granted by the Spirit. In the United States, where no church was established, each denomination competed equally for standing and respect. The potential impact of such bourgeois aspirations upon women's leadership was reflected in the history of the divisions within British Methodist communion during the first half of the nineteenth century. The Wesleyans, who placed a premium upon respectability, banned women preachers in 1803, while others, such as the Primitive Methodists and Bible Christians, mirrored their American counterparts in supporting many women among local and itinerant preachers.[25]

This devotion to order was tied in to Asbury's system of Methodist organization, as was his concern about "fraternity" among his preachers. Asbury built the church upon itinerant ministries and did not really approve of settled pastors. He himself did not shy away from these duties, but rode an amazing set of circuits all his life and preferred ministers who rode circuits as well. During his tenure as head of the American church, only circuit riders had voting privileges at the Annual Conference. For Asbury, families represented competing loyalties that would divert the minister from complete dedication to God. As Russell Richey argues, "it was commitment to Christ and to one another that mattered. The hedges around that commitment – celibacy, whiteness, maleness, mobility – only reinforced the primary commitment." Essentially, he gathered around him, at one time or another, literally thousands of young, unmarried men willing to withstand the rigors of weather, terrain, and the risks of solitary travel.[26] It was a life Asbury did not make available to Methodist women, but, considering its hazards, undoubtedly increased if the traveler were female, what woman would dare take on the labor?

Yet the answer cannot lie solely in the risks; Nancy Towle and Nancy Cram did take those same risks onto themselves, as did several African-American Methodist women. The answer only partly lies in Asbury's lack of encouragement. True, he actively divorced the leadership from settled congregations and built up ranks of circuit riders out of local class leaders and preachers. Any particularly gifted man might demonstrate his gifts and be confirmed in a larger ministerial call. Lay preaching, the core of the Methodist network, was an important symbol of the common-man ministry that denied special status to education and wealth. Asbury asserted that a ministerial vocation required that one give up any aspect of being a gentleman, including dress, manners, and financial security. "We must suffer *with* if we labor *for* the poor."[27] Asbury may have envisioned only common men among his preachers, yet his very agenda had built within it the potential for women's activity. Who better to call to women than women preachers? What of women's extraordinary calls? Asbury and his successors did not generally recognize such calls to women, but understanding their reasons is less important then explaining the willingness of people to accept those restrictions. Most white Methodist women who felt a call either parlayed that call into a domestic leadership, that is Christian housewife, or took on the lesser local leadership roles of testifier or class leader. Those who persevered left the Methodist communion, but they were very few indeed.

The problem was not restricted to Methodists. Baptists, who fifty years before had offered opportunities for female authority and influence, were themselves retracting their promises. In upstate New York, Presbyterian James Carnahan denounced itinerant preacher Martha Howell and the Baptist Church that permitted it: "They suffer that woman Jezebel which called herself a prophetess, to teach and to seduce the servants of the Lord." He was also scandalized that Baptists allowed women to participate in disciplinary actions. The Baptists quickly responded that she only witnessed her own experiences and faith, and that she did not preach or teach. The Baptist respondent also dismissed the charges of women's involvement in church affairs, explaining "a majority of the brethren present shall perform the business and the sisters are consulted only to avoid grieving them immeasurably."[28]

Susan Juster has noted that at the beginning of the nineteenth century, despite their growing predominance in Baptist congregations, women had lost most of their congregational authority. Most Baptist men now judged that women had no authority to preach, teach, or pray aloud. One anonymous writer in the *Baptist Magazine* claimed that the prohibition on women's speech was "unlimited."

> I conceive it to be unscriptural for them to speak in the church *at all*, not only by teaching, or by prayer, leading the devotions of the church, but by professing their repentance toward God, and faith in the Lord Jesus Christ, or their future contrition and confidence; by imparting necessary information on any matter; in giving testimony to confirm any fact; in asking or answering any question; or by verbally assenting to or dissenting from, any proposition there...

Obviously, women who, many thought, were not allowed to witness, could no longer vote in congregational affairs. And their voices were heard far less frequently in church meetings. As Baptists moved from ad hoc groups addressing problems on a case by case basis to standing committees, women were systematically excluded. Moreover, when women did speak, they were likely to be silenced or labeled "disorderly."[29]

Betsy Luther of Warren Baptist Church, for example, protested the changed treatment and usage of women in her congregation. Because she had criticized the church, a deacon had said "she was mad," and "she was brass mounted"; he responded to her complaints against him "with levity." Luther bitterly observed that "sisters were formerly capable of executing the business of Committees, and if they were not now, they had better be cut off from the church." A Providence congregation excommunicated Joanna Gano because she had challenged her husband and several other men about their connections with freemasonry. She protested that "my ideas of our Brethren joining the Masonic Society, and the labours I took with them, I thought scriptural, and do still think," but the church "did not exclude Mrs. Gano on account of her opinions...but on account of her hard and unchristian language and conduct." The church granted Gano no place in theological dispute, just as another church denied Luther the right to admonish leaders. Both congregational leaderships, now entirely male, excommunicated these women not for their theological opinions, but for expressing those opinions.[30]

Baptists, like the Methodists, were in part experiencing the polarization that follows an institutionalization process. Just as Asbury created an itinerant ethos that, in its very organization and conceptualization, excluded women, so the Baptists in their search for respectability as a denomination affirmed their status by taking on the nation's views of women and gender difference. Yet if respectability was sought, why were class boundaries still crossed? For many clerics of the old school – Presbyterians, Congregationalists, Episcopalians – maintaining class, racial, and gender differences provided the foundation of order. Many new evangelicals, especially the more organized churches, found maintaining gender difference to be essential even as they worked to eradicate class differences. This assignment of women to subordinate roles despite a language and rhetoric privileging the spiritual call indicates in and of itself a changed meaning of and lesser import given to the concept of spiritual calling. If all depended upon divine grace, there would have been a continued recognition of women's potential equality. That women were usually not perceived as equal participants reveals that the basis of common-man ministry no longer lay entirely in the actions of God, but now owed some debt to the actions of man. This reflected the changing theology that placed more responsibility upon the shoulders of believers and denounced passivity, a feminine characteristic, as a viable pathway to salvation. In short, the crossing of class boundaries had less to do with a faith in the Spirit than with changing perceptions of human nature and human capacity.

In this sense, the answer lay beyond the parochial world of preaching and congregations to the changing social climate and its impact upon evangelical communities. This gender/class counterpoint was neither contradiction nor coincidence. Rather, these two ideological forces combined with other beliefs and circumstances to constitute the popular, democratic ethos that would characterize turn-of-the-century politics and insinuate itself into religion. As Gordon Wood has argued, the American Revolution transformed the ideological framework within which individuals were judged and the boundaries around which their relationships were formed.[31]

When the framers of the constitution established the new government, they expected to involve the populace in extremely limited ways while a small elite ran the nation. Most leaders distrusted the people as, at best, stupid and gullible. The populace could turn into an uncontrollable mob, as demonstrated by urban riots during the decade preceding the war, and the new leaders, fearing all tyrannies, ultimately feared tyranny of the majority. Some men were suited to lead, while most followed, yet any assumption that some naturally rose to join the elite while others remained fixed among the masses was no longer accepted uncontested. The phrase "all men are created equal" was not mere rhetoric but the expression of a commitment to an equality of nature shared by all before circumstances interfered. Physician Benjamin Rush noted that

> Human nature is the same in all ages and countries, and all the differences we perceive in its characters in respect to virtue and vice, knowledge and ignorance, may be accounted for from climate,

country, degrees of civilization, forms of government, or accidental causes.[32]

While the republic's creators valued the improving forces of education, taste, and manners, many believed that common sense and experience was needed to counterbalance the conceit and arrogance that easily arose from a privileged background. Among his pseudonyms, John Adams sometimes argued in the persona of "Humphrey Ploughjogger," a semi-illiterate farmer whose clear insights were not cluttered by superfluous education. Ploughjogger sneered at the "better sort," who considered "talents to excel as extreamly scarce, indulged by Nature to very few, and unattainable by all the Rest." This he compared to the Calvinist doctrine of election, a "vanity" that suggested that "God elected a precious few...to Life eternal without regard to any forseen Virtue, and repro-bated all the Rest, without regard to any forseen Vice." And while he was not well read in political philosophy, Adams's Ploughjogger believed himself to have more sense.[33]

Adams, Jefferson, and others believed not in a leveled human condi-tion, but in a range of talent and intelligence that appeared across the spectrum of classes. What was necessary was that opportunities were available for all men to test their mettle and pursue their goals, for the good of the men and the good of the nation. They denied neither the value of learning nor the reality of differences among men; indeed, the founders of the republic believed that the nation should be governed by those who were both knowledgeable and virtuous. They merely noted that the chance to become knowledgeable and virtuous should be avail-able to all, a concern reflected in the debates about individual liberties and the creation and ratification of the Bill of Rights.

However, discussions of rights soon gave way to discussions of abili-ties and responsibilities. Those first representatives quickly discovered that they did not agree on key government policies, and as competing programs and philosophies captured competing interests, political parties appeared. In order to serve the nation, leaders had to win elec-tions, and in order to win they needed votes. In this electioneering, people began to hear of their own ability to choose governors and deter-mine policies. The franchise was expanding ever outward until, in 1824, almost all states had universal white manhood suffrage. A stunning anti-intellectual tone overarched much of the political debate, and human equality was reconstructed with a leveling thrust: the equality of all men was assumed in their natural human condition.

Theories of humanity grounded not in political argument but natural philosophy appealed to Enlightenment minds rejecting the privilege of birth and to ordinary minds unwilling to grant others any superior ability to rule over them. This rhetoric empowered the social inferior by denying either the reality or the significance of differences and, instead, embracing a model of baseline similarity. Nevertheless, such a language need not eradicate all differences characterizing the human condition; it could, by naturalizing key distinctions, discount entire classes of persons. Race, for example, became a prime target of debate. Thomas Jefferson has become famous for his own convoluted writings on racial inequality and his failure to consider native Americans and, especially, Africans as the natural equals of Europeans.[34] Africans provided much food for discussion, for, as some Enlightenment writers argued, the inequalities and constrictions of slavery could easily account for any supposed intellectual or moral inferiority. Gender was, apparently, an easier target. Women's essential difference from and inferiority to men was hardly debated by male intellectuals, merely assumed and invoked to rationalize the continued subordination of women. (This natural philosophy framework was so pervasive through the first two-thirds of the nineteenth century that when women such as Sarah Grimke, Elizabeth Cady Stanton, and Susan B. Anthony began to argue for women's equality, they challenged the assumption that women and men were naturally different, arguing instead that they shared the basic essence of humanity.)

The rhetoric of citizenship was from the beginning a white, masculine language. The racial inferiority of African Americans was judged to make them mentally and emotionally unfit for citizenship. The social and economic needs of the white moneyed classes, north and south, resulted in a 1787 constitution (and its 1791 Bill of Rights) that, amidst all its discussion of representative government and individual liberties, implicitly excluded African Americans from that government and explicitly protected the institution of slavery. Before the law, most Africans not only had no personhood – no humanity, but as slaves, their status was chattel under the complete control of an owner. Free African Americans, while enjoying limited personal freedoms of movement, labor, and property ownership, were often excluded from basic privileges of citizenship such as voting. In similar fashion women were made dependents within the republic. Just as wives enjoyed no legal identity under coverture, but had their being subsumed under their husband's, so women had no political personhood apart from men who represented them. As in the case of African Americans, this was explained in terms of women's natural mental and emotional unfitness to participate in government. It was not that the lives of women or African Americans had changed: their circumstances had not changed, and that fact pointed up the progress that had been made by non-elite white men in the cause of republican liberty.[35]

In opening the political arena to all comers regardless of class or wealth, that is, in expanding white manhood suffrage, participation in government at any level from holding national office to merely voting in local elections became a signifier of manliness. Debating politics, organizing parades, and running for office were performances of civic duty and, by extension, performances of masculinity. While slaves, free Africans, and white women might enjoy patriotic celebrations and election parades, their attendance as non-participatory observers pointed up the citizenship of white men. They were, in effect, an audience for the public performance of white masculinity and civic virtue. In the new republic all free, white men were citizens, employing their talents for the good of the nation; women were reconstructed (and praised) as producers of citizens – republican mothers.[36]

This Enlightenment language of the natural equality of men, the political realities of increased popular participation in elections, and the flattering language used by candidates to attract support all infected religious discourse. Nathan Hatch writes of the "democratization" of American Christianity, arguing that these cultural and political forces undermined the significance of class and education as ideological organizers of human society. The rising Arminianism reflected this new reluctance to set apart an "elect" community of saints while the common-man ministry of the evangelicals accompanied the increasingly anti-intellectual bias of a nation that sometimes sneered at learning and taste as effete and useless. This perception of education as irrelevant was also apparent in a growing faith in the individual's ability to interpret the Bible for himself. The educated ministry, like the virtuous citizenry, earned significantly less respect and deference than had been the case even eighty years before.[37]

Evangelicals considered themselves children of the Spirit; they were, in fact, children of the Enlightenment and the democratic revolution. In granting the role of human activity in pursuing spiritual fulfillment, evangelicals simply followed the guidance provided by eighteenth-century culture. They also differed from their Puritan ancestors in that they no longer respected as natural ranks of birth, wealth, and education. In other words, evangelicals rejected both predestination and providence. However, they retained a surprising similarity with their forbears in two respects. First, in perceptions of women and gender difference. Their analytical framework may have differed, but both seventeenth-century Puritans and nineteenth-century evangelicals understood women to be by nature essentially different from and inferior to men. Second, despite the contrary cultural forces of a high regard for social rank or a new respect for human ability, both communities believed in the actual working of the Spirit among individual believers. The new democratic ideology and the solidifying denominational structures could easily account for the new opportunities offered to lower and middling class white evangelical men, as well as closing down similar options for African Americans and women. However, the insistent appearance of women and African Americans among the preaching leadership reflected a legacy, however grudgingly recognized, of the continued work of the Holy Spirit among the people of God.

Like the Baptists, the Methodists experienced extraordinary success among African Americans, enslaved and free, at the turn of the century. Itinerant Thomas Rankin wrote of one meeting:

> I preached from Ezekiel's vision of the dry bones: "And there was a great shaking." I was obliged to stop again and again, and beg of the people to compose themselves, But they could not: some on their knees and some on their faces, were crying mightily to God all the time I was preaching. Hundreds of Negroes were among them, with the tears streaming down their faces.

The Holy Spirit was active indeed, and in Petersburg Rankin had no problem identifying his grace. "Such power descended that hundreds fell to the ground, and the house seemed to shake with the presence of God. The chapel was full of white and black, and many were without that could not get in." Francis Asbury's journal is filled with notices of large African-American communities experiencing grace at his sermons. So many slaves became Methodists that advertisements for runaways often described slaves as Methodist exhorters. By 1800, the conference estimated that 20,000 African Americans were Methodist, representing a third of the American Methodist population.[38]

The appeal of evangelicalism in 1800 had remained the same over fifty years. Evangelicals continued to pursue converts from all classes, regions, and races. Indeed, Methodist theology required that itinerants seek after the dispossessed. As early as 1787, the Annual Conference required preachers to try everything "for the spiritual benefit and salvation of the Negroes." Asbury felt great joy that experiential religion again flourished among Africans, and he reminded preachers that "these are the poor, these are the people we are more immediately called to preach to."[39] Of significance, too, was the culture surrounding the work and lives of the itinerants. With their meager salaries, abstemious conduct, and modest worldly attainments, Methodist preachers appeared and behaved as men who knew poverty and valued the virtues of those who survived. Additionally, several notable black preachers and exhorters were found in the Methodist ranks, accomplishing two goals at once. The church put forward those best able, through common experience, to communicate successfully with slaves and free blacks and, at the same time, signified their commitment to spiritual equality.

Most important, however, was the continued fit of evangelical religiosity to African-American culture. Methodists did not reject the emotional enthusiasm of the people: Asbury himself ordered the conference to "attend to preaching, prayer, class meeting, and love feast; and then, if they will shout, why let them shout."[40] Methodists highly valued music in both prayer and education, and Africans were a deeply musical people. Moreover, among Baptists and Methodists, this encouragement of religious sensibility was accompanied by a style of preaching that was simple, clear, and therefore immediately understood as well as experienced. Richard Allen knew of "no religious sect or denomination that would suit the capacity of the colored people as well as the Methodist…" In his own experience,

> The Methodists were the first people that brought glad tidings to the colored people…We are beholden to the Methodists, under God, for the light of the gospel we enjoy; for all other denominations preached so high-flown that we were not able to comprehend their doctrine. Sure am I that reading sermons will never prove so beneficial to the colored people as spiritual or extempore preaching. I am well convinced that the Methodist has proved beneficial to thousands and ten times thousands.[41]

The appeal of Methodism was in a simplicity that could engage the uneducated and unsophisticated and a religiosity that appealed to many African-American communities. Just how many is unknown. Albert Raboteau believes that, as late as 1820, the majority of slaves "remained only minimally touched by Christianity," with evangelical religion having made its greatest strides among house servants, artisans, and urban slaves. Gary Nash, on the other hand, has argued that in Philadelphia the membership of the African evangelical churches represented at least a third of the black population and probably much more.[42]

As early as 1800 race politics appeared to destroy the simple equality presumed by the evangelical ethos. The Methodists had taken credible anti-slavery stands, with many white converts freeing their slaves. However, the Conferences of 1804 and 1808 omitted the chapter on slavery from the new version of the *Discipline*. The first Methodist *Discipline* limited the office of class leader to white persons. Among Baptists, the decline in authority felt by women was echoed in the black community. For example, the Portsmouth Baptist Association had, in 1794, allowed free black men to represent churches in association meetings; in 1828 the association ruled that black churches must be represented through white men.[43] The denominations were changing, but at the same time a black theology and community ethos was developing parallel to, rather than out of, white evangelical church and thought. Slaves David George and George Liele founded a separate Baptist church in Silver Bluff, South Carolina, and one of their converts, Andrew Bryan, gathered a separate church near Savannah that by 1790 boasted 225 full members and 350 potential converts. Separate black churches in Williamsburg and Petersburg (Virginia) and Lexington

(Kentucky) all spoke to the ability of African Americans to pursue their Christian vision independent of their masters.[44]

The most extensive, separate African church network was the African Methodist Episcopal (AME) Church, founded by Richard Allen in the wake of discrimination and hostility black congregants experienced at Philadelphia's St. George's Methodist Church.[45] One of the leaders who established the first African Church in Philadelphia, Richard Allen left the congregation when they decided to affiliate with the Episcopal Church. In summer 1794, he and other black Methodists, with the blessing of Asbury, built the church of Bethel as a separate black congregation within the Methodist denomination. Allen, ordained by Asbury, was the first black deacon. For more than twenty years, battles were engaged between Bethel and the ruling elders of the Methodist conference who refused to grant Bethel the same autonomy enjoyed by white congregations. Thus, in 1816, Bethel met with delegates from churches in Baltimore and elsewhere, and "taking into consideration their grievances, and in order to secure the privileges, promote union and harmony among themselves," they voted to create the AME Church.[46] Richard Allen was elected as the denomination's first bishop.

The authority of women in black Methodist communities is difficult to discern. The attitude of the black male leadership could probably be best described as ambivalent. For example, at one moment early in the history of Bethel, Allen described a key decision to amend their charter in order to regain authority over their own affairs, and noted that the new supplement was unanimously accepted, "by both male and female." Yet, in the same decade, he had refused to let Dorothy Ripley, an English visitor, preach in the church, and had discouraged the black preacher Jarena Lee. Allen told her that one

> Mrs. Cook...had also some time before requested the same privilege; who it was believed, had done much good in the way of exhortation, and holding prayer meetings; and who had been permitted to do so by the verbal license of the preacher in charge at the time. But as to women preaching, he said that our Discipline knew nothing at all about it – that it did not call for women preachers.

Yet Allen allowed her to hold meetings and exhort as she felt called. Eight years later, after the AME Church had separated, Allen had again the chance to consider her call. Inspired by the Spirit, Lee stood up and preached extemporaneously, and Allen gave her his unqualified support. From that point forward, Allen would support her, despite protests from within his denomination that women should not preach. An excellent reflection of the ambivalence in the church as a whole was that, in 1850, at the annual meeting of the Philadelphia Conference, women who believed themselves called to preach were so numerous that they formed an organization. The association did not last, but at the 1852 General Conference a resolution to license women preachers was defeated by the significant majority of delegates, all of whom were male.[47]

From the time that African Americans joined the evangelical churches in significant numbers, that is from the 1780s onward, black women felt called to preach. How many women actually sought leadership roles or attempted a preaching ministry cannot be known, nor do we have a clear sense of how many women took on local leadership responsibilities. Still, the number of black women who developed serious reputations as preachers remains astonishing. These women converted in a flash of light, heard voices that summoned them to the preaching desk, and felt irresistible impulses to embark upon the itinerant trail, sometimes into great danger. Two of the earliest black female preachers, Jarena Lee and Zilpha Elaw, were members of the AME Church. A third woman, a generation older than Lee and Elaw, published her story under the simple name, Old Elizabeth. That her religious work was performed among Methodists is clear from the language that she used describing the community; whether African Methodist or as a member of the original denomination is not known.

Elizabeth, the oldest of the three children, was born a slave in Maryland in 1766. She was sold twice more, the final time to a Presbyterian who did not believe in permanent slavery. He freed her when she reached thirty years. She did not begin preaching until she was 42, and although her tale is brief it chronicles a successful career as an itinerant preacher who frequently toured the northern states, traveling as far west as Michigan and back again to Pennsylvania when she was 87. There she lived at least ten more years. Jarena Lee and Zilpha Elaw were both born to free parents on the mid-Atlantic seaboard, and each, as a child, was in service in Philadelphia. Both were drawn fairly early to the Methodist Church, and each felt the commission to preach years before she actually embarked upon her first mission around her thirtieth year. As has been noted, Lee waited eight years for denominational approval while Elaw herself tarried for several years.

Two themes dominated the stories all three women told. First, all three emphasized the work of the Spirit in their hearts. Their exceptionally strong connection with the supernatural first exhibited itself in their personal experiences of conversion and sanctification. Elaw experienced conversion while milking a cow, the very ordinariness of her activities pointing up the divine intervention:

> I turned my head, and saw a tall figure approaching, who came and stood by me. He had long hair, which parted in the front and came down on his shoulders; he wore a long white robe down to the feet; and as he stood with open arms and smiled upon me, he disappeared.

She originally thought that the vision may have only been in her mind, except that the cow "bowed her knees and cowered down upon the ground."[48] Elizabeth had the far more terrifying experience of having been left "standing upon the brink of this awful pit...Still, I felt all the while that I was sustained by some invisible power." She continued to struggle, crying for mercy, until she felt herself being raised higher. "Then I thought I was permitted to look straight forward, and saw the Saviour standing with his hand stretched out to receive me...I felt filled with light and love." She was then granted a glimpse of heaven's door, through which she saw "millions of glorified spirits in white robes."[49]

The voice of the Spirit became most insistent in its charge to preach the Gospel, speaking both in direct, verbal instruction as well as in signs and providences. Lee heard a distinct voice say "Go Preach the Gospel...I will put words in your mouth, and will turn your enemies to become your friends." Elaw reported that at a camp meeting "the Lord opened my mouth in public prayer." At one point she was commissioned to go to the family of Elias Boudinot, one of the richest men in Burlington, and, as if in spiritual confirmation, she had great success there. Moreover, she explained, the Spirit not only called, it instructed, "for I enjoyed so intimate and heavenly an intercourse with God, that I was assured He had sent an angel to instruct me in such of His holy mysteries as were otherwise beyond my comprehension."[50] Elizabeth opened a Bible to the text "Gird up thy loins now like a man, and answer thou me. Obey God rather than men." Many people, including church leaders, told her that nothing in scripture sanctioned women preaching, and that the labor was too difficult for women; yet, as she struggled, "there seemed a light from heaven to fall upon me, which banished all my desponding fears, and I was enabled to form a new resolution to go on to prison and to death, if it might be my portion...."[51] Like Sarah Osborn, they read the success of their meetings as signs of divine approval of their labors, and both Lee and Elaw brought tears and joy to listeners in churches, private meetings, and the deathbed. In those moments when they failed to follow God's will, they suffered physically and emotionally. Elaw especially seemed a nineteenth-century Jonah, enduring several long periods of illness, which she interpreted as God's response to her failure to answer the charge.[52]

A second theme that resonated in all the texts was the importance of women's encouragement along the discovery of the vocational path and, afterwards, in facilitating the preacher's meetings. When Elizabeth sought a place for her first meeting, the Spirit sent her to the home of a widow who happily agreed to sponsor her and gathered a meeting of women in the neighborhood. At another point, when she was feeling quite demoralized by the negative comments from the elders, she "felt much moved upon by the Spirit of the Lord, and meeting with an aged sister, I found upon conversing with her that she could sympathize with me in this spiritual work." Elaw was urged toward her call by her sister Hannah who, before her death, had "seen Jesus, and had been in the society of angels." The angel instructed Hannah to tell Zilpha "that she must preach the gospel." Hannah had insisted that the call be taken up that very night, and would have no peace until Elaw left her room. Even as Elaw continued to resist, she received a visit from a female minister who urged her, believing that "god has provided a real work for thy employment." Upon her extraordinary visits to convert a dying man, Lee was accompanied by two women, and even after Allen had encouraged her call, Jarena Lee remained uncertain until the Spirit directed her to the house of a sister, who gathered a small meeting.[53]

None of these women challenged traditional roles for women; Elaw wrote rather heatedly about woman's proper place.

> The boastful speeches too often vented by young females against either the paternal yoke or the government of a husband, is both indecent and impious – conveying a wanton disrespect to the regulation of Scripture:…That woman is dependant on and subject to man, is the dictate of nature; that the man is not created for the woman, but the woman for the man, is that of Scripture.[54]

Yet all of these women traveled unencumbered by family responsibilities. As far as her autobiography shows, Elizabeth was unmarried and childless. Both Elaw and Lee were young widows, and each one left her children in the care of others so that she could travel. Lee told of traveling thirty miles from home even though her son was extremely sick. However, the Spirit upheld her, for "not a thought of my little son came into my mind; it was hid from me, lest I should have been diverted from the work I had to, to look after my son."[55] And, in the very public nature of their labor, they overturned traditional expectations. Elizabeth recorded that her meetings gave great offense, and the town tried to shut down the assembly. "Even the elders of our meeting joined with the wicked people, and said such meetings must be stopped, and that woman quieted. But I was not afraid of any of them, and continued to go, and burnt with a zeal not my own."[56]

Perhaps the most astonishing evidence of spiritual authority was the vast numbers of white men and women that came to hear and were moved by these women. Despite the pretensions of evangelical networks to equality, the United States was thoroughly dominated by a racial ideology buttressed by exploitative economic and disabling legal relationships. Both Elizabeth and Elaw preached in slave states, risking the very real possibility of capture and resale into slavery, yet they continued in the Chesapeake as long as God commanded. After surprising people that "a coloured woman can preach," Elizabeth directly confronted injustice, so that "they strove to imprison me because I spoke against slavery."[57] Lee recorded the success of "a poor coloured woman" through whom the Spirit poured forth: "Though, as I was told, there were lawyers, doctors, and magistrates present, to hear me speak, yet there was mourning and crying among sinners, for the Lord scattered fire among them of his own kindling. The Lord gave his handmaiden power to speak...."[58] Elaw claimed some of her greatest successes among white persons. Her extended work in New England and her later travels in England all pointed to a person of amazing charisma and power. At one point in her travels, she described preaching in a Maryland chapel filled with white proprietors in the main body of the building, and slaves in the gallery. Although the Methodist trustee had asked all listeners to refrain from demonstrating their feelings,

> the powerful operation of the Holy Spirit disdained the limits prescribed by man's reason...the coloured people in the gallery wept aloud and raised vehement cries to heaven; the people below were also unable to restrain their emotions; and all wept beneath the inspiration of the Spirit of grace. I was obliged to stop in my discourse, and give vent to my own feelings, and leave it to God to preach in His own more effectual way.[59]

The language of these preachers clearly lays all responsibility for their labor and their success to the Holy Spirit; all problems or shortfalls are naturally laid to their own failures to follow God's will. They present themselves as vessels through which the Spirit can pour his grace, and in their very passivity they gain power, "for as unseemly as it may appear now-a-days for a woman to preach, it should be remembered that nothing is impossible with God."[60] But they were not trance speakers, and in their battle for recognition of their right to labor, they demonstrated a personal power of their own. They blamed the human actions that denied them their place and, perhaps inadvertently, displayed themselves as women actively following the call of grace. Elizabeth looked "upon man as a very selfish being, when placed in a religious office, to presume to resist the work of the Almighty; because He does not work by man's authority." Jarena Lee warned the church, lest through its bylaws and discipline, they brought "into disrepute even the word of life." And, in direct response to someone's citation of the Pauline position, Elaw engaged in a knowledgeable, perceptive scriptural discussion on women in the early church.

> It is true, that in the ordinary course of Church arrangement and order the Apostle Paul laid it down as a rule, that females should not speak in the church, nor be suffered to teach, but the Scriptures make it evident that this rule was not intended to limit the extraordinary

directions of the Holy Ghost, in reference to female Evangelists, or oracular sisters.

This assertion was followed by a catalogue of female evangelists, including Phebe, Tryphena, Priscilla, the sisters of Nereus, the mother of Rufus, and the four Virgin daughters of Philip. She also noted the prophecy of Joel, that God would pour out his Spirit upon his servants and handmaids. In the book of Acts, Peter asserted that this prophecy was fulfilled on Pentecost, and if this was so, she argued, then "the Christian dispensation has for its main feature the inspirations of the holy prophetic Spirit, descending on the handmaids as well as on the servants of God."[61]

It is important to remember that, while female evangelical preachers might have been recognized, they were permitted to travel and speak as unpaid evangelists, leading onetime meetings or delivering haphazardly scheduled sermons. There was no question of accepting these women into the ordained ranks; they were not even permitted to serve as delegates to the regional conferences. Their relationship to the AME leadership was similar to the relationship of black deacons and preachers to the Methodist Conferences before the separation. Black deacons were recognized as spiritually gifted and were permitted to do a lot of work, but they were not paid, and they had no place in making policy. After the separation, the AME opened the doors more widely to female preachers, but they provided no recognized status; they certainly did not ordain women.

The activity, authority, and success of these early African-American preachers raises again the question of white women. The male leadership of the AME behaved no differently from that of the white Methodist connections, but many black women who heard the call of the Spirit to preach went off and did so while white women accommodated themselves to the male leadership. While there may have been differences in the way women and men, white and black, understood evangelical religiosity, I suspect that the answer lies in republican ideology and the gender politics of the early republic. White women lived in a world thoroughly enmeshed in a habit of obedience to male authority. The rule of fathers and husbands was generally unchallenged, and it was reinforced by a sharply gendered political culture that rewarded women for their own, peculiarly female contributions to the male citizenry. From white women's perspective as subjects, their masters were men, and they had accepted that reality a long time ago.

African-American women lived in a world in which their fathers and husbands had no social or political authority: power lay in the hands of white masters or the white elite. The manhood of citizenship had no meaning for Africans, since black men were, because of their race (if not their slave status), explicitly excluded from the citizenry. In this bifurcated society, black men and women knew that white men held the power, but they did not grant the justice of that authority, for theirs was a relationship of force rather than consent. African Americans split off from white evangelical churches, first into separate congregations within denominations, and then, when excessively controlled, into separate denominations. Once separate, the AME Church established its own lines of institutional hierarchy, with male leaders claiming the same privileges exercised by white men in the general Methodist Church, accepting as given patriarchal assumptions about church networks. Out of the habit of distrusting authority, many women countered those assumptions. Men only were ordained, and controlled the reins of church power, but women were called as preachers. They did preach and were greatly respected. Men as well as women discovered that the Spirit would not be denied, and soon black preaching women were crisscrossing the nation and the ocean, carrying the Gospel message.

# 7 Domestic piety
## Mothers, missionaries, and the Holiness movement

Settlement moved west at a remarkable pace, but this was not the only frontier to transform the young nation. The first decades of the new republic and its increasingly democratic politics were accompanied by industrialization and the rise of market capitalism. While the southern states continued to eat up land with cotton plantations, producing raw staples for an economy inextricably tied to European trade and industry, the free-farm settlements of the northern areas were key producers in a growing domestic economy. During the first half of the nineteenth century, the nation was crisscrossed by new transportation networks of roads, canals, and, by the 1840s, railroads. Southern transporters carried cotton to the ports and returned with manufactured imports, but, in the north, industrial products made in the cities were shipped to the hinterlands which, in turn, shipped foodstuffs back to towns no longer able to feed themselves. As the northern frontier continued to move, cities arose on transportation lines, initially as market centers accommodating the new settlement, but soon as industrial producers. The development of farm machinery nurtured the growth of commercial agriculture, and the demand for this technology created particular industries sensibly located in the west and further expanding urban development.

The new market capitalism brought with it a new middle class. By 1850, numerous towns had sprouted along northeastern canals, rivers, and railroads, and growing numbers of artisans, shopkeepers, clerks, and managers augmented what had been a small, elite urban class of professionals – lawyers and physicians, merchants, and factory owners. These men held positions and worked in offices away from their homes, their children attended school, and their wives managed households staffed by servants and provisioned by small producers and vendors, such as bakers or grocers. These women produced pleasant homes for husbands and contributed citizens for the next generation; that is, they were domestic caretakers and republican mothers – both honorable callings. It is important to refrain from seeing too much too quickly: in 1850 most families in the United States, including the northeast, still lived on farms and most women were exhaustively engaged in clothing and feeding their families. However, with the advent of industrialization and the transportation revolution came this new middle class – white, largely Anglo-American and Protestant, the descendants of New Englanders with New York and Pennsylvania thrown in. With so many services provided by shops and so much labor performed by servants, middle-class women enjoyed more leisure time to consume, self-improve, socialize, and entertain themselves.

The increase in leisure time was accompanied by an outpouring of literature for the female reading public – periodicals, novels, instructional guides, and inspirational and religious tracts. Through explicit directions and literary examples to be emulated or eschewed, these works prescribed the proper focus and labor of women from girlhood to widowhood, portraying images of an ideal woman who shunned the public arena in favor of the domestic hearth. Such women, by means of their modest virtues and gentle care, nourished spousal devotion and filial affection. Hers was neither a wasted nor peripheral effort, but rather a productive enterprise in and of itself.

> It is at home, where man...seeks a refuge from the vexations and embarrassments of business, an enchanting repose from exertion, a relaxation from care by the interchange of affection: where some of his finest sympathies, tastes, and moral and religious feelings are formed and nourished; – where is the treasury or pure disinterested love, such as is seldom found in the busy walks of a selfish and calculating world.[1]

Husbands found pleasant retreats from the anxieties of the world, sons absorbed the moral qualities that prepared them for future responsibilities of work and citizenship, and daughters grew in the knowledge needed to raise, in their own turn, future generations.

Barbara Welter has summarized the qualities embodied in this "Cult of True Womanhood" as piety, purity, submissiveness, and domesticity.[2] The concerns, anxieties, and labors of the true woman were entirely domestic. She maintained the house, ensuring that the daily needs of food, clothing, and cleanliness were met, either through her own labor or, more likely, through supervising servants. Domestic duties also included the care and education of children and nursing the sick. The excellent housewife attacked these duties with skill (doubtlessly learned from her mother) and diligence. Although many women effectively managed the routine and finances of the household, the husband, in fact, held the authority to set household allowances, hire servants, and make decisions about the children. The true woman submitted herself to his rule and guidance in all things, great and small, accepting his judgments on moral and monetary matters with equal fervor, and was, in the words of one southern Presbyterian, "ennobled" by her subjection.[3] In the practice of these two virtues, the literature promised a woman success in house management and happiness in marriage. Her house would run smoothly, her husband would respect her, and her influence would thrive.

Yet, while these practical virtues would ensure her success in family relationships, two other attributes qualified women to be wives and, especially, mothers. In highlighting the superior piety and purity of women, writers had completely reversed themselves on the nature of womanhood. No longer were women considered at risk to become overwhelmed with dangerous passions. In contrast, women were judged far less likely than men to fall into sexual sin. Women were now characterized by innocence, with this concept of innocence representing a change in and of itself. Puritans might not have denied the innocence of women, but the words they might use to clarify "innocent" were "credulous," "gullible," and "ignorant." Innocence could be a fatal weakness, opening women who knew no better to the wiles of Satan. In the romanticism of the nineteenth century, innocence was transformed into an essential goodness. Still, an intimation of weakness remained. Women needed to be strong enough to protect that innocence from unscrupulous men. The average woman was no longer feared as a potential seductress; she was more likely to be seduced, since men were now seen as those more likely to indulge in sexual sin.

In the advice literature of the era, young women's temptations reflect this changing perception of their nature. The primary sins, or indulgences, of femininity grew out of women's intellectual weakness and their excitability, combined with the leisure time and surplus income so valuable to the construction of the middle class. As early as 1793, Presbyterian John Ogden had decried the "increasing luxurious stile of living in America," a practice especially prevalent among the "privileged and promoted orders."[4] The specter of idleness and frivolity was never far from these texts, and cautionary tales about fashionable, empty-headed spendthrifts haunted the stories. The single girl, who should have been a housewife-in-training but usually was not restricted by domestic cares, was instead running about in society having unwholesome fun, symbolized by the ball and the dancing school.[5] Women of all ages opened the door to temptation with novel-reading and followed this up with endless rounds of social visiting. One writer of *Letters to a Young Lady* wrote that "some of your sex spend their time in a continual rotation of these visits, and have so many preconcerted engagements on their hands, as require a very orderly arrangement upon paper," and he found such a social life "a most useless and insipid life." Such parties, he noted, encouraged women to devote excessive time and money on dress and appeared to work against any sort of female delicacy. Guests spent far more time exchanging "gossip" and "scandal," than in edifying conversation.[6]

Of course, novel-reading, visiting, parties, and consumption were certainly as much a practice of married women of leisure as of single women, but the literature pointed up the unmarried. Young, unmarried women were thought to be at especial risk, since women's gentle, senti-mental, innocent, and uncritically affectionate natures, deemed untempered by judgment or understanding, required guidance and restriction within domestic pursuits and through submission to the reasonable and experienced will of a father or husband. Many of the particular feminine sins had remained the same across two centuries: sins of words, gossip and slander; sins of vanity, fashion without taste or prudence; selfishness, spending on the self without regard for the family needs; and sexual dalliance, from novel-reading to flirtations at balls. The difference lay in the ultimate fate that lay in store for such sinful women. In the seventeenth century, such women dallied with Satan; they risked eternal damnation, if not demonic possession or even an accusation of witchcraft. By the nineteenth century, these women risked a hell on earth: lost reputations, isolation, and poverty.

However, the rewards of industry and virtue were also great. In one notable mid-nineteenth-century tale, a merchant complained of his two eldest, useless daughters who did nothing all day but loll about on sofas and try on clothes. Warned by the author, the father apprentices them out to a dressmaker and a milliner. They object, but must go, and later, when the father loses his business and then has a stroke, the girls are able to return home, provide domestic comfort for their father, and supply the household's material needs as well, establishing their own business.[7] Clearly, the remedy for those weaknesses had also remained the same across the centuries, namely submission to a strong, by nature superior, father or husband. The reward, as well, had remained the same. Those very fathers and husbands reaped the harvest of their female depen-dents' virtue. The iconography of the always domestic, self-sacrificing, submissive wife, mother, and daughter remained intact.

Yes, the language had changed, but the gender politics remained the same. Women were innocent; women were tempted; and women were responsible for men's purity and, apparently, solvency. In the seven-teenth century, women were active agents of evil who seduced men who would not, presumably, have fallen into sin otherwise. In the nineteenth, women were given the added responsibility of protecting men from themselves by deflecting and fighting the inevitable sexual advances of men and by salvaging the family income through household industry and frugality. Any failure to act for good allowed male sin. In both cases, he sinned, she was blamed, and the greater punishment was hers.

Accompanying these qualities of virtue and moral goodness was the assignment of piety to femininity. Writers had begun to naturalize what had been noticed time and again, namely that women constituted the majority of church members. From this, they concluded that women were more inclined toward religion than men. This perception was tied with the Enlightenment construction of basic, natural gender differences, where men became associated with rational, intellectual activity while women remained creatures of the heart, governed by sentiment and emotion. Man thinks; woman feels. That men were competitive individualists involved in rational economic enterprise and political machinations while women became cooperative family members dedicated to home, hearth, and church surprised no one. As one minister explained, "'women are happily formed for religion' by means of their 'natural endowments' of sensibility, delicacy, imagination, and sympathy."[8] As early as 1850, a few female voices, like that of Elizabeth Cady Stanton, would decry this reality as the result of training and limited opportunities. However, during most of the nineteenth century, the image of woman as loving caretaker guided by emotion, not reason, remained unchallenged. Women who did not fit this image were frequently judged unwomanly, or unnatural.

This construction of gender became an important factor for those religionists working to understand the nature of spiritual experience. Beginning with Jonathan Edwards during the Great Awakening and continuing into the revivals of the turn of the century, religion was dissociated with the mind and connected with the heart. For evangelicals, true faith was not about clear thinking or doctrinally correct beliefs, but holy love and spiritual sensation. While Edwards and his colleagues saw this as a central aspect of human nature, within a century it had become associated with female humanity. It was not that men were incapable of religious involvement or spiritual commitment, but that exercises in piety did not come naturally to them. This superior piety of women in part explained the superior purity of woman, and the two together made women the ideal choices for motherhood, raising the next generation of virtuous citizens.

> Not that I would derogate from the prerogative of the father, or depreciate the influence which he is capable of exerting upon the character of his family; but the mother's appropriate sphere and pursuits give her a decided advantage in the great work of laying the foundation of future character; inculcating those principles and sentiments [which] are to control the destiny of her children in all future time.[9]

The cult of true womanhood assumed a structure of basic gender difference, but this idealized, dualistic characterization was neither universal nor unambiguous. Not only were these virtues at risk among the young and prominent among matrons, such qualities were also specific to race and class. While Anglo-American middle- and upper-class women may have been inscribed with these features, others did not fare so well. For example, white women might be judged capable of extraordinary piety, but black women were often not granted that potential. John Taylor was so disturbed by the religious fervor and holiness of a female slave convert, Letty, that he denied her womanhood and portrayed her in masculine terms:

> Her masculine strength made her equal to any black man on the plantation, her high spirit and violent temper, often brought her in contact with them in bloody blows; as her body was strong so was her mind; nature had done more for her than common."[10]

African-American women, because of their race, continued to be stereotyped in caricatures that denied their affections, the strength of their emotional commitments, and, especially, their morality; they were often described as sensual, promiscuous creatures who sought out sexual connections.[11] To a lesser extent, working-class women, especially immigrants, were denied the same femininity. In other words, rather than give up the uncontrolled, passionate coquette or the evil seductress, the dominant culture reconstructed womanhood on the basis of race and class, placing one group upon a pedestal while keeping the others in the mire – the well-known madonna and virgin vs. whore trope, with a racist and classist slant. Such conceptions of natural, racial inferiority served to rationalize the ownership of slaves and excuse the particular evils of the system, including the separation of families and the sexual abuse of women.

The impact upon lower-class women was not quite as destructive in the early decades of the century, but only because most of these women were Anglo-American and Protestant, and because class lines were somewhat fluid. By 1850, however, with the arrival of millions of immigrants and the ethnic and religious differences overlaying class, the placement of poor working women in a separate, unprotected category would stand uncontested. Black women as well as poor white women would always represent a comparison female community. The unwomanly depravity of poor women in the cities, working as prostitutes or afflicted with alcohol, might shock the "delicate sensibilities" of middle-class women, but their presence pointed up the nature of virtuous womanhood even as they became the appropriate focus of middle-class Christian benevolence.[12] In the south, the genteel femininity of planters' wives marked their husbands as masters, signaling male authority over slaves as well as women.[13] As Christine Stansell has explained, "the language of virtue and vice" had become a "code of class."[14]

Into this white, industrialized, genteel world, evangelicalism finally arrived. It had been delayed in the northeast, where the Congregationalists and Presbyterians were particularly well-established. Although the Baptist and Methodist organizations did originate in New

England and the mid-Atlantic, respectively, the astonishing growth of these evangelical networks occurred in the south and west along the constantly moving frontier. Still, during the first two decades of the nineteenth century, Baptists and especially Methodists made significant inroads into the northeastern states, and their success had disturbed the established church leadership. In response to the dying fervor afflicting Congregational and Presbyterian churches, Timothy Dwight, grandson of Jonathan Edwards and president of Yale, led a series of revivals among his students. These young candidates for ordination then went out into New England's congregations bringing the Gospel message of human depravity, Christ's atonement, and the irresistible offer of saving grace. There young preachers experienced great success in leading many persons to conversion. Their progress has been labeled the beginning of the Second Great Awakening, although the enthusiasm and excitement of the 1740s and the turn-of-the-century frontier was not seen. Instead, ministers reported new waves of Christian commitment to salvation, personal reformation of morals, and dedication to social reform.

The efforts of the Yale graduates had been rather tranquil, and many were proud of that fact. But the enthusiastic revivalism that charged through the frontier did finally arrive about twenty years later in the northeast, coinciding with the rise of Charles Grandison Finney of Oneida County, upstate New York. Originally a lawyer, Finney experienced a transformative conversion in 1821 and embarked upon an impressive career converting others. He was so successful that, although he had no formal theological training (and no intention of getting any), he was licensed to preach by the St Lawrence Presbytery. His career as a preacher and revival leader began with notoriously effective revivals in towns along the Erie Canal. He then performed in Philadelphia and New York, after which he returned to Rochester. Finney was an excellent revivalist who used his own adaptations of Methodist methods. He led meetings that might last all night or several days, encouraged those struggling to sit upon an "anxious bench," and encouraged all laypersons, women as well as men, to testify publicly. He advertised his meetings and published his successes, gleaning communication and media methods from political campaigns. Like his Methodist colleagues, he believed that revivals could be made. A "revival is not a miracle, or dependent on a miracle in any sense. It is a purely philosophical result of the right use of the constituted means." Finney published instructional manuals on how to start and promote a revival.[15]

Nathan Hatch has argued that Charles Finney served as a transitional figure in the religious development of the industrial United States. Greedy for conversions, he borrowed and stole any ideas that worked, and the ideas that he saw working all came from politicians and Methodists. He adapted the styles, tools, and rituals of the evangelicals and applied them to the middle classes. He abandoned Calvinist election and predestination, instead preaching the evangelicals' Arminian theology. He softened the vulgar excesses and eased the emotional intensity: a kind of revivalist immediacy with a genteel veneer. Finney claimed that his revivals were most productive among "the highest classes of society...My meetings soon became thronged with that class. The lawyers, physicians, merchants, and indeed all the most intelligent people, became more and more interested, and more and more easily influenced."[16] His converts included future women's rights activists Elizabeth Cady Stanton, Paulina Kellogg Wright, and Antoinette Brown Blackwell, the first woman ordained to the ministry.

Not even Quakers were safe from the spread of evangelicalism. A rising sector of the Quaker community, supported by English Friends who had been influenced by the Wesleyans, had grown anxious that commitment to the inner light, expressed within the ideologically unrestricted meetings of silence, were leading participants away from scriptural authority and committed belief in Christ's atonement as the means to salvation. But, as important as theology may have been, questions concerning orthodoxy are usually connected with social order and control, and the debates among Quakers reflected increasing efforts on the parts of leading Friends and key Meetings in the urban areas to exercise control over smaller groups outside the northeastern cities. The first schism focused upon Elias Hicks, an outspoken opponent of the new evangelicalism and proponent of anti-slavery reform who valued the inner light before the scriptural orthodoxy. When Hicks rose to speak at the Philadelphia Yearly Meeting, the evangelical leadership tried to prevent it, shocking many traditionalists, who may not have agreed with Hicks but certainly believed in the ideological freedom of the Meeting. This first division, in 1827, was followed by several others in both the orthodox and the Hicksite movement as Quakers struggled with their devotion to the light, their attraction to evangelical models of salvation, and their need for order.[17]

Further, conflicts about social order are also about gender, and the evangelical Quakers questioned the forceful presence of women within the community. Apparently, Quakers were not free from aspirations of respectability, and, like their non-Quaker middle-class neighbors, urban Quakers had come to espouse the construction of separate spheres and the exclusion of women from the public arena. In the 1830s, for example, English Quaker Joseph Gurney spoke to orthodox meetings in the United States to great applause. As he called for Bible study and further attention to education, he questioned the public presence that American women enjoyed:

> I do not approve of ladies speaking in public, even in the antislavery cause, except under the immediate influences of the Holy Spirit.

Then, and then only all is safe. Should my dear ladies have to speak in this way, I have no objections.[18]

While forced to grant, by his own doctrine, that women must speak if moved by the Spirit, he challenged any other public role for them. Among the regrets he expressed was the predominance of women among the ministry. Although all branches of the Quaker community produced great female leaders in the nineteenth century, it is perhaps not surprising that such activist women as Lucretia Mott and Susan B. Anthony were Hicksites.[19]

In the northeast, the nineteenth century had continued the trend of the numerical dominance of women on church membership rolls. In Oneida County, Mary Ryan discovered that in the 1810s churches were dependent upon female members. More than 90 percent of all families enrolled in the Presbyterian church in Utica included a wife and/or mother. Nearly half were represented by mothers only, while less than 10 percent were represented by men alone. In Whitestown, 70 percent of the communicants were women, and, while twenty solitary women sponsored children for baptism, only one solitary man did the same. This pattern held during the revivals. At the very least, women always represented at least half the converts, but the percentages could go as high as 72 percent. Nancy Cott found similar figures for New England, where three-fifths of all converts were women, while Sean Wilentz has noted that in the First Presbyterian Church of New York City 70 percent of the converts were women.[20] Certainly no one seemed surprised at the high numbers of women: their presence and response to the intensity of revivals matched both their knowledge of women as religious devotees and cultural assumptions about the attraction that religion held for women. The English skeptic Harriet Martineau rejected such explanations in favor of boredom or a "resource against vacuity," but she did not deny the reality of women's involvement in church: "in New England, a vast deal of [women's] time is spent in attending preachings, and other religious meetings: and in paying visits, for religious purposes, to the poor and sorrowful."[21]

In these revivals, white bourgeois women found a quiet authority located in their piety. Women brought their male relatives, brothers and sons as well as their husbands and fathers, to conversion. In Oneida, almost one-third of all converts had been preceded into the church by relatives, mostly women acting alone. That mothers brought in their children was acknowledged and applauded by evangelicals like Beriah Green, who noted that it was the love and care of mothers, not the authority and responsibility of the father, who would bring children to God. The *Mothers Magazine* waxed particularly eloquent on the spiritual nurturance mothers provided their children: "The church had her seasons of refreshing and her turn of decay; but here in the circle of mothers, it is felt that the Holy Spirit condescends to *dwell*. It seems his blessed rest."[22] Southern evangelical pastors frequently expressed their own dependence upon women as the bearers of the next generation of evangelicals. Seemingly the Holy Spirit, source of divine grace, had been replaced with "the 'virtuous love of a pure woman.' "[23]

Women's influence also extended to adult men. Evangelical magazines contained fictional accounts of women who, forbidden by fathers or husbands to attend a revival meeting, went anyway. These women regretted their defiance, but they saw themselves as obeying Christ before man. The hostile men then turned them out of the house, or followed them, or continued the harassment; ultimately, the harasser became overwhelmed with guilt. The inevitable conclusion of all these stories was the ultimate conversion of the husband or father.[24] The genre served the revival cause well, for women remained true to their female virtues and challenged men quite gently, and only in the area of piety. They did not undermine the comprehensive power structure lodged in separate spheres, but exercised authority in the only place it had been granted, religion, and guided men back into the one arena shared by both sexes, the church. At this level, such stories reinforced the cultural construction of gender. More to the point, the genre reflected the era's real trends: the pews overflowed with converts, women outnumbered men, and many of those men who had joined the church came through the persuasion of women.

Of course, not all women were able to lead their men to true faith, and in this lay seeds of gender conflict. Lyman Beecher noted that religion could seriously trouble the family of the newly converted. A wife or a daughter, he explained,

> is reproached, chided, scolded, and it may be *beaten*, by the hands of her husband or father...and thus having distracted and disturbed his whole house, he now sallies forth, to curse revivals of religion, and to tell how they...disturb and destroy domestic peace.[25]

Yet Beecher and others could not have missed the subversion of domestic authority inherent in this ideology. Many men continued outside the churches, while their wives attended and brought their children with or, as has been suggested, without their consent. An evangelical wife may have been described as rejecting her husband's commands with gentle pleadings and tears. Still, she was defying her husband's authority, and she was honored for it. Southern evangelical ministers recognized the conflict and frequently refused to allow any woman to join their congregations without her husband's permission.[26]

At a deeper level, those persuasive fictional episodes that delineated women's conflict and ultimate success were more disturbing than the presence of unsympathetic but ineffective husbands. In these stories women defied husbands and fathers, and, far from suffering for it, emerged victorious in battle over men's hearts because they shared a cause with God. It may be that these "anointed lords of the creation" would be converted not through direct confrontation but through wifely devotion, prayer, and example.[27] Nevertheless, in this arena they had, with the assistance of grace and domesticity, mastered their male masters.

In 1835 Finney accepted an appointment as professor of theology at the new Oberlin College in Ohio. His departure coincided with the decline of enthusiasm in upstate New York and its replacement with a development that Mary Ryan has called the domestication of religion. In the evangelical popular culture, children, husbands, and other relatives were converted through the prayers, actions, and intercession of women alone. Ministers were no longer needed, except, perhaps, as functionaries to preach and preside over the sacraments. The work of pastoring lay in the realm of wives and mothers. Throughout the mid-Atlantic and New England states, this trend was reflected in the development of Female Missionary Societies and Maternal Associations established to foster revivalism and continue the work of conversion within families. Here women discussed methods and strategized over revivals; they printed pamphlets, distributed tracts, read the *Mothers Magazine*. They even opened Sunday Schools designed to provide Gospel education for poor children who had not the advantage of a Christian education in their homes.[28]

Some women continued to feel a call to a preaching ministry. Harriet Livermore continued along the pathway of preaching women of the previous generation, claiming no denomination, but calling herself the "Pilgrim Stranger." She preached before Congress four times during her twenty-five-year career as an itinerant, each time warning people to attend to the social disruptions and spiritual decline afflicting the nation. She is one of sixty women Catherine Brekus has found who began a preaching career between 1820 and 1845. Like almost all of these women, Livermore was focused upon the second coming of Christ, delivering a millennialist warning to her listeners. Also like most of these women, Livermore was not a member of a mainstream denomination. In addition to Freewill Baptists, African Methodists, and Christians, several women had arisen among the Millerites, those followers of William Miller who anticipated the second coming in 1843.[29] All of these sectarian communities, along with those few women preachers who denied any denominational affiliation, emphasized the call of the Spirit over the demands of religious structure or the social order. They took pride in their differences from other, more staid evangelicals. In their separateness and egalitarian ideology, including the acceptance of women and African-American leaders, they found their identity and their strength.

Mainstream evangelical women who felt a stronger call to the ministry might have entered the mission field. From the beginning of the nineteenth century, young eager religionists and their expanding churches began to consider their responsibilities to the non-Christian world. Although a few communities and individuals had worked within native American communities during the previous century, with new waves of revivalism missionary energy exploded ever outward. Each evangelical denomination sent men and women into the field, following examples set in England. Primary leadership in the United States came from the American Board of Commissioners for Foreign Missions, founded in 1813 as the missionary organization of the Congregationalist, Presbyterian, and Dutch Reformed churches. Only two years later, the Baptists would establish their own mission-sponsoring organization. These Boards recruited missionaries, financed expeditions, and maintained lines of authority, communication, and supply.

During its first fifty years, the Board of Commissioners for Foreign Missions established overseas mission stations in Gabon, south Africa, Greece, Cyprus, Armenia, Palestine, Syria, Persia, Turkey, India, Ceylon, China, Siam, Singapore, Borneo, Hawaii, and Micronesia. They also supported extensive efforts in North America among the Cherokees, Choctaws, Chickasaws, Creeks, Pawnees, Dakotas, Ojibwas, Osages, Maumees, Mackinaws, and peoples in Oregon and New York. Additional stations throughout North America, Asia, and Africa were established and staffed by Baptists and Methodists. Into the arena the American Board of Foreign Missions alone sent more than 1,250 preachers, pastors, catechists, physicians, and schoolteachers. More than half of these missionaries – 691 – were women.

Both overseas and native American missions were founded and overseen by ordained ministers. With rare exceptions, these ordained men and their male assistants were accompanied by wives. This reflected the opinion of Board members, who believed that wives were "a protection among savages, and men can not there long make a tolerable home without them." From their own decisions and organization, Baptists and Methodists obviously agreed with the Commissioners for Foreign Missions that, when "well selected in respect to health, education, and piety, wives endure 'hardness' quite as well as their husbands, and sometimes with more faith and patience." In addition to wives, more than a hundred unmarried women joined mission work, primarily among native Americans, as the Board cited difficulties in housing and protecting women overseas, along with "well-defined and appropriate spheres of labor in no danger of failing...."[30] In the mission field, wives worked as unofficial counselors in the same manner as a pastor's wife. Additionally, wives and single women would nurse the sick, catechize women, run day schools for children at the smaller stations and female boarding schools at the larger ones, and, in extraordinary cases, engage in their own itinerant ministry.

Once the Reformation had opened marriage to the clergy, ordained ministers had found in their wives not only household managers and mothers of their children, but staunch supporters of their work and, sometimes, exemplary models of piety. As early as the Great Awakening, but especially after the arrival of the Methodists, pastors' wives became more significant contributors to the spiritual prosperity of the community. They hosted itinerant preachers and incorporated outsiders into their domestic congregations. Sometimes they held private meetings of women in their homes. Missionary wives followed in these footsteps, and they should not be mistaken for passive, submissive helpmeets to husbands who decided one day to travel for the Gospel. A few women, such as Anna Maria Ward, must have been caught by a husband's delayed call.[31] But the men were, on average, quite young when they embarked upon their work, and they usually married just before they set out. Women who married these men often had missionary careers in mind and sought husbands whose missionary call would allow their wives to pursue a Christian vocation in the field. The intentions and methods were clearly seen in the lives of women like Sarah Hall, who joined the Burma mission as the wife of George Boardman and, at his death, continued her labor by marrying the recently widowed Adoniram Judson, still in Burma.

Ann Hasseltine Judson, the first American woman to join an overseas mission, had recorded in her journal her own interest in such work. Inspired by the life of David Brainerd, an eighteenth-century missionary among native Americans, she "Felt my heart enlarged to pray for spiritual blessings for myself, my friends, the church at large, the heathen world, and the African slaves. Felt a willingness to give myself away to Christ, to be disposed of as he pleases." Sarah Lanman Smith demonstrated an interest in missions long before she embarked upon her work in Syria. She saved up her money for the missionary cause, subscribed to the *Missionary Herald*, joined the Foreign Missionary Society, and taught Sabbath school among the Mohegans. Three years before she married Eli Smith, she wrote: "I have thought, lately, that if individuals from what are called 'the first families,' of both sexes, were to consecrate themselves to the work, it would give a new impulse to the cause." A year later she herself made "the resolution, that whenever my dear parents want me no longer, if unfettered as I am now, I shall devote myself personally to a mission among the heathen."[32]

Harriet Lathrop Winslow, a member of the Ceylon mission for thirteen years, also recorded early inclinations toward missionary work in her diary, even as she denied her call:

When I reflect on the multitudes of my fellow-creatures who are perishing for lack of vision, and that I am living at ease, without aiding in the promulgation of the Gospel, I am almost ready to wish myself a man, that I might spend my life with the poor heathen.

She would later note in 1816 that,

> For *four and a half years*, my prevailing desire has been to spend my life in the service of Christ...My plans for future enjoyment always centred in giving up all for Christ, and spending my days in a pagan land. Such plans, however, appeared like idle dreams, to cheat life of some of its dull hours...

After reading the memoirs of Harriet Newell, a woman who accompanied Ann Judson on the first missions to India and died soon after arrival, Harriet Lathrop wrote that "No situation in my native land could I imagine so capable of affording me substantial happiness..."[33]

   These early missionaries were not so crass as to admit that they actually sought husbands in order to get overseas. Ann Hasseltine tried hard to divest her affections from her duty, since "female delicacy and honour would forbid her to bestow her hand, merely as a preliminary and necessary arrangement." Yet, after Adoniram Judson had proposed, she devoted her spiritual efforts to discerning whether it was her duty to accept the "opportunity [that] has been presented to me, of spending my days among the heathen, in attempting to persuade them to receive the gospel." In seeking her father's consent, Sarah Lanman presented a similarly calm exposition regarding Eli Smith's proposal of marriage: "Now a field seems opened before me, more desirable than any other upon a foreign soil, with a fellow-laborer whose previous knowledge of the station, and other qualifications, give him a high rank in this department."[34] Not all families easily consented to daughters and sisters traveling overseas among the dangerous "savages". Lucy Allen Lindley experienced such opposition from her father and brothers that she was ever estranged from her father, while Annie Safford saw in her parents' vehement opposition to her desire to marry missionary Sexton James a divine signal that God's will for her lay in supporting her parents. Fortunately, they changed their minds, and Safford quickly interpreted their decision as an acquiescence to God's true will for themselves and, thus, for her.[35]

   However, as early as 1819 one finds the breakneck-pace courtships that reflect the centrality of a missionary vocation over a call to conjugal love and partnership. The American Board had recruited Asa Thurston and Hiram Bingham for their new mission to the Sandwich Islands (Hawaii). Neither wanted to serve alone and celibate. Thurston solved the problem first. Having learned of a student colleague's eligible cousin, pious schoolteacher Lucy Goodale, he arranged a meeting, met the family, proposed marriage, and married Lucy eighteen days later. At his own ordination, Hiram Bingham met Sybil Mosely, also a schoolteacher. Bingham quickly introduced himself, and the two were married one week later. Undoubtedly both women were committed to mission work prior to meeting their husbands, and knowledge of the women's interests had encouraged the men in their marital pursuit. An even more explicit example of marriage as missionary contract was the case of Charlotte Fowler. Known locally for her charitable work in New York and New Jersey, and for her interest in missions, she was "courted" by a medical doctor going to the Sandwich Islands. After an initial meeting, Fowler spent some days considering a reference from one of the doctor's professors. At the end of a week she agreed to marry him.[36]

Women did not realize their callings in isolation. Throughout their journals and autobiographies the importance of a spiritual community appears. For some, it might be a locally organized prayer group, but for others the academy began to foster such ambitions. In her history of the Judson family, Joan Jacobs Brumberg relates the importance of Bradford Academy, and other such schools, to the spiritual development of young women like Ann Hasseltine and Harriet Atwood.[37] When Mary Lyon opened her own academy in 1837, she believed that she was fostering the spiritual as well as intellectual development of young New England women, who might well utilize their gifts as ministers' wives. The community soon experienced the missionary fever of the age. Students at Mt. Holyoke kept mite boxes to support the foreign missions as the first steps in their education toward vocations as missionary wives.[38]

From the beginnings of their spiritual journeys, missionary women described themselves as passive receptacles for divine grace and obedient followers of divine will. Both Winslow and Judson had recorded in the diaries of their youths sudden convictions of their own sinfulness and equally sudden realizations of God's grace. While the period of repentance and lamentation was long and arduous, the experiences of illumination were of a moment. Winslow described one Sabbath noon, when

> I nearly lost all my encouragement, and I believe ceased speaking; but soon recommenced, feeling that I could do nothing else. I seemed then to have new confidence in God, and the language "All things whatsoever ye shall ask in prayer, believing, ye shall receive," caused me to open my mouth wide, and I trust to plead with that faith which is never rejected. A sweet peace was shed abroad in my soul.

So, too, Ann Judson, having at last realized the depths of her sinfulness, came to understand that "I had feelings and dispositions, to which I was formerly an utter stranger. I had sweet communion with the blessed God...." She firmly asserted that "Nothing but the power of God can keep me from returning to the world, and becoming as vain as ever."[39]

Harriet Atwood Newell experienced two sequential encounters with the Spirit, the first approximately three years before the second, primary one. In describing her early engagement with God, at the age of 13, she noted that "My convictions of sin were not so pungent and distressing, as many have had, but they were of long continuance. I was brought to cast my soul on the Saviour of sinners, and rely on him alone for salvation." She felt neither ecstasies nor raptures, but "I was filled with a sweet peace, a heavenly calmness, which I can never describe." In this account, Atwood's admission that this first encounter lacked a deep emotional crisis hinted that this was not a true conversion, an implication made more explicit by her note that she failed to join the church at this time and that she relapsed. Fortunately, three years later she was brought to a true sense of her sins: "My past transgressions rose like great mountains before me. The most poignant anguish seized my mind; my carnal security fled, and I felt myself a guilty transgressor, naked before a holy God." Once again, she found her salvation and strength in God, and resolved to dedicate her life to him: "This resolution produced a calm serenity and composure, to which I had long been a stranger. How lovely the way of salvation then appeared! – Oh, how lovely was the character of the Saviour!"[40]

They traced their mission call directly to God, working to convince themselves and others who were concerned – parents, friends, and funding boards – that they were following God's will. Providence was a most important indicator of divine will, and parental consents, physical well-being, particularly supportive friends, or the romantic attachment to a candidate for the mission field were read as promising signs. Harriet Winslow prayed that "my motives may be simple and my eye single to the glory of God…nothing do I dread so much as that God should leave me to think or act for myself." Winslow's search for the voice of the Spirit was finally rewarded with an experience that she interpreted as a clear call.

> in pouring out my soul on this subject to the Father of light, I realized more of that sweet peace which "my willing soul would stay" – and, finally, in so drawing me to the throne of mercy, that I could not leave without a blessing; and at length dissipating every doubt, and enabling me by the eye of faith to discover the finger of God pointing to the East, and with the affection of a Father, and the authority of a Sovereign, saying, "Come, follow me."

Ann Judson had similarly concluded "That if nothing in providence appears to prevent, I must spend my days in a heathen land. I am a creature of God, and he has an undoubted right to do with me, as seemeth good in his sight." Sarah Lanman Smith was deeply interested in traveling overseas, noting in a letter to her father that

You know I have always cultivated a spirit of enterprize, which mamma's influence has tended to increase; and her disregard of those trifling things which many women esteem so highly, has insensibly led me to value the stronger points of character more...I have been hedged up of late, and my circle of duties continually narrowing, until my field is circumscribed by the walls of my father's house.

Yet, in this same letter, she would rejoice in her proposed marriage to Eli Smith that the "leadings of Providence and the coincidences which accompany the present event lead me to feel that God not only permits, but is *calling* me to leave all and follow him."[41] Much of what these women did and said reflected an active interest in, and preparation for, the only pastoral vocation available to women in established denominations. Nevertheless, these women consistently reconstructed themselves as passive, submissive souls feeling the pull of spiritual grace. Their inclinations and active preparations became providential signs from God that such work was meant for them.

These women played key roles in the mission field, where the segregation of women and men in many areas required female missionaries to educate and evangelize women. As Ann Judson once noted, a wife "in her sphere, can be equally useful with her husband. I presume Mrs. Marshman does more good in her school than half the ministers in America." During her career, Judson gathered a group of women into a Sabbath Society to learn of the Bible; built with her husband a *zayat* for religious conversation; began a school for three young girls; translated several tracts and sections of the Bible into Burmese; wrote a catechism in Burmese; translated the Book of Matthew into Siamese; and translated a Siamese sacred book into English.[42] And Judson was not the only woman to accept the extraordinary opportunities in Burma. Sarah Hall Boardman remained there after the death of her first husband, preaching in Burmese. She was said to have "conducted the worship of two or three hundred karens, through the medium of her Burmese interpreter; and such was her modest manner of accomplishing the unusual task, that even the most fastidious were pleased."[43] Deborah Wade worked for forty-five years as a preacher and teacher with such extraordinary success that the she and her husband were each paired with a younger missionary of the opposite sex as an assistant in order to increase the harvest of conversions. In 1833, she and her husband trained future Baptist missionaries at the seminary in Hamilton, New York. And Eliza Grew Jones, who crafted a Siamese–English dictionary and translated significant sections of the first five books of the Bible, nevertheless most enjoyed her work as an evangelist. She found the work of preaching and fostering belief delightful and exciting, and resisted the expectation that as a woman she was destined to teach small children.[44]

The mission work itself and the experiences and efforts of these women as recorded in diaries and letters differed markedly from the hagiographic literature published about them. In journals and letters, the women seemed intent upon stripping the vocation of its idyllic over-tones, though their early writings reek of the romance and adventure of converting the "heathen", planting the seed of the Gospel in virgin soil, and bringing the truth to just one soul. The realities were quite dreary. Women and their partners experienced extended isolation from any who shared their language and culture. They had to struggle with alien cultures, foreign foods, and tropical climates that were far beyond their experience and practical knowledge learned in New England. Throughout her letters from the mission field, Sarah Smith lamented her need for the language of the people surrounding her. In describing her trials, she noted that they were not the sort of hardships that she had imagined: "...there is a taking to pieces, if I may so speak, of all former habits and associations, and modes of action; and the constructing of new, which shall be adapted to the circumstances of a people totally diverse from those with whom we have been educated." In fact, she felt it impossible to make much progress without developing a sophisticated understanding of manners and hospitality: "Externals have an important place in the regard of the inhabitants of these countries, and hospitality [and] politeness are very essential. The sincerity of plain American manners, falls far short of the suavity demanded by the habits of the East. I feel quite deficient in Malta...."[45]

Death and disease were a constant threat. Within a year of her arrival, Harriet Newell, the "proto-martyr" who had accompanied Judson, died from the complications of childbirth; Elizabeth Hervey died within three months of reaching Calcutta. While others lived for several years, it was common to die in the field without ever seeing families and friends again. Added to this was the tragedy of infant death. Every child born to Ann Judson died; she herself died in 1826 at the age of 37, and her thir-teen years in the field represented an impressively long one. Missionaries were sometimes trapped in colonial wars, as the nations in which they lived either attacked or defended themselves against European colonial authorities (usually British). The Smiths warned friends not to be alarmed by war raging in Syria, as they were placed fairly safely. The Judsons did not fare so well. During the 1824–1826 war between Burma and the British in Bengal, Adoniram Judson, along with other foreigners, was taken prisoner and kept incarcerated by the Burmese until the victo-ries of the British forced the liberation of British and American prisoners. Ann Judson spent seven months pleading for and caring for her husband and two other missionaries, following the prisoners after they had been taken from the city of Ava – a long trek during which she was accompa-nied by one servant, two Burmese girls, and her three-month-old daughter.

These were, of course, hardships that hopeful missionaries had considered, but what they seemed not prepared for was the indifference, sometimes hostility, of those they had come to convert. Many of the "heathen" were not ready and excited about conversion; many followed religious systems, Buddhism and Islam, that they found quite satisfactory. Judson noted that she was in Burma seven years before she felt the joy of her first convert. Smith lamented that in Malta the missions made so very little progress because the entire island was dominated by the Roman Catholic Church. In visiting a home housing about 250 girls, "all of whom looked cheerful and well, as they were most industriously employed in every variety of work," she had been thoroughly pleased until entering a chapel, "where I unexpectedly beheld at one end, pictures, crucifixes, confessionals, and all the apparatus of Romanism. My heart sickened at the sight...." Within Sarah Smith's world, all these young women were doomed to perdition, unless the missionaries could bring the true sense of the Gospel to them: "The work which mission have to accomplish in these countries, is far more formidable than among pagans."[46]

Still, long after hearing from women who lived and died in the field, long after all but the least sensible could entertain any romantic hopes, more and more women were measuring their strength and listening for the Spirit's call. The work required a unity with God. As Smith advised a woman contemplating a missionary career,

> you must secure some of your most valuable hours; and so occupy yourself in them as to get *near* to God; and so as to bring eternal things near to you, that you may throw your entire self into the work which engages his infinite mind; and that every thing may dwindle to a point.[47]

Smith, who began her career several years after the first wave of missionaries had died, had acknowledged the risks:

> I do not forget, that the life of a missionary is usually short; and that even before I reach the field of labor, I may find a watery grave. Should I arrive there, my prevailing impression is, that I shall live but a few years, and that those few may accomplish but little for the benefit of those immediately around me. But if only a "cup bearer" to him who seeks my aid, by helping him to work successfully, I should not go in vain.[48]

Thus she happily embarked upon a typically brief career in Syria, dying only three years after she had arrived. Esther MacComber taught at the school in Burma for only three years before her death in 1840; Sarah Comstock (who died in 1843) worked with her spouse in Burma for nine years; Sarah Boardman Judson was among the longest lived, surviving one husband to marry Ann Judson's widowed husband, completing nineteen years in Burma in 1845. Yet, throughout the nineteenth and well into the twentieth century, women kept choosing missionary work. They endured hardship, isolation, sickness, and death in order to bring the Gospel to women and children and, through them, their husbands. Like their husbands, missionary women sought conversions. During an era that prescribed feminine perfection as not only pious and pure, but domestic, submissive, and passive, these proselytizing women were the "Stars Amid Darkness."[49]

Not all evangelical women traveled overseas to realize their preaching vocations, for the 1830s witnessed the birth of a Methodist revitalization movement that would involve significant numbers of women as it transformed the nature of American evangelicalism. Methodists had continued to expand their congregations and influence, but in the changing nation they were losing their intensity. Camp meetings had fallen to the Methodist penchant for organization, and the enthusiasm of the frontier took on a formulaic pattern that even participants could see. The planning worked more to control rather than open the door for the spontaneous experience and expression of the Spirit.[50] Even as preachers and pastors continued to keep most avenues to religious leadership closed, Methodist women had been following the tracks of their Congregationalist and Presbyterian sisters. Joining evangelical societies, working in Sunday schools, and hearing their superior feminine piety praised in sermons and tracts, Methodist women found the same support for their efforts.

Yet some among the Methodists were regretting the loss of the strong, committed religiosity that had been replaced with the accommodation to the realities of nineteenth-century society. They proposed a return to a godly life, a discipline of personal virtue, or Holiness, that marked a continuous commitment to the spiritual quest. They returned to Wesley's concept of sanctification, or Christian perfection, through which the believer, through the grace-filled assistance of the Holy Spirit, became a new person, marked as a true saint whose very thoughts and behavior strove toward perfection in Holiness. As in the seventeenth century, sanctification was evidenced in outward appearance and behavior, but the inward transformation that recreated the sanctified was the work of the Spirit. God was ever-present facilitating the process, but the pathway toward perfection was a struggle that had to be actively embraced by the believer.

The primary leader in the movement to return Methodists to the perfectionist vision of John Wesley was Phoebe Palmer. The daughter of devout Methodist parents, she came to maturity obediently following the directives and wishes of her parents; that is, as a child and young adult, she never considered any other church or belief system, and she adhered with exemplary fidelity to virtuous behavior. She spent her childhood in New York City, married, and then invited her newly married sister and brother-in-law, Sarah and Thomas Lankford, to live in the Palmer household until the Lankfords left the city in 1840. During this decade, both women struggled spiritually with their inability to experience the emotional conversion revered and demanded within the Methodist community. Having always been prayerful followers of Methodism, their experiential history lacked that period of sin and despair that necessarily preceded any realization of the assurance of salvation. Lankford, when a child, had once at a camp meeting " 'burst into tears' and gone 'to the altar as a penitent,' there falling into a kind of swoon during which she felt her sins forgiven," but the assurance that should have followed disappeared in a few days.[51] Palmer herself never experienced even that level of emotion, although she spent many hours during revival meetings sitting on the mourning bench.

Both women came to realize that a person could not strive for an emotional experience. All that potential saints could do was actively adhere to belief and perform their outward duties. Lankford made this discovery almost two years before Palmer, and it was probably through her guidance that Palmer finally resolved her spiritual difficulties.[52] They were not replacing the work of the Spirit with active belief and godly behavior, but simply recognizing the possible and profitable venues for human endeavor: "I never made much progress in the career of faith, until I most solemnly resolved, in the strength of the Lord Jehovah, that I would do every duty, though I might die in the effort."[53] Palmer later described and deprecated her initial false, useless struggles as interfering with the Spirit's work. At times, she claimed, her faith "became almost victorious," yet she could not hold on with steadfast confidence due to her "proneness to reason." She also deeply regretted her inclination to measure "my experience by what I imagined the experience of others"; in other words, the drive for an emotional conversion was a drive to follow other people rather than God. Once she stopped judging herself against the appearances of others, and began listening to the Holy Spirit through the Scriptures, she experienced the transformative grace of sanctification: "As I had resolved that I would abide by the decisions of Scripture, the Holy Spirit did not leave himself without a witness in my heart. Quietness and assurance now took possession of my breast, and an undisturbed resting on the promises became my heritage."[54] In pondering her relationships with her husband, her children, and her God, she could finally proclaim herself prepared to sacrifice all for God and know that her statement was true. She now lived only for God: "Let this body be actuated by the Spirit, as an instrument in thy hands for the performance of thy pleasure in all things." And she realized that she had at last found the Spirit.

> While thus glorying in being enabled to tell and know that I was altogether for the Lord's, the question, accompanied with light, power, and unquestionable assurance, came to my mind, "What is this but the state of holiness which you have so long been seeking?" It was enough! I now felt that the seal of consecration had in verity been set. God, by the testimony of his Spirit, had proclaimed me wholly his![55]

Palmer had discovered a new pathway to Holiness. Rather than the Wesleyan model of constantly striving to emulate the ways of virtue and discipline, Palmer threw herself upon the altar, sacrificed her person to the Spirit, and received the blessing of sanctification.

Throughout the 1830s, Palmer and Lankford had joined female missionary societies and done charity work, and in 1835 Lankford had combined two women's prayer groups that she led into a single meeting that met weekly in their home. During the three years after her own sanctification, Palmer rose to leadership within the Methodist community, taking her colleagues toward a revitalized commitment to Holiness. In 1837, she began teaching a young ladies' Bible class that grew to some fifty members under her guidance; in 1838 she spoke at her first camp meeting; and the next year she became the first woman in New York City appointed to lead a mixed Methodist class. Lankford had been the undisputed leader of the Tuesday meetings, now attended by men as well. When she moved out of the city in 1840, Palmer assumed sole leadership of the "Tuesday Meeting for the Promotion of Holiness," the gathering that has often been described as the foundation of the Holiness movement. Over the next two decades, Palmer toured as an itinerant, speaking at more than a hundred places in New England and the mid-Atlantic. She then traveled to England for four years and, upon her return, renewed her travels. Her reputation was enhanced by the publication of articles in the Holiness journal founded by colleague Timothy Merritt, *Guide to Christian Perfection*, which she and her husband finally purchased in 1863. She also wrote theological texts that sold amazingly well. Her first treatise, *The Way of Holiness*, went through three editions in its first year of publication.[56]

Phoebe Palmer's success as a preacher at camp meetings indicates a woman of rhetorical skill and palpable virtue, a person in whom the Spirit was perceived to thrive. Although the ranks of lay exhorters remained open to all, most formally invited preachers at camp meetings, the individuals on the preaching stand, were men. However, a few women regularly participated in meetings and sometimes even sponsored their own, and they were widely known and universally recognized for their spiritual gifts. In other words, Palmer traveled within a Spirit-focused evangelical network that recognized the "extraordinary call" of a lay preacher. Like Jarena Lee and Zilpha Elaw, Palmer needed no ordination in order to get a pulpit, and she found her authority not in any official naming, but in the recognition of ordinary believers (and even Methodist officials) that she was filled with the Spirit and had important things to reveal. This they knew through her writings and the reputation that grew out of the "Tuesday Meetings." Members met weekly for about ninety minutes, following a fairly loose pattern that included hymns, prayer, and a brief presentation on a scriptural text. Most of the meeting comprised unstructured testimonials of personal religious experience.[57] The meeting attracted a vast number of people – men and women, clerical and lay – from a range of denominations. Many individuals who visited her meetings, for quite early the meetings became known throughout the northeast, returned to their homes and instituted meetings modeled after Palmer's, thus establishing a network of Holiness communities. Many more, unable to follow her leadership path, considered themselves indebted to her advice, spiritual guidance, and support.[58]

Palmer was among the first women to defend in public the right and duty of women to speak at religious meetings. Unlike her other writings, characterized by spiritual exploration, assertive exhortation, and a dependence upon illumination, Palmer's *Tongues of Fire on the Daughters of the Lord* was a closely reasoned discussion that incorporated scriptural exegesis, citations of texts by early church fathers, and detailed reviews of church history.[59] Palmer expounded at length upon Old Testament prophets, women preachers identified in the Book of Acts, and the writings of Paul. Her authorities included biblical scholars whose translations of the texts explicitly noted women preachers, historians of the Christian church during its first three centuries, early church fathers who had witnessed women leaders, and the founding mothers of Methodism. She referred to the large numbers of women who occupy the pews of churches throughout Christendom, denounced the church as "a Potter's Field, where the gifts of women are buried," and pointed to women's natural abilities: "God has eminently endowed woman with gifts for the social circle. He has given her the power of persuasion, and the ability to captivate. Who may *win* souls to Christ, if she may not?"

Yet, throughout this extensive intellectual and polemical discourse, the center of the discussion remained the prophetic voice of the Spirit. Women must speak because the Holy Spirit demanded it; with souls filled with the loveliness of grace, they were impelled to spread the Gospel word:

> how cruel to woman it is to compel her to stifle her convictions, to grieve the Holy Spirit, to deny the Saviour the service of her noble gifts, because the pleasure of the Church (not surely the world, for it favors woman's liberty) must be regarded above that of God.[60]

Palmer called upon the church to dismiss the restrictive constraints placed around the field of ministry, and again open the pulpit to all those, women as well as men, whom the Spirit had called. The official rubrics and authority of ordination was at best meaningless: unnecessary among those who respected the call of the Spirit and destructive of those who enforced their own qualification against the Spirit's direction. Holiness "is the ordination which Christ gives his disciples, by the reception of which they are empowered to go forth and bear much fruit."[61]

Phoebe Palmer came to spiritual maturity during these same unpredictable years in the early nineteenth century, and she, too, began her spiritual career within an evangelical world. Nevertheless, she pursued a narrow pathway missed not only by the overwhelming majority of white evangelical women of her generation, but even by those outstanding female leaders who heard a call to minister. Pious mothers, enthusiastic Sunday school teachers, and missionary women shared with Palmer and women in the Holiness movement a reliance upon the call of the Spirit. But, there was a difference. Phoebe Palmer, alone of these women, appears to have been liberated as well as empowered. That is, she pastored and preached to her community without a rationalizing status or the mask of domestic piety. Most evangelical women built upon an authority claimed through their female virtue in combination with their influence as wives and mothers; missionary wives certainly prepared for a special kind of evangelical leadership, but their position was legitimated through their nuptial relationships. Palmer left all of those worldly trappings behind, laying claim to her authority solely through the extraordinary call of the Spirit. She certainly believed that women's intellectual and rhetorical abilities were equal to those of men. Yet, while she argued for women's worldly capacities, her call was not grounded in (and thereby not restricted by) the world's appointments. In this, Phoebe Palmer, unlike her more conventional sisters, was beyond the demands of men's institutions.

# 8    The reformer's pulpit

During the forty years before the Civil War, many women channeled their spiritual energy through voluntary associations, particularly those focused upon reform. From the beginning of the century, various societies and associations arose to solve particular problems, largely in towns growing so quickly that government could not adequately address the needs of the population. Initially these groups included organizations dedicated to services such as fire protection, charitable associations working to facilitate poor relief, and mutual benefit societies providing widows' pensions, insurance, and burials for subscribing members. With the spread of evangelical culture, new associations arose to further the cause of religion, including Bible societies, tract societies, and Sunday school unions. The associations were connected in hierarchical networks of local, state, and national groups and managed by officers and trustees, usually ministers and prominent laymen. Though men retained the decision-making authority, the work was conducted by massive numbers of female volunteers who sold bibles, distributed tracts, and taught Sunday school classes. They also did much of the actual fund-raising, providing money for male officers to spend, as they saw fit, on projects that women would then complete. By the end of the 1820s, women and men were devoting greater efforts to reform, and women were expanding their autonomy. Women formed their own societies, elected own officers, and made policy decisions about goals, methods, fund-raising, and expenditures.

In *Women and the Work of Benevolence*, Lori D. Ginzberg has noted that the annual reports of these organizations reflected the clear assignment of labor according to gender propriety. Women and men met in single-sex business meetings led by single-sex boards. Reports also emphasized that women avoided the limelight as "unfeminine," demurely asking men to chair public meetings, deliver speeches, and manage the financial details. Yet, while benevolence associations directed by men generally conformed to these lines on paper, it would be wrong to conclude that women exercised no power within the benevolence community, or even that they left all of these details to men. As the primary laborers, and often essential fund-raisers, these women could and did require that the associations' goals and strategies conform to their own expectations. When associations appeared to move in other directions, female leaders were quite prepared to withhold labor or funds from the enterprise. Moreover, women did exert extraordinary, if behind-the-scenes, control in charity finances. In small tract societies, called "cent societies," women raised hundreds of dollars through small contributions; yet even significant projects, such as the building of asylums, which required enormous funds, were largely financed through the financial efforts of women.[1] As Elias Cornelius said of Salem's Society for Moral and Religious Instruction,

> Not only have [women] rendered very important personal services by visiting the poor, by instructing a large part of the Sabbath scholars, and taking the entire charge of the female adult school, but they have formed themselves into an Auxiliary Society, which affords annually a valuable addition to the funds.

Interestingly, this factor was noted in a footnote to the sermon and was not included in the sermon itself, reflecting, perhaps inadvertently (he claimed it should have been mentioned), the hidden reality of women's essential involvement.[2] Clearly, whether publicized or not, women found in this arena an alternative pathway to authority. The church, in its sponsorship of benevolence work, became a world in which women could exercise their leadership abilities. It was a space between the public world of the marketplace and the private world of the home, a safe and appropriate space for women, but one through which they could move onto the public stage.

In the wake of the incredible social and cultural changes brought by political democratization, industrialization, urbanization, and immigration, there was very little that people did not try to reform, and most of these programs were initiated during the 1820s and 1830s. Evangelical theology, with its Arminian encouragement of individual effort toward personal salvation, helped drive the fatalism of unchangeable providence out of the national mind and replace it with an optimistic faith in the ability of individuals to change society for the better. Efforts were afoot to develop public education, move the insane into decent asylums, improve prisons, end capital punishment, shut down businesses on Sundays, clean up cities, control public health, and encourage people to eat grains and eschew meat. Most of these movements were organized in the same way, with local, regional, and national structures prescribed in written constitutions, officers elected at all levels, and focused efforts that usually involved print media and public speeches. Many men and women joined more than one cause, and these memberships overlapped, not only with each other, but also with mutual-aid societies and the new self-improvement associations such as literary societies. Most members were Anglo-American, Protestant, and middle-class. While those who held the greatest authority and were most active tended to be urban dwellers, membership in societies was often rural. Many farmers and their wives felt connected with the larger community via their correspondence with benevolence and reform organizations.

The extraordinary number of women who invested their energies in reform movements may well have been seeking activity or authority. Just as perceptions of female piety had accompanied and supported women's contributions to the spread of evangelicalism, the romantic construction of female morality rationalized, even mandated, women's involvement in reform work. Yet, while some women were undoubtedly motivated by benevolent desires and spiritual impulses, this work must have been personally gratifying as well. If bringing children, husbands, and fathers to church gave women some authority in their private worlds, reform work acted out female authority in a public space. The movements tapped the skills and intellectual resources of some incredibly gifted persons who, due to their sex, had been denied the opportunity to use those gifts. As the one respectable outlet for the exercise of women's non-domestic skills, reform work engaged some of the brightest minds, most powerful orators, eloquent writers, astute planners, sophisticated thinkers, and skillful organizers of the early nineteenth century.

Additionally, women may well have expected that these movements would improve the conditions of their own lives. Domestic ideology may have promised comfortable homes and happy families to all wives who embraced its ideals, but the realities were far different. Although much was said about the influence of women in the household, wives had no legal standing and no control over the economic or social conditions that governed their families. Some husbands and fathers drank; some spent money recklessly with no concern for their dependents; a few were violent; too many were licentious. Women worried that they had no legal or custodial rights to care for their own children. They were frequently isolated on farmsteads by their husbands' decisions, with little opportunity for conversation with any other adult women, including their own sisters and mothers. In other words, in addition to responding to "social evils," some women were challenging the limitations and sufferings of their own lives.

Any involvement represented an opportunity to act in the public sphere and to connect socially with other women. But the particular causes chosen often directly affected women's relationships, homes, and domestic labor. Health reform might well fascinate women, since women were the primary health-care providers in households. The sabbatarian movement's efforts to honor the Lord's day by closing down businesses, especially taverns, on Sundays helped keep men at home. Schools educated their children while the sanitation and public health movements kept the household environs clean and wholesome. The female segment of the temperance movement took a decidedly partisan tone, for men drank and women did not. Evangelicals had always been strong advocates of abstinence for themselves, and by mid-century they worked to demand similar virtue from others. Interestingly, temperance was one of the very few reform efforts to have a strong association in the southern states, not surprising in light of the region's evangelical climate. In their efforts to control other people's drinking, the temperance movement became a fairly strong anti-immigrant voice. Women's temperance societies, however, were dominated by the picture of the drunken man who consumed the family's savings, lost his job, neglected his home, and physically abused his wife and children. Drinking became a symbol of the imbalance of power between men and women, and, after the Civil War, the Women's Christian Temperance Union would stand out as a staunch supporter of women's rights.[3]

The Moral Reform Movement arose in New York City in the 1830s in the wake of Finney's revivals. As Finney called upon his converts to wage war against all sin, several women decided to address the problem of sexual sin, forming the New York Female Moral Reform Society in May 1834. Their short-term goal was the eradication of prostitution, and to this end the association hired men as missionaries, an interesting turnabout from the male-dominated tract societies that used female volunteers. These male missionaries, sometimes accompanied by female members, would seek out the city's prostitutes in the jails, almshouse, and hospitals as well as brothels, where they would distribute Bibles and lead prayers. Also, standing by their belief that women became prostitutes because of stringent economic conditions and a flawed moral sense resulting from their poor upbringing, the Society operated a House of Reception, where young women learned trades while being taught appropriate moral and religious sensibilities. (It failed rapidly and dramatically due to lack of prostitutes' interest.) Beyond efforts to attack prostitution, the Female Moral Reform Society wanted to eliminate all sexual licentiousness, even lewd behavior and speech. To fight what they saw as the pervasive moral climate of lasciviousness and carnality, a climate created by men, the society purchased a newspaper, the *Advocate of Moral Reform*, peddled subscriptions, and sent female missionaries on tours throughout the northeast to organize branch societies. By 1839, the *Advocate* was an unqualified success with a subscription list upwards of 16,500. Approximately 445 auxiliaries to the New York Society had been founded, and the society voted to reorganize itself as a national society, with the New York Society as one of many regional branches.[4]

The remarkable expansion of the Society reflected women's widespread identification with the objectives and ideology of the movement's leadership. Undoubtedly, many women were attracted by its uncompromising moral focus as well as its concern for young women lured into prostitution. However, in addressing the general problem of unbridled male sexuality, reformers touched a core of gender frustration and resentment that fueled this movement for years. Women may have been moral and sympathetic, but they were also angry, and, as Carroll Smith-Rosenberg has demonstrated, they utilized a stereotypical understanding of gender difference to claim moral and domestic authority for women and justify attacks upon the prerogatives and power of men. The vast chasm separating good and evil took the form of female purity against male debauchery. These women deplored the double standard that judged the errant man indulgently while wholeheartedly condemning his victim to humiliation. They agreed that the guilty woman should be held accountable, "But let not the most guilty of the two – the deliberate destroyer of female innocence – be afforded even an 'apron of fig leaves' to conceal the blackness of his crimes." The *Advocate* maintained the notion of the innocent woman, but here innocent became synonymous with trusting and affectionate, one who would plight her troth to a crafty, convincing deceiver. The publication's attack upon the character of men was striking in the monolithic, violent language employed. Predatory, lascivious men "robbed," "ruined," and "rioted"; they were "reckless," "mad," and "drenched in sin." Labels like "The Destroyer" and "Murderer of Virtue" wove through stories and letters, revealing among the *Advocate*'s readers a deep fear of and fury against male power over women's reputations and women's happiness.[5]

In addition to the camaraderie that arose from naming and vilifying the source of women's predicament, men, the association worked to build a coalition of women. Through the formation of a vast network of local moral reform societies staffed by women and the publication of a newspaper written, edited, and published entirely by women, the association united women in a common endeavor to exert their superior moral influence and pressure the men in their circles, especially their husbands. Like the evangelical Mothers' Union, the Moral Reform Society argued that women, as the more moral sex, should be responsible for the sexual education of their children, especially their sons.[6]

Smith-Rosenberg's analysis of female moral reformers is extremely compelling. Although many women were impelled toward this work by altruistic desires stirred by evangelical enthusiasm, they found within the association and through its journal a company of women who shared their experiences of powerlessness and isolation. Discussions of prostitution and sexual depravity flowed easily into the realm of gender politics, and women blamed their sexual vulnerability, economic dependence, and political disabilities on men. They vented their frustrations in language reverberating with rage and invoked contemporary ideas of gender to grant themselves some authority in the home. When male outsiders asked whether this indelicate subject was an appropriate arena for women, the organizers talked of women's natural position as society's moral arbiters, pondered the courageous piety of women who braved taverns and brothels in order to distribute tracts and Bibles, and reassured their critics by organizing their societies through evangelical churches.

Unarguably the most significant reform movement of the early nineteenth century was abolitionism. The anti-slavery movement differed from most of the other reform efforts in size, methods, the diversity of membership, and the absence of a united philosophy. Abolitionism was probably the early nineteenth-century movement that had the greatest impact upon American society, actively pushing the national agenda to engage the moral question of slavery and moving the nation closer to civil war. While many evangelical converts did participate at all levels of anti-slavery work, from the extreme radicals who favored complete political equality to the fairly conservative African colonization societies working to free slaves but send them someplace else, others eschewed abolitionism, particularly during the movement's early years. One need only remember the prevalence of evangelical religion throughout the south to realize the difficulties any evangelical network would experience when addressing slavery. Northern evangelicals would remain uneasy about slave ownership, while white Southerners asserted that slavery was a political issue inappropriate for religious debate, and, in any case, Old Testament patriarchs had owned slaves.

This is not to say that evangelicalism was unimportant to the rise of abolitionism. Nancy Hardesty has presented an overwhelming list of female reform leaders, primarily abolitionists and women's rights activists, who were affected by the evangelical work of the era.[7] Many had been converted in revivals led by Finney or one of his colleagues; others had attended Oberlin college. Oberlin itself was founded by evangelical students and faculty from Lane Seminary dissatisfied with the seminary's resistance to the anti-slavery cause. Nevertheless, I find it misguided to credit evangelical sensibilities, rather than other ideological factors such as a long-standing dedication to republican ideals and an increasing romantic repugnance at cruelty, for devotion to reform efforts as radical as women's rights or abolitionism.

The Oberlin connection does not lead to a legitimate conclusion that female activists were evangelicals. As Lucy Stone, never sympathetic to evangelicalism, once said, "Men came to Oberlin for various reasons, women because they had nowhere else to go."[8] The key connection between radical women reformers and evangelicalism seems to have been the opportunities provided. At evangelical meetings, leaders often encouraged women to participate publicly as exhorters. They taught at Sunday schools, ran Mothers' Meetings, and were praised as central participants in their families' spiritual lives. Oberlin was the first college to open its doors, and then its regular curriculum, to women. But the opportunities were not unrestricted. Women were not accepted into the ordained ministry, and they were not accepted into Oberlin's theology curriculum, nor even permitted to debate in public forums on the campus. What is most telling is that so many of these women, once touched by the evangelical call, turned against evangelicalism fairly quickly. The Grimke sisters, for example, converted from the Episcopal to the Presbyterian church, but in their growing dissatisfaction they switched again to the spiritual openness and relative freedom of the Quaker community. Elizabeth Cady Stanton, baptized Presbyterian and converted during a Finney revival, later turned sharply against evangelical religion. Describing her own conversion as a period of extreme terror, she later declared that Finney's "preaching worked incalculable harm to the very souls he sought to save."[9] Evangelicalism opened some doors and provided some training in the public arena, but the tunnel vision of evangelicals placed individual conversions above all social agendas and undermined their contributions to the anti-slavery cause. The staunchest white supporters of radical abolitionism came not from evangelical ranks, but from among Quakers and the fairly intellectual Unitarians.

Abolitionism attracted both white and black women. While African-American women were concerned with an evil that threatened the lives and well-being of themselves and their families, the moral imperative expressed by many white women may have grown out of a vicarious identification with the sufferings of enslaved women. They may well have felt anguish on behalf of all slaves, but they were especially drawn by the plight of slave children separated from their mothers, the agonies of those mothers, and the humiliation of women who were abused by male masters. One need only look at Harriet Beecher Stowe's *Uncle Tom's Cabin*, a template of evangelical women's anti-slavery philosophy. Although composed as a rhetorical response to the Fugitive Slave Law of 1850, Stowe must have had her female readership in mind as she crafted a sentimental novel that owed much of its effectiveness to her extensive and compelling treatment of women, slave and free, through the lens of domestic piety.

Stowe's primary hero is a Christlike Tom: an illiterate, virtuous, non-violent slave preacher who suffers and dies to save others, but who does not stand up to the system and fight for his own freedom. He does not even escape when opportunities are provided. Beyond the gentle and honorable Tom, beloved of all children, the female reader would grieve over the plight of the enslaved Eliza protecting her child who has been sold, the severe (undeserved) physical abuse suffered by the good-hearted child Topsy, and the beautiful slave women subjected to the aggressive sexual violence of Simon Legree. The offhand cruelty of slave-holder Marie St. Clair appeared unnatural, while the pathos of Mrs. Shelby's inability to stop the sale of Eliza's child underlined the domestic powerlessness of women. There was even a New England spinster whose drive to do right by Topsy was initially hampered by her own racism, while Topsy herself became a missionary to the African colony of Liberia – a nice evangelical touch. Finally, the Quaker matriarch Rachel Halliday created a serene haven for fugitive slave and free alike, gently directing her family through her formidable power of goodness and love.

Stowe's placement of Quakers at the center of the underground railroad reflected the extensive involvement of Quakers against slavery. Unlike other reform movements discussed, anti-slavery agitation predated the American Revolution, and Quakers took the lead freeing their own slaves and challenging state governments to liberate the rest. Many of the laws enacted freed slaves gradually rather than immediately, but by the first decade of the nineteenth century all states from Pennsylvania northward had set emancipation in motion, and the importation of slaves from outside the United States was illegal. After these victories, the anti-slavery societies quieted down, working to protect individuals who risked or had been wrongfully enslaved and calling for the amelioration of the slaves' condition. The anti-slavery movement was reborn in the reform climate of the 1830s. William Lloyd Garrison and his *Liberator*, first published in 1831, led the charge. Garrison brought a new universalism and urgency. He transformed the movement into abolitionism, a moral crusade against the sin of slavery, and he called for the immediate emancipation of all slaves across the nation. While more conservative anti-slavery societies continued their work, abolitionism took the front page and the imagination.

Quakers did not universally embrace abolitionism, although their theology and ethics were adamantly (and consistently) anti-slavery. Among the earliest religious communities to denounce the institution of slavery, Quakers had already removed all slaveholders from their community, if not by suasion than by exclusion, or "reading them out of meeting." Pennsylvania Quakers had taken the lead in advocating the gradual emancipation of the state's slaves; most Quakers who had lived in the southern states had since relocated north. Quakers had even begun campaigns to boycott sugar, tobacco, rice, and other products that were produced through slave labor. However, there is a significant difference between opposing slavery for yourself and your community and committing yourselves to ending the slaveholding of others. In other words, focused inwardly upon their own perfection, Quakers had purged themselves (and their regions) of the sin of slaveholding as they delivered "quiet testimony" within meeting. Many had little time to engage in what they judged a political battle involving other people and other states, and they feared that supporting radical abolitionism might compromise their pacifist principles.[10]

Like their peers, evangelical Quakers steered clear of the more public and disruptive efforts, focusing instead upon fostering the growth of religion through Bible and tract societies, promoting missionary efforts among native Americans, and enforcing a stricter discipline. Not until the 1840s did a significant number of Quakers in both the orthodox and Hicksite branches openly "come out" for abolitionism as well as a range of reform causes, including temperance and women's rights. Many Friends began to criticize their communities' quietist position, calling instead for a more activist position for emancipation and equal rights for free blacks.[11]

And yet, the Quakers, particularly the liberal branches, had opened the door to and encouraged women's leadership within the community. Hicksite Quakers Lydia White and Sydney Ann Lewis, of the District of Columbia, operated stores that sold only produce grown with free labor. Connecticut Quaker Prudence Crandall ran a school for girls. When she attempted to admit a black pupil to her school, the remaining students were withdrawn. Crandall then opened a school for black girls, spending almost a year successfully battling the town for the right to operate such a school.[12] Many leading women abolitionists had once been affiliated with the liberal branches of the Quaker community. These included Abby Kelley Foster, disowned by the Uxbridge, Massachusetts meeting because she had critiqued the Society of Friends and their weakness on anti-slavery activism in a public forum, the *Liberator*, and Lucretia Mott, an outspoken voice opposing slavery and advocating women's rights.

A friend and supporter of Garrison, she and her husband James joined Garrison's efforts to explore and utilize nonviolent methods of resistance to slavery. Mott managed to remained a member of her Hicksite meeting in good standing, despite her advocacy of unpopular causes and methods, probably because she consistently envisioned herself as an itinerant preacher; that is, a Public Friend. She always received the Meeting's permission to travel before she set out, and although she generally spoke of abolitionism in her sermons, it was not always at the center. In other words, she always spoke as the Spirit guided her and ardently supported the right of other women to speak as they were moved. Although most Quakers had taken on fairly conventional social attitudes, including support for civil government and acceptance of natural hierarchies of rank and gender, their belief in the power of the inner light restrained their censorship. Quaker leaders could, and did, censor political speech and women's public speech. However, they could not interfere with the voice of the Spirit. A woman such as Lucretia Mott, who spoke from the Spirit, would always be heard and honored.[13]

Abolitionism was not the sort of movement that would normally appeal to most evangelicals. The evangelical imperative, promoted through the construction and maintenance of communities of believers, was, in the end, a personalized focus upon conversion: the relationship between the individual believer and God. Certain that the perfection of society would follow the sanctification of individuals, many evangelicals concentrated upon the Holiness of themselves and their own communities, and evangelical reform often focused upon saving someone from his or her own sins. Abolitionism had little to do with personal holiness, the holiness of a believer's family, or anyone's holiness. Abolitionists committed themselves to the destruction of a system that exploited and brutalized persons largely unknown to and living far removed from themselves; persons whose conditions were unimaginably different from their own. The rhetoric of abolitionism, though deeply moralistic, was often structured by the language of natural philosophy or political rights rather than religion. They attacked a system and a government rather than individuals. They did denounce slaveholders, but they looked to rescue not sinners but those sinned against.

Evangelical leaders sympathetic to the cause were frequently discomfited by abolitionists. When anti-slavery speakers continued their lectures at Oberlin during a revival, Finney objected that they distracted students from the more important work at hand. He was shocked that some students considered joining the abolitionist cause rather than the ministry. When they joined, evangelicals tended to work with the more conservative anti-slavery groups that tried to eradicate slavery through political means, as if to separate religion from politics. Conservatives also excluded women from the movement's work and women's inequality from the movement's agenda. On the other side, abolitionists were disturbed by the willingness of evangelicals to ignore slavery. During camp meetings no one ever demanded that slaveholders repent and free their slaves; few even discussed it. Abolitionists found this the highest hypocrisy.[14]

Evangelicals' ability to commit to anti-slavery was hampered not only by a philosophical concentration upon personal salvation but also by their commitment to Christian unity and fellowship. The work of the Spirit should not be interrupted by the problems of the world. Yet even moderate abolitionists, who did not insist that churches join radicals in denouncing the government for its tolerance of slavery, grew increasingly disgusted by the failure of denominations to condemn slaveholding itself as a sin. Interdenominational organizations such as the American Tract Society or the American Bible Society were not even moved by pleas that owners were neglecting the spiritual needs of their slaves. Not all evangelicals joined in such compromises. Several smaller groups, such as the Wesleyan Methodist Connection, the American Baptist Free Mission Society, and the Free Presbyterian Church, separated off from their churches in order to come out as abolitionists. And both the Methodist and Baptist communions experienced dramatic schisms in 1844 and 1845 over the denominations' position on slavery. Still, as John McKivigan has argued, this division owed less to the anti-slavery sentiment of northern evangelicals than to the abrasive pro-slavery actions of southerners. Even after separation, northern

Baptists and Methodists did not discipline slaveholders, and thousands of slave-owners remained in communion with the northern churches.[15]

A revealing example of this dedication to fellowship was the behavior of American representatives to the convention of the Evangelical Alliance that met in London, 1846. American participants included several slave-holding ministers, moving several of the meeting's sponsors to propose barring slaveholders from the meeting. Many northerners objected to such a resolution, convincing the convention to allow the American community to restrict its own membership. The American and Foreign Anti-Slavery Society denounced the convention's acceptance of slave-holders, calling it "a complete triumph of the American policy of building up religious institutions, which shall be precluded, by their very constitution, from bearing an effective testimony against slavery."[16]

Yet, as the abolitionist movement expanded its membership, its leaders used not only strategies and techniques learned from political campaigns, but also rhetoric and methods employed by evangelicals to initiate and nourish revivals. The concept of the lecture circuit mirrored the Methodist preaching network. Meetings were often held outdoors, with orators sheltered by tents. They included testimonials from ex-slaves, who called all listeners to shed their ignorance and apathy and take on the task of reform. Listeners also heard sermons of inflammatory political oratory and had opportunities to subscribe to the truth by signing petitions. The lecturers had often been trained by Theodore Weld and Henry Stanton, who incorporated many of Finney's revivalist tech-niques into abolitionist operations. They created an anti-slavery equivalent of Finney's Holy Band, a corps of speakers called the "Seventy," a reference to the seventy disciples sent out by Jesus.[17]

Among the seventy were Sarah and Angelina Grimke, and their extraordinary popularity underscored the evangelical character of aboli-tionism. The Grimke sisters were raised in South Carolina, daughters of a large rice planter. Uncomfortable with her life as a slaveholder, Sarah moved to Pennsylvania, converted to Presbyterianism, then Quakerism, and embarked upon a career fighting slavery. Her younger sister Angelina joined her several years later. The Grimkes were obviously charismatic speakers, and an 1837 series of lectures advertised for women was widely attended by men as well. (So many men that the New England clergy published a formal letter denouncing the Grimke women for publicly speaking before men.) Sarah and Angelina were model evangelical witnesses: repentant sinners and newly sanctified saints. They had once owned slaves, but they realized that this was evil, and so they had stopped supporting this system and called upon others to join their campaign.

Even when directly attacked, as in the 1838 riot that destroyed Pennsylvania Hall during the Convention of American Women Against Slavery, anti-slavery women never doubted that they had a right and an obligation to fight in this movement. Anti-slavery was a moral cause, and morality fell squarely within women's sphere. Because many men were uncomfortable with women's involvement, women formed their own parallel network, and the American Female Antislavery Society crisscrossed the northeast in correspondence, newspapers, and circuits. Unlike other reform organizations, abolitionism vastly expanded the forum and audience for women's voices. Previously, when women spoke, it was generally before children, in committee meetings, or in print. Scotswoman Frances Wright was the first woman to speak from a lecture platform in the United States, and that was not until 1828. In abolitionist circles, women following the Grimkes embarked upon the lecture circuit, appearing before "promiscuous" audiences of men and women.

This was a moment when black and white women worked together toward the same cause. African American women alone founded the first female anti-slavery society in Salem, Massachusetts in 1832, and they were involved in the initial organization of racially integrated female societies in Boston, Philadelphia, and New York. These cooperative efforts were sometimes difficult to maintain, for white and black women organized for different reasons and spoke from different social and economic positions. Many African Americans remained personally entangled in slavery – if not fugitives themselves, they had left behind children, spouses, parents, and friends. Black women abolitionists were relatively poor, supporting themselves as teachers, seamstresses, laundresses, and domestic servants. While many black women who wrote and lectured had been born into free families and raised with some formal education and economic comfort, volunteer work had to be balanced against black women's needs to support themselves and their families. Some women, such as the underground railroad guide Harriet Tubman or the lecturer Sojourner Truth, were occasionally dependent upon white abolitionists' patronage in order to continue their work or avoid financial embarrassment. Black reformers sometimes supported themselves by selling their writing, here again dependent upon white abolitionist editors to facilitate the publication of such books as Harriet Jacobs' *Incidents in the Life of a Slave Girl*, Sojourner Truth's *Narrative*, and Maria Stewart's *Productions*.[18] Ideologically, all but the most radical white abolitionists maintained a limited focus upon ending slavery; they often gave little thought to the welfare of emancipated slaves. Black women sought community improvement, political equality, and economic opportunity as well as freedom.

Not all white women were willing to work with black women. Some female anti-slavery societies tried to exclude black women members, and several succeeded, prompting the formation of alternative associations in the large cities. Yet even in these integrated societies the relationships between white and black anti-slavery women were often afflicted by the differences of class and education, and the prejudices of privilege. The patronizing attitude of white activists and their frequent refusal to heed black women's voices or include them in policy decisions drove many black women to join with black men to create separate anti-slavery societies. Still, white and black women activists shared a cause, a language, a network, and a lecture circuit. Many became women's rights activists as well. Even as they joined separate organizations, black women maintained their personal and professional ties with white abolitionists; for, despite their limitations, many white abolitionist women had actively supported the local free black communities.[19]

Black women shared with many white women a formative evangelical background. Maria Miller Stewart stood out among the early activists for her courageous public presence and her effective, eloquent style. Born of free black parents and orphaned at the age of 5, Maria Miller worked as a servant in a New England minister's family. At 15, she left them to support herself; at 23, she married James Stewart, shipping master of Boston's waterfront. During the three years of her marriage she educated herself, but she was widowed in 1829 and left penniless, defrauded by the two white men her husband had named as executors of his will. She entered the public arena through Garrison, who published two of her essays in 1831. In 1832, five years before the Grimkes lectured in New England, Stewart became the first American woman to deliver a speech. She initially addressed the Afric-American Female Intelligence Society, but over the next year she spoke at least four times before mixed audiences in Boston.

Stewart's lectures engaged the common self-improvement themes of education, economic independence, and personal responsibility, all grounded in a strong commitment to faith. She called upon community members to build and patronize their own businesses and fund schools for their children. And, while she argued that improved education would help end prejudice by overturning racial stereotypes, she also directly challenged white women's prejudice, a prejudice she clearly tied to the privilege of race and class.

> O, ye fairer sisters, whose hands are never soiled, whose nerves and muscles are never strained, go learn by experience! Had we had the opportunity that you have had to improve our moral and mental faculties, what would have hindered our intellects from being as bright, and our manners from being as dignified as yours? Had it been our lot to have been nursed in the lap of affluence and ease, and to have basked beneath the smiles and sunshine of fortune, should we not have naturally supposed that we were never made to toil?

She also publicly criticized black men for their failure to work for the community and against slavery:

Is it blindness of mind or stupidity of soul or want of education that has caused our men never to let their voices be heard nor their hands be raised in behalf of their color? Or has it been for fear of offending the whites?...If you are men, convince them that you possess the spirit of men. Have the sons of Africa no souls?[20]

Verbally attacking black men in a public forum was a dangerous occupation, and she received taunts, jeers, and rotten vegetables. Two years after she had begun speaking, she became so disenchanted that she delivered a farewell address and left for New York. There she joined a literary society and worked against slavery, and while she continued to write she gave up the public speaking.

Stewart's own writings trace her strength and commitment back to an extraordinary religious experience after the death of her husband. Her conversion had transformed her:

I found myself sitting at the feet of Jesus, clothed in my right mind. For I before had been like a ship tossed to and fro, in a storm at sea. Then was I glad when I realized the dangers I had escaped; and then I consecrated my soul and body, and all the powers of my mind to his service ...[21]

Within the confidence of her new prophetic role, Stewart expressed complete trust in divine justice and power, even to a willingness to accept martyrdom: "the God in whom I trust is able to protect me from the rage and malice of mine enemies, and from them that will rise up against me; and if there is no other way for me to escape, he is able to take me to himself...." The fires of the Spirit inflamed rhetoric that took on the rhythms of revivalist preachers: "O, ye daughters of Africa, awake! awake! arise! no longer sleep nor slumber, but distinguish yourselves." But the Spirit moved her to speak to inequality and slavery, for "never will the chains of slavery and ignorance burst, till we be united as one, and cultivate among ourselves the pure principles of piety, morality and virtue." When she directly confronted the American populace about slavery, she employed the terrifying language of the divine vengeance.

Oh America, America...Thou art almost become drunken with the blood of her slain; thou has enriched thyself through her toils and labors; and now thou refuseth to make even a small return....ye rich and powerful ones, many of you will call for the rocks and mountains to fall upon you...whilst many of the sable-skinned Africans you now despise, will shine in the kingdom of heaven as the stars forever and ever.[22]

Her language toward African Americans alternated between outrage and coaxing, at one moment demanding that men and women stand up and embrace their own cause of abolitionism, at others pleading with her listeners to improve themselves and build the community for their children. Her advice to women at first seems to reflect the cult of piety so strong among white evangelicals: "Could I but see mothers in Israel, chaste, keepers at home, not busy bodies, meddlers in other men's matters, whose adorning is of the inward man, possessing a meek and quiet spirit...." Later comments belie this interpretation, demonstrating instead that she referred to sins that disturbed the harmony of the community. Her confidence in black women appears in the rhetorical question, "How long shall the fair daughters of Africa be compelled to bury their minds and talents beneath a load of iron pots and kettles?" She urged women to unite and promised that they would build a future.

> Shall it any longer be said of the daughters of Africa, they have no ambition, they have no force? By no means. Let every female heart become united, and let us raise a fund ourselves, and at the end of one year and a half, we might be able to lay the corner-stone for the building of a High School...Let each one strive to excell in good housewifery, knowing that prudence and economy are the road to wealth.[23]

In her farewell address to Boston, as she defended her right to speak, she stood at her strongest. She employed religious language and rhetorical forms, and incorporated arguments from secular history, church history, and the scripture:

> Be no longer astonished...that God at this eventful period should raise up your own females to strive, by their example, both in public and private, to assist those who are endeavoring to stop the strong current of prejudice that flows so profusely against us at present....[24]

She reminded her hearers of medieval women who studied law and wrote poetry, and invoked female oracles and prophets among Greeks and Romans. But her strongest claims were formulated in the same language used by Zilpha Elaw and Jarena Lee. Her words were the gift of the Holy Spirit, and, while Paul may have commanded women to keep silent in the churches, Jesus did not:

> What if I am a woman; is not the God of ancient times the God of these modern days? Did he not raise up Deborah to be a mother and a judge in Israel? Did not Queen Esther save the lives of the Jews? And Mary Magdalene first declare the resurrection of Christ from the dead?

In the end, she spoke as a prophet, had been tried by fire, and now believed "that a rich reward awaits me, if not in this world, in the world to come."[25]

Despite her brave words, Maria Stewart removed herself from the public platform, although she continued to agitate and write on the need for African Americans to unite together, build their communities in the north, and fight slavery in the south. Yet, while Stewart was building her career, another woman, born into slavery rather than freedom, was experiencing similar struggles with God. While she never described herself as a prophet, she did become a powerful preacher, and she believed that she spoke with an authority that came from the Holy Spirit. For many years she shunned the political/social cause of slavery in favor of alarming her hearers that the last days were at hand. In the end, she, too, turned to abolitionism and women's rights as the central cause demanding her commitment.

The outspoken abolitionist and feminist, Sojourner Truth – her life, speeches, and persona – is the stuff of myth, a myth created in part by Frances Dana Gage in an essay in the New York *Independent*, 1863. Gage recounted Truth's speech to a women's rights convention in Akron, 1851, emphasizing her power, her humor, and her authority as a former slave. Gage quoted Truth's words, erroneously, in a southern dialect, and she placed Truth in a hostile, white environment to emphasize Truth's powers of oratory, although other evidence indicates a sympathetic audience. Gage provided Truth's ringing rhetorical question, "ar'n't I a woman," thus creating the icon that feminists have memorialized.[26] Sojourner Truth's power, intelligence, and eloquence were balanced against an objectified image of an earthy, illiterate, black woman culturally distant from her white audience. The portrait overwhelms the reader with the charisma and authority lodged in such a surprising figure, but it reveals little about this woman's history as the slave Isabella, and almost nothing about the experiences that transformed her into Sojourner Truth.

Isabella was born into slavery in New York just before the end of the eighteenth century. When she was 9, she was separated from her parents upon the death of their master. She served as a slave of the Dumont family for eighteen years, until the emancipation laws freed her in 1828. During her enslavement she bore at least four children, and when she left the Dumonts she still had her infant daughter with her. Upon gaining her freedom, Isabella's narrative tells an extraordinary story of her successful efforts to free her son. Five-year-old Peter had been illegally sold and transported to Alabama, and she brought the case to court, hired lawyers in her behalf, raised money to pay them, and, with their assistance, effected the return of her son to New York and and her care.[27]

Interestingly, her challenge before the courts occurred after she had directly experienced the power of God. Truth's account of her early religious beliefs portrays a simple, unwavering faith in a God that could provide comfort but mainly worked in a barter fashion: she made promises; God provided help. The account of her conversion carried many marks of the evangelical conversion: "God revealed himself to her, with all the suddenness of a flash of lightning, showing her, 'in the twinkling of an eye, that he was *all over*...'. " This language of immediacy was accompanied by images of omnipresence and omnipotence as she described the characteristic terror before divine majesty. Like many converts during this era, she saw a vision. In her need for a mediator between herself and God, "a friend appeared to stand between herself and an insulted Deity...all 'bruises and putrifying sores,' like herself." She described the vision as "beaming with the beauty of holiness, and radiant with love," and at length realized that this was Jesus. Like many before her, she was now filled with joy rather than terror and despair, pondering "the union existing between herself and Jesus – Jesus, the transcendently lovely, as well as great and powerful." Before her conversion, Truth claimed that she had very little theological understanding of Jesus, "but had received from what she heard no impression that he was any other than an eminent man, like a Washington or a Lafayette." Following this experience she began to attend religious meetings, where she heard intellectual discourses upon the incarnational nature of Jesus. Her response to such sermons reveals a woman confident in her own spiritual knowledge, unimpressed by learning or rhetoric: "Of that I only know as I saw. I did not see [Jesus] to be God; else, how could he stand between me and God? I saw him as a friend, standing between me and God, through whom, love flowed as from a fountain."[28]

For several years she seemed a convert in search of a community. Initially she joined Methodists, then, in New York City she changed her membership to the Zion African Church. While there she became involved with a group of Methodists who met together in intense, Spirit-filled meetings. Members took on the disciplines of Holiness and sharing with each other spiritual gifts. During these years, Isabella established a reputation as a preacher. James Latourette, one of the founders of this group, reported that "she was remarkable for bringing about conversions, that the effect of her preaching was so 'miraculous' that 'even learned and respectable people were running after her.'"[29] In 1833 she moved into a very small perfectionist community, and, for two years she was a member of the Kingdom of Robert Matthias, a powerful man who saw himself as a prophet directed by the Spirit to usher in the millennium. It was after fifteen years of searching, in 1843, that Isabella felt called to leave New York City. She began her travels as a preacher, renaming herself Sojourner Truth.[30]

As an itinerant, Truth traveled from meeting to meeting, speaking to any who would listen, finding shelter and food among them. As her reputation grew, she advertised her own meetings and attracted large audiences. The sermons she recounts in her narrative and her descriptions of the meetings indicate that she moved among millennialists who expected the end of the world any moment. She impressed her audiences with her spiritual authority, her wit, and her sense. In these final pages of her narrative, an interesting transformation has occurred. While Truth began her itineracy at the behest of the Spirit, she was soon making decisions about what to say and where to go; she began speaking in her own voice. At one point she agreed to work for a family but accepted very little money; at another she refrained from lecturing a rowdy, drunken crowd. She decided to accept an invitation to live in Northampton with the anti-slavery community, and, while she still spoke at camp meetings, she would soon embark upon a career as an anti-slavery lecturer. She was learning how to speak, and, by her own account, she had grasped the methods of quieting an excitable crowd, stirring a lethargic one, and countering hecklers, lessons that served her well when she moved onto the political lecture circuit.

Even as she turned to political advocacy, the evangelical cast of her rhetoric and her spirit was present. The famous speech memorialized by Gage was first reported by Marius Robinson in the *Anti-Slavery Bugle*. His record included not only Truth's common-sense claims to equality on the basis of her human capacity, but an interesting range of biblical references. She noted Eve's temptation of Adam; she commented upon Mary and Martha, the grieving sisters of Lazarus, and Jesus, who "never spurned women from him." She also spoke directly to the nature of Jesus: "And how came Jesus into the world? Through God who created him and the woman who bore him. Man where is your part?" In a later address on women's rights she spoke of Esther, the queen who successfully defended her people against the machinations of fraudulent courtiers, and warned of women's ultimate victory. Esther was an excellent example here, for, as Nell Painter has noted, Esther was also a Jew, one of the outcast race. Truth did not fear to name the gender of the enemy in her apocryphal pronouncement: "I do not want any man to be killed, but I am sorry to see them so short minded. But we'll have our rights; see if we don't; and you can't stop us from them; see if you can. You may hiss as much as you like, but it is comin'." Through the 1850s, Truth became well known as an antislavery speaker, delivering millennialist denunciations, peppered with scriptural examples and quotations, about the coming of emancipation justice, when whites would suffer and black Americans would be free: "The promises of Scripture were for all the black people, and God would recompense for all their sufferings in this world."[31]

The legendary charisma and strength of Sojourner Truth has been built upon fleeting glimpses told years afterward. What many reformers remembered was a tall, striking woman with a deep voice, a woman who retained the attention of any audience, and turned the most negative climate around: "The power and wit of this remarkable woman convulsed the audience with Laughter."[32] She overwhelmed listeners with prayer, oratory, and hymn-singing, and she had a flair for the dramatic. When a group of unsympathetic men attacked her authenticity, demanding that she prove her femaleness by showing her breasts to the women in attendance, she bared her breasts to all, and effectively shamed those men who made such a demand.

Many reformers seemed embarrassed by her deep relationship with the Spirit, but Sojourner Truth's communion with God grounded her persona and her strength. She had seen visions of Jesus, maintained an intense relationship with the divinity, and opened herself to the inspiration of the Holy Spirit. Sometimes she followed the Spirit's guidance, and sometimes she spoke the Spirit's words. At other moments she made her own decisions and crafted her own sermons. She displayed the authority of the spiritually gifted, but she spoke in her own voice. Sojourner Truth personified the two trends in women's public activism in the nineteenth century. As a reformer, she attacked the oppressive systems of patriarchy and slavery with the authenticity of her own experiences and arguments constructed through her own knowledge and good sense. However, before she spoke on behalf of slaves or women, Sojourner Truth experienced the joy of Holy Spirit, worshiped with a small Holiness sect, preached among millennialist enthusiasts, and won conversions. Considering her personal religious history and her chosen Spirit-oriented communities, it is not surprising that she became one of the best-known preachers in her region, and that she carried a charisma into reform work. She was obviously an intelligent and talented woman. However, women were given little space to exercise such abilities. Like Anne Hutchinson, Sarah Osborn, Zilpha Elaw, and Ann Judson, Sojourner Truth had reached the Spirit. Only then did she find her own voice.

# 9 Voices and silence

## Women, the Spirit, and the Enlightenment

This exploration of the first two centuries of American religious history has examined the relationship between the sociopolitical environment, gender politics, and a particular kind of religion. The environment was British North America: colonies founded by English settlers who displaced the native inhabitants through negotiation, warfare, and, inadvertently but most effectively, disease. Having established prosperous, secure settler communities, the expanding colonies wearied of their colonial status and, through declaration and war, freed themselves from British rule. The new nation constructed a constitutional republic and expanded popular participation in the government. While the society and its customs came directly out of village practice and the common law, this proto-English community was transformed by the people's distance from England, the rigors and opportunities of the constantly moving frontier, their contact with the native population, and their importation and exploitation of Africans.

The gender politics were lodged within English patriarchy, an integrated social, cultural, and political system whose power structure assumed hierarchies of class and gender. The basic unit of inequality, male over female, sat at the center of the common-law construction of the family as a single entity under the legal and economic headship of the male householder. The British colonies added race to this dynamic, adding two underclasses to the social hierarchies. All slaves, male and female, were the property of their masters, with neither protection nor status before the law. Slave women and men usually worked as agricultural laborers, although in urban areas slaves worked in households and as artisans. Africans who gained their freedom, either through purchase or flight, had significantly fewer citizenship rights than free whites. Free white women were expected to marry, from which point they became legally invisible under the coverture of their husbands. Throughout, women were denied any participatory role in the government. Freewomen's contributions to the economy were restricted to the household economy. The boundaries circumscribing women were justified through an ideology that essentialized gender difference and understood women as systematically inferior to men. Between 1600 and 1850 the language and paradigms for understanding humanity and gender changed, but the hegemonic ideologies consistently retained convictions of women's physical, intellectual, and emotional weakness.

The religions in question, Puritanism and Evangelicalism, embraced the direct involvement of the Holy Spirit in people's lives. Believers used their engagement with the Spirit to support their own claims to authority. Initially, these religious groups were dissenting sects whose membership expanded by the recruitment of adult believers, and they defined themselves in part by opposition to established churches, which they characterized as legalistic and spiritually dead. As nonconformist communities, Puritans and Evangelicals had more space for experimentation in structuring their community, leadership, and, consequently, theology. Most members of these Spirit-based movements lacked power and influence, and they actively resisted the efforts of establishment churches to control their minds, hearts, and pocketbooks. Puritans and Evangelicals argued that the authority of the Spirit empowered believers to challenge official authorities, and spiritual experience justified their claims to cultural, social, and political authority.

Of course, spiritual charisma did sometimes empower poor as well as rich, common as well as noble, ignorant as well as educated, and women as well as men. Puritan leaders were not always comfortable extending that power to anyone who had experienced the Spirit, but in the beginning this was unimportant. As English nonconformists, these men could safely allow the presence of the Spirit to reinforce their arguments for expanding their own power, for they could depend upon the government and society at large to keep women and the underclasses under control. However, once they accessed real authority, through the establishment of their own government and church institution in Massachusetts, they became disinterested guardians of the social order and the self-interested guardians of their own power. At this stage, theologians began to reconsider their views of the Spirit. They moved to restrict the Spirit's possible actions and revise their interpretations of those actions. They needed to disempower the inappropriately charismatic, female prophets and artisan preachers, who by their very charisma undermined the hierarchy.

The Puritan leaders' response to women who challenged the religious hegemony illustrates this pattern clearly. During the first decade of settlement, while colonists were still in transit between English nonconformity and Congregational establishment, Anne Hutchinson attracted an impressive following. Scarcely twenty years later, Quakers brought a similar spiritual challenge to the government, attracting many followers by their intense piety, their sincerity, and their refusal to grant any authority except that established by the Holy Spirit. In both cases, the sacred and secular government identified a threat to the social order and patriarchal structure. In both cases, the troublemakers were charged with subversion of the familial and social order. Also in both cases, they were charged with heresy, particularly their beliefs about the power and accessibility of the Spirit that many Puritans had shared at the beginning of the century. Initially, there were also suggestions that spiritually charismatic women were deluded by Satan, and during the second half of the seventeenth century the demonic moved to center stage as accusations of witchcraft became a means of controlling powerful women.

The next century saw this same dynamic worked out among Evangelicals, for the same reasons but within a different ideological frame. In eighteenth-century revivals and nineteenth-century camp meetings, Evangelicals emphasized the progress of the Spirit among their participants. Promoting divine grace as the force that empowered participants to reach salvation and lead others, Evangelical preachers emphasized that God extended grace to all, and that any person, regardless of class, education, sex, or race, could be tapped by the Spirit for especial service. This assertively egalitarian thrust pushed many Baptists to place black converts in positions of lay authority and to recognize, as did Methodists, the call of many slaves and free black men as preachers. Initially, this spirituality also pushed Evangelicals toward an anti-slavery position, and, while neither community ever excommunicated a man for owning slaves or agitated for emancipation, Baptists and Methodists had begun questioning the morality of slavery, challenging masters to free their slaves, and demanding of Evangelical masters moral conduct toward their slaves.

Unfortunately, rather than progress further in fighting for racial equality, Evangelicals regressed. Among the upwardly mobile southerners, many Evangelical Presbyterians (as well as Baptists and Methodists) became slaveholders, thus changing their attitude toward the morality of slavery. Baptists, Methodists, and Presbyterians all divided sectionally over the slavery issue. Additionally, white Methodists found that, while they could still recognize the call of black exhorters, they were far less comfortable with the formal ordination of black men to the ministry. Moreover, they actively opposed granting black Methodist congregations autonomy in governing their own business and spiritual affairs. While African Americans remained within the Evangelical fold, they left these networks for institutional structures of their own making and authority.

Women, too, struggled with Evangelicals' failure to follow the Spirit. Across the century Baptist women, initially recognized as potentially charismatic, were silenced as preachers and congregational leaders. Methodist women also lost spiritual authority across the century and the ocean. Once again, Evangelical men throughout the eighteenth and early nineteenth century were aspiring, through the Spirit, to power that they did not have. However, with the American Revolution and the democratization of American politics, political citizenship was expanded downward across class lines. All free white men were, at least rhetorically, offered equal access to power. The importance of wealth in this early national society was masked by the political rhetoric of the time: opportunity was highlighted, and, to be fair, the opportunity provided by the frontier was a reality for white men. But once these men had acquired power to their own satisfaction, they had no intention of offering it to others. They began to shut down the Spirit system.

From the medieval period, through the Reformation, and forward, institutional Christian churches had joined their destinies to European systems and cultures. They believed God was male, the ministry should be male, and the social order as prescribed by the Bible represented a patriarchal hierarchy. Christianity's patriarchy was thus tied to parallel economic and political systems invested in maintaining the wealth and power of men and to an ideological system of science that constructed woman as inherently inferior to man. With few expectations for power or influence, unless one was of the nobility (and even that was not much), women found two hopes in religion. First, sanctity was recognized as power in and of itself. Several medieval women exercised influence over powerful men because they were holy; Reformation women were honored for piety and devotion to family. In the eighteenth and nineteenth centuries, theologians praised women as the pious sex and granted them, sometimes explicitly and sometimes by implication, authority over their families, even husbands and sons, out of their superior piety and purity. While preachers expected women to exercise their authority in a private, familial environment, female reformers co-opted this language and justified their entry onto the public stage.

Women also followed a second religious pathway to power – the door opened by the Holy Spirit. God remained the ultimate authority, and if a person could lodge her claim within a divine call or revelation, then she could lay some claim to leadership, regardless of rank, gender, or education. Religions that privileged the Spirit's call were particularly attractive to women, and within these communities women, heeding the call, assumed an authority that would not be outside this protected circle. Undoubtedly many Puritan and Evangelical women, originally empowered by their community's religiosity, experienced frustration as their church's devotion to mystical spirituality waned, but they had other choices available. During this era, several Spirit-oriented religions explored mystical communion and recognized the charisma of all their practitioners.

In the seventeenth century, many small sectaries arose out of the Puritan ethos, opening further spiritual opportunities to Puritan women. The best known, most successful, and longest lived were the Friends, or Quakers, who emphasized the believer's communication with the spirit, "the inner light." Because the Quakers placed the inner light at the center of religious identity and affirmed that every person had access to this inspiration, they recognized an equality among all souls. This connection with the Spirit became the primary qualification for leadership within the community, thus opening the doors to all persons in touch with the Spirit, including women. In the early nineteenth century, this pattern was repeated. As Evangelicals began to set boundaries around congregational authority, individuals and small communities left the institutional networks to devote more attention to the Spirit and less to other peripheral considerations. The Holiness movement descended directly from the Methodist movement and its understanding of sanctification. While American Methodists grew extremely interested in institutional aspects of religious authority, the Holiness movement remained committed to recognizing the Spirit and the discipline of the individual as the sole criteria upon which to judge and appoint leaders.

The Quaker and Holiness movements, as well as many smaller sectaries and utopian groups throughout these centuries, concentrated on the Spirit to the exclusion of any other consideration, including biblical injunctions to maintain the social order. Where some order was required, a group might judge it as a necessary accommodation to the misguided hierarchy of the surrounding society. Or, a community might construct a new order, a radically egalitarian one, such as the discipline of the Holiness movement. These groups remained unconnected with other institutions. They rejected governmental interference or support of their congregations' affairs, and they ignored institutional churches, except to use them as a counterpoint to define themselves. Consequently they were able to retain a stronger commitment to the Spirit and a wider door to women's religious leadership. On the other side, in closing the door to women's leadership, church leaders forfeited their mystical relationship with God. Had Puritan or Evangelical men been willing to risk their privileges as ordained ministers, elders, and citizens, they might have retained the intimacy with God that accompanied attendance upon the Spirit's word.

In the seventeenth century, women and men used many of the same terms to describe their spiritual relationships with God. Both were familial conceptions, growing out of people's primary experiences of close, loving interpersonal relationships. A common portrayal of the divine–human relationship was father/child. Those more mystically inclined spoke of God erotically as their lover and themselves beloved; or, in a more contained sense, God as bridegroom and the self as bride. These can easily be understood as metaphorical descriptions, but it should also be realized that, in painting a relationship with God, believers were explaining as best they could their own emotional attachment to God and their sense of God's extraordinary love for them. In other words, Puritans were not saying God is similar to a father, but God is my father; so too, they were not analogically expounding that God is like a lover, but God is my lover, and I am his beloved.

In both cases, the gender of God was male, and both constructions were hierarchical. Here the similarities end. The language of the parental relationship established a God who ordered and judged and a believer who obeyed or was condemned, thus rewarding activity, a "masculine" trait. The sexual construction implied complete passivity, a "feminine" characteristic, on the part of the believer – God loved and enraptured the individual unable to resist the overpowering embrace of God. Moreover, the believer could be male or female in the parental relationship, but only female in the erotic one. Puritan men as well as women wrote of themselves as brides, as seduced, as ravished, meaning that Puritan men reconstructed themselves as female when they used this language to describe their relationship with God. While the sexual metaphor under-lined the believer's intimate love relationship with God, the language itself threatened the structure of cultural authority. Women may have had fewer problems in developing their communion with the Spirit, for they had no gender identity to overcome, while men were, at moments, asked to envision themselves as essentially different and powerless; that is, female. Paternal language, as Ben Barker-Benfield has pointed out, was more comfortable for the male leadership since it emphasized the male believer's superior likeness to God – father/son as opposed to father/daughter – and therefore gave superior place of authority to men. By the end of the seventeenth century, the erotic language gave way to the more predictable, comprehensible language of patriarchy.[1]

In the rising Evangelicalism of the eighteenth and early nineteenth centuries, the erotic language came back, briefly. Many Great Awakening converts returned to the image of bridegroom and marital love as the best expression of their newfound connection with God. After the Revolution, however, this sense of God as lover was disappearing, to be replaced, again, by God the father. The difference, however, was in the understanding of fatherhood. With the rise of romanticism and a new value placed upon parenting and personal relationships within the family, the father of nineteenth-century women converts was a benevo-lent, compassionate, and protective individual; no longer the awaited, exciting bridegroom, God had become a "cosy Person." Inequality remained, but there was still an assumption of God's personal commit-ment to the individual. Men also spoke of God as father, but this was father as immense patriarch, a God of wrath, an unyielding lawgiver and judge. Male converts were initially wary of God, but their godlikeness surmounted other fears as they developed relationships with God that, in the Arminian world, began to look like contracts.[2]

Following the Revolution, and the new premium placed upon the frontier, economic opportunity, and popular participation in govern-ment, the ethos of resignation to divine providence was replaced with a conviction that persons could control their own fate. This growing confidence in human ability infiltrated individuals' theologies, and the passivity of the believer was being replaced with activity. Individuals were doing something about their salvation – something more than preparing for grace. Men and women actively sought God, and as the years progressed their conviction grew that their salvation depended upon their own actions. However, in the transformations of the early nineteenth century, the opportunities and democratic participation were offered to men, not women, and this difference in social and political reality was reflected in significant gender differences in personal spirituality.

While men and women used many of the same descriptions, labels, and formulas in their testimonies, their spiritual autobiographies were not telling the same story. Women often spoke of themselves as living in a state of sin, while men talked of committing sins. In their conversions, both men and women were guided, led, swept up, convinced, but the male believer quickly regained an active role by making choices, talking to people, praying for strength, embracing faith. Just as women were wives and mothers whose interests and destinies were represented and controlled by others, spiritually they continued to describe themselves as persons driven by God. This became especially clear in the language used by religious leaders. Men spoke of hearing the Spirit, embracing their call, and heeding God's will. They were freeing themselves from their bonds with the Spirit and finding their own Arminian way and their own voice. Women's language in this regard had remained largely unchanged. Women preachers spoke not in their own voices, but in the voice of the Spirit, who spoke through them. They did not assume leadership; they were the willing, or even unwilling, subjects who could not resist the Spirit.

As decades passed, the words women leaders used to describe their faith and their calls grew increasingly distinct from the evidence of their behavior. These women denied that they made choices or challenged their subordinate position in a patriarchal society; they spoke of themselves entirely in the passive voice as vessels filled with the Holy Spirit. But whether they actually believed themselves the captives of the Spirit or deliberately manipulated language to justify fulfilling their desires, their very activism belied this construction of passivity. Mary Dyer may have been inspired by the Holy Spirit, but what she did with that inspiration was return to Massachusetts Bay twice, daring the authorities to keep their promise and execute her. Zilpha Elaw was led by the Spirit to risk her freedom traveling and preaching in Maryland, a slave state. And what is to be made of Ann Judson or Harriet Winslow who, seeking careers in ministry, found themselves embarked upon missionary work through calls to marry missionary husbands?

In the nineteenth century, women were rethinking their understanding of themselves in relationship with God and reconsidering their abilities to act rather than be acted upon, even by God. When Sarah Osborn wrote of her leadership in the Newport revivals of the 1760s, she may have described herself as impelled by God. However, in her self-defense she invoked not only the vague language of passive vessel but also concrete descriptions of her successes and an assertion that if she did not offer her home and her guidance, no one else would take up the work, and certain souls would be left outside the Gospel. Missionary women talked of the Spirit's call, but they also wrote of their own efforts to discern the Spirit's voice. To an outsider, their actions seem clearly directed toward identifying and wedding a missionary.

Women had begun to use their own voices and act out of their own desires. By mid-century, Congregationalist Antoinette Brown and Universalist Olympia Brown became the first women to achieve ordination, and unmarried women were working as missionaries among native American communities. By the end of the century, unmarried women would train and travel as missionaries throughout the world, providing stability and continuity in missions in which the ordained personnel changed regularly. Evangelical women like Frances Willard would attend the Moody Bible Institute and prepare themselves to be lay preachers. When denied pulpits, they would find, in reform movements like the Women's Christian Temperance Union, outlets for their spiritual and moral leadership.

Although women still attained greatest authority through their connection with the Holy Spirit, even among the most mystical religiosities the changes came. Ellen Gould White, pioneer leader of the Seventh Day Adventists, and Mary Baker Eddy, founder of the Church of Jesus Christ, Scientist, established churches following the guidance of the Spirit. White claimed more than two thousand revelations and visions, and her writings were treated as inspired, sacred texts. Yet her focus upon health led her upon the activist path of building health missions around the world. Mary Baker Eddy also produced a sacred text, *Science and Health*, that she kept revising as she reconsidered its meaning, and she created the Metaphysical College for the training of spiritual healers. In one sense, White and Eddy look just like Anne Hutchinson, Mary Dyer, Jarena Lee, and Ann Judson. Their entire claim to religious authority rested upon neither their intellectual abilities nor their pastoral skills, but in their connection with the divine. The differences, however, are quite striking. Puritan and Evangelical women, even those as radical as Hutchinson and Lee, worked within institutional systems that privileged the spiritual connection, or at least claimed to. To deny authority to these women, church networks had either to accuse individuals of fraud or to find some way to discount spiritual charisma. White and Eddy founded new religions, and, while their theology may have been divinely inspired, their work to establish institutions clearly falls into the realm of human endeavor. Like Charles Finney fifty years before, Eddy believed that human effort could impact spiritual forces.

The same force that pushed Charles Finney was pushing women, although women were taking longer to arrive at the same place. Women who sought a public platform to accomplish transformative good had initially turned to the church to provide a legitimate forum through which they could act and speak. A corps of female reformers embraced causes that included Evangelical societies, Sunday-school unions, moral reform, temperance, sabbatarianism, and abolitionism, many of which began through involvement in church congregations. For many female congregants and reformers, particularly those involved in abolitionism, the resistance of male leaders to include women in the leadership of churches and associations brought women to reconsider their position and role. Demonstrating their own descent from the Enlightenment, women of the Spirit like Sarah Grimke, Quaker, and Phoebe Palmer, Holiness leader, began to use the tools of scholarship and reason to challenge the scriptural foundation of women's subordination.[3]

Susan Anthony, Elizabeth Cady Stanton, Lucy Stone, and many others challenged the construction of gender difference as essential and natural. They argued for equal political rights and social and economic opportunities on the grounds that all human beings were essentially the same, and that, with the exception of physical capacity and reproduction, the differences between the genders were a matter of education. Women's voices were soon heard in their own right, proclaiming their abilities and strengths to pursue knowledge and careers. The Arminian theology that had overwhelmed American Evangelicalism appeared in the writings of women believers who came to understand that they, too, could control their moral behavior, make theological decisions, and achieve their own salvation.

Sojourner Truth probably stands as the best example of a Spirit-led woman discovering her own, independent voice. She first spoke publicly while a member of a small Holiness congregation, developing her oratorical skill and style and earning a strong reputation as a preacher. From the moment of her conversion to her assumption of the name Sojourner fifteen years later, she described herself as a follower of the Spirit. In the late 1830s and early 1840s, she was preaching her own vision of the Gospel while African Americans all around her were engaged in abolitionism. But by the end of the 1840s, she, too, chose the abolitionist movement and the women's rights movement. She may have constructed her speeches within her millennialist cosmology and invoked Evangelical rhetoric, but Sojourner Truth knew what other women would discover – that the voice belonged not to the Holy Spirit, but to herself.

# Notes

## 1 Women, the Spirit, and the Reformation

1 On Margery Kempe, see Louise Collis, *Memoirs of a Medieval Woman: The Life and Times of Margery Kempe* (New York: Harper & Row, 1983).

2 Julian of Norwich, *Showings*, trans. and ed. Edmund Colledge and James Walsh (New York: Paulist Press, 1978), 176: 204–205.

3 Caroline Walker Bynum, *Fragmentation and Redemption: Essays on Gender and the Human Body in Medieval Religion* (New York: Zone Books, 1992); Eleanor McLaughlin "Women, Power, and the Pursuit of Holiness in Medieval Christianity," in Eleanor McLaughlin and Rosemary Ruether, eds., *Women of Spirit: Female Leadership in the Jewish and Christian Traditions*, (New York: Simon and Schuster, 1979), particularly in terms of her discussion of the power that holiness gave to individual, unmarried women.

4 *The Geneva Bible: A Facsimile of the 1560 Edition*, Introduction by Lloyd E. Berry (Madison: University of Wisconsin Press, 1969), I Corinthians 7:1; commentary to I Corinthians 7:1; 7:28, leaves 78–79. In several margin notes to this chapter, the commentator reiterates the conclusion that celibacy is preferred only because marriage brings worldly cares.

5 William Gouge, *Of Domesticall Duties, Eight Treatises* (London: John Haviland for William Bladen, 1622), 183.

6 Francis Cheynell, *A Plot for the Good of Posterity* (London: for Samuel Gellibrand, 1646), 11.

7 On the strength and power of the convent as a female institution, see Caroline Bynum, *Holy Feast and Holy Fast: The Religious Significance of Food to Medieval Women* (Berkeley: University of California Press, 1987).

8 See Amanda Porterfield, *Female Piety in Puritan New England: The Emergence of Religious Humanism* (New York: Oxford University Press, 1992), especially Chapters 3 and 4, for her argument on the relationship between the rising importance of the domus and the influence of women.

9 Anne Bradstreet, "An Epitaph on my Dear and Ever-Honoured Mother, Mrs. Dorothy Dudley, Who Deceased December 27, 1643, and of Her Age, 61" (1678), in Jeannine Hensley, ed., *The Works of Anne Bradstreet* (Cambridge: Harvard University Press, 1967), 204.

10 Margaret Cavendish Newcastle, *Orations of Divers Sorts, Accommodated to Diverse Places* (London, 1662), 226–227.

11 John Winthrop, *A Short Story of the Rise, reign, and ruine of the Antinomians, Familists & Libertines*, in David D. Hall, ed., *The Antinomian Controversy, 1636–1638: A Documentary History* (Middletown, Conn.: Wesleyan University Press, 1968), 268.

## 2 Wives and mothers in the colonial New England landscape

1 John Winthrop, "Common Grevances Groaninge for Reformation," in *The Winthrop Papers*, 5 vols. (Boston: Massachusetts Historical Society, 1929–47), February–March, 1623/4, 2:295–297.

2 Virginia DeJohn Anderson, *New England's Generation: The Great Migration and the Formation of Society and Culture in the Seventeenth Century* (New York: Cambridge University Press, 1991), appendices, 222–226.

3 For a good overview, see Mary Beth Norton, *Founding Mothers & Fathers: Gendered Power and the Forming of American Society* (New York: Alfred A. Knopf, 1996).

4 Laura Thatcher Ulrich, *Good Wives: Image and Reality in the Lives of Women in Northern New England, 1650–1750* (New York: Oxford University Press, 1980), 35–50 develops this concept of "deputy husband" in some detail.

5 Ulrich, *Good Wives*, 167–183; 202–235; Mary Rowlandson, *A Narrative of the Captivity of Mrs. Mary Rowlandson* (Boston, 1682). For another account of captivity, see John Demos, *The Unredeemed Captive: A Family Story from Early America* (New York: Alfred A. Knopf, 1994).

6 On church membership, see Edmund S. Morgan, *Visible Saints: The History of a Puritan Idea* (Ithaca, N.Y.: Cornell University Press, 1963).

7 Perry Miller's great work mapping the Puritan's intellectual world, *The New England Mind: The Seventeenth Century* (Cambridge: Harvard University Press, 1939), begins with two chapters on Augustinian piety. This piety, he insisted, was the foundation of Puritan culture.

8 Morgan, *Visible Saints:*, 66–73; Perry Miller, "The Marrow of Puritan Divinity," in *Errand into the Wilderness* (New York: Harper & Row, 1956), 48–98; Charles E. Hambrick-Stowe, *The Practice of Piety: Puritan Devotional Disciplines in Seventeenth-Century New England* (Chapel Hill: University of North Carolina Press, 1982), 76–90; Charles Lloyd Cohen, *God's Caress: The Psychology of Puritan Religious Conversion* (New York: Oxford University Press, 1986), 5–11.

9 George Selement and Bruce C. Woolley, eds., *Thomas Shepard's Confessions* (Boston: Colonial Society of Massachusetts, 1981), 61; 65–69, citations 68, 69.

10 The best literary analysis of the conversion narrative is Patricia Caldwell, *The Puritan Conversion Narrative: The Beginnings of American Expression* (Cambridge: Cambridge University Press, 1983). Although Caldwell does not use the term "performance," she traces the movement of the narratives toward formulaic consistency, the means by which this was accomplished, and the insights revealed despite the paradigmatic restrictions.

11 Thomas Hooker, *The Soules Humiliation* (London: T. Cotes for Andrew Crooke, 1640), 18; 134; Hooker, *The Soules Preparation for Christ* (London: T. P. for A. Crooke, 1632), 108; "Elders Reply," Manuscript in the Massachusetts Historical Society, in David D. Hall, ed. *The Antinomian Controversy, 1636–1638: A Documentary History* (Middletown, Conn.: Wesleyan University Press, 1968), 73.

12 Hooker, *Soules Humiliation*, 59; see also 8–12; Hooker, *Soules Preparation*, 90; 36. See also Peter Bulkeley, *The Gospel Covenant; or the Covenant of Grace Opened* (London: Matthew Simmons, 1651), for an even more detailed blueprint.

13 Galatians 3:28, citation from *The Geneva Bible: A Facsimile of the 1560 Edition* (Madison: University of Wisconsin Press, 1969), NT 88.

14 Kenneth A. Lockridge, *Literacy in Colonial New England* (New York: W. W. Norton, 1974), 38–42.

15 John Cotton, *A Conference Mr. John Cotton Held at Boston With the Elders of New-England* (1646) in Hall, ed., *The Antinomian Controversy*, 177.

16 John Brinsley, *Mystical Implantation: or, The Great Gospel Mystery of the Christian's Union and Communion with and Conformity to Jesus Christ* (London: for Ralph Smith, 1652), 21; 28.

17 Selement and Woolley, *Shepard's Confessions*, 102; 91; 102.

18 Ibid., 104; 140; 51; 40.

19 Ibid., 41; 143; 63; 135.

20 Ibid., Brother Jackson's Maid, Testimony, 120; 177; 41; Edward Taylor, *Meditation. Cant. 4.8. My Spouse*, in *The Poems of Edward Taylor* (New Haven: Yale University Press, 1960), 39.

21 Brinsley, *Mystical Implantation*, 32. On the mystical nature of the conversion experience, see Miller, *The Seventeenth Century*, Book I. See also Michael McGiffert, Introduction to *God's Plot: The Paradoxes of Puritan Piety: Being the Autobiography and Journal of Thomas Shepard* (Amherst: University of Massachusetts Press, 1972), 3–29; Cohen, *God's Caress*.

22 William Hill, *A New-Years Gift for Women Being a true Looking-Glass* (London: T.N. for author, 1660), 2. Ulrich, *Good Wives*, uses these two characters (along with Jael) in her portrayal of Puritan women's lives. As the biblical book Proverbs became the model for domestic manuals, Bathsheba, believed to be the worthy housewife discussed, became a model for women.

23 See, for example, Hill, *New-Years Gift for Women*, 22–31; (J). S., *A Brief Anatomie of Women* (London: E. Alsop, 1653), 5; [R. Aylet], *Susanna, or the Arraignment of the two Unjust Elders* (London: for A. R., 1654); Elizabeth Jocelin, *The Mothers legacie, To her unborne Childe* (London: John Haviland for William Barret, 1624), 38–50.

24 Thomas Foxcroft, *A Sermon Preached at Cambridge, after the Funeral of Mrs. Elizabeth Foxcroft* (Boston, 1721), 4; 14; Cotton Mather, *Diary of Cotton Mather* (New York: Frederick Ungar Publishing Co., 1951), 1:185–186.

25 *The Acts and Monuments of John Foxe*, ed. Josiah Pratt (London: George Seeley, 1870), 5:551; 550. Askew's own record of the examinations can be found in Anne Askew, *The first examinacyon of Anne Askewe, lately martyred in Smythfelde, by the Romysh popes upholders, with elucydacyon of Johan Bale* (Wesel, 1546), and Anne Askew, *The lattre examinacion of the worthye servaunt of God mistres Anne Askewe* (Wesel, 1547).

26 Foxe, *Acts and Monuments*, vols. 7 and 8. Not all of the individuals that Foxe discusses were executed. Historians have found that fifty-five, or 20 percent, of the Marian martyrs were female. A. G. Dickens, *The English Reformation* (New York: Schocken, 1964), 364–65; Retha Warnicke,*Women of the English Renaissance and Reformation* (Westport, Conn.: Greenwood Press, 1983), 74.

27 John Bale, Preface to Askew, *Lattre Examinacion*.

28 Mary Ellen Lamb, "The Cooke Sisters: Attitudes toward Learned Women in the Renaissance," in Margaret Patterson Hannay, ed., *Silent But for the Word: Tudor Women as Patrons, Translators, and Writers of Religious Works* (Kent: Kent State University Press, 1985), 107–125.

29 Richard Hooker, *Works*, ed. J. Keble, 1:152–153 as quoted in Patrick Collinson, "The Role of Women in the English Reformation Illustrated by the Life and Friendships of Anne Locke," in his *Godly People: Essays on English Protestantism and Puritanism* (London: Hambleden Press), 274.

30 Hutchinson, Dyer, Moody, and other female religious leaders are discussed in Chapter 3.

31 Cotton Mather, *Ornaments for the Daughters of Zion* (Cambridge, 1692).

32 Joseph Hopkins Twichell, ed., *Some Old Puritan Love-Letters – John and Margaret Winthrop – 1618–1638* (New York: Dodd, Mead, and Co., 1893).

33 Anne Bradstreet, "To My Dear Children," in Jeannine Hensley, ed., *The Works of Anne Bradstreet* (Cambridge: Harvard University Press, 1967), 241.

34 See Ulrich, *Good Wives*, 126–145 for a good discussion of pregnancy, labor, and women's rituals surrounding birthing during the late seventeenth and early eighteenth centuries.

35 Bradstreet, "Of the Four Ages of Man," *Works*, 53.

36 For example, Hannah Sewall bore fourteen children and lost seven in infancy; Cotton Mather's wife bore thirteen children and lost seven as well. Bradstreet, by comparison, was a lucky mother, with all children surviving infancy, and only one dying before she did.

37 John Demos, *A Little Commonwealth* (New York: Oxford University Press, 1970), 66, and Philip Greven, *Four Generations* (Ithaca, N.Y.: Cornell University Press, 1970), 27; 110, both suggest that the number of women who died in childbirth in Plymouth and Andover, respectively, was as high as 20 percent.

38 Bradstreet, "Before the Birth of One of Her Children," *Works*, 224.

39 Cotton Mather, *Memorials of Early Piety: The Memoirs of Jerusha Oliver* (Boston, 1711), 28.

40 Sarah Goodhue, *A Valedictory and Monitory Writing*, cited in Ulrich, *Good Wives*, 154–155. Goodhue did die in childbirth.

41 Bradstreet, "In Memory of my Dear Grandchild Elizabeth Bradstreet,"*Works*, 235. See also "In Memory of my Dear Grandchild Anne Bradstreet," *Works*, 236; "On my Dear Grandchild Simon Bradstreet," *Works*, 237.

42 Bradstreet, "To the Memory of My Dear Daughter-in-Law, Mrs Mercy Bradstreet," *Works*, 238–239.

43 Bradstreet, "A Letter to Her Husband, Absent Upon Public Employment," *Works*, 226.

44 Bradstreet, "Meditations When My Soul Hath Been Refreshed with the Consolations Which The World Knows Not," *Works*, 250.

45 Bradstreet, "Upon a Fit of Sickness, Anno 1632 Aetatis Suae," *Works*, 222; "Meditations When My Soul Hath Been Refreshed," 251.

46 Bradstreet, "To My Dear Children," 241–242.

47 Bradstreet, "Meditations When My Soul Hath Been Refreshed," 250.

48 Bradstreet, "To My Dear Children," 240–245; citations 242; 243.

49 Bradstreet, "As Weary Pilgrim," written 31 August 1669, *Works*, 295.

50 Introduction to "An Excellent Song which was Salomons," *Geneva Bible*; John Cotton, *A brief exposition with practical observations upon the whole book of Canticles* (London, 1655); John Winthrop, *A Short Story of the Rise, reign, and ruine of the Antinomians, Familists & Libertines*, in Hall, ed., *Antinomian Controversy*,273, also quoted in "The Examination of Mrs. Anne Hutchinson at the Court at Newtown," in Hall, ed., *The Antinomian Controversy*, 337; Thomas Hooker, *The Unbelievers Preparation for Christ* (London. 1638), 72; Shepard, *God's Plot: Autobiography of Shepard*, 45. Amanda Porterfield, *Female Piety in Puritan New England: The Emergence of Religious Humanism* (New York: Oxford University Press, 1992), has identified a superfluity of these sexual allusions in the writings of Cotton, Hooker, and Shepard.

51 Ben Barker-Benfield, "Anne Hutchinson and the Puritan Attitude Toward Women," *Feminist Studies* 1 (1972), 65–98 provides an excellent outline of the changing Puritan focus from Christ the Bridegroom to God the Father.

### 3 Prophesying women: pushing the boundaries of patriarchy

1 John Winthrop, *A Short Story of the Rise, reign, and ruine of the Antinomians, Familists & Libertines*, in David D. Hall, ed., *The Antinomian Controversy, 1636–1638: A Documentary History* (Middletown, Conn.: Wesleyan University Press, 1968), 268.

2 John Winthrop, *Winthrop's Journal, "History of New England" 1630–1649*, ed. James Kendall Hosmer (New York: Barnes and Noble, Inc., 1908), 2:126.

3 Richard D. Pierce, ed., *The Records of the First Church in Boston 1630–1868* (Boston: The Colonial Society of Massachusetts, 1961), 46; 55; 56; Sarah Keayne was later excommunicated, possibly for continuing in her prophesying, but the records, acknowledging the sin of "irregular prophesying," noted an additional sin: "odious, lewd, and scandalous uncleane behaviours with one Nicholas Hart an Excommunicate person …" 24 October 1647, 49. It is difficult to consider the sexual sins separate from the "irregular prophesying," since outspoken women were so often automatically tied to sexual deviance.

4 Petition of the women of Malden to the General Court, 28 October 1651, Massachusetts State Archives.

5 Winthrop, *Journal*, 1:285–286.

6 Thomas Welde, *An Answer to W. R.* (London: Tho. Paine for H. Overton, 1644), 19. On the importance of this testimony and the general practice among congregations, see Edmund S. Morgan, *Visible Saints: The History of a Puritan Idea* (New York: New York University Press, 1963); Patricia Caldwell, *The Puritan Conversion Narrative: The Beginnings of American Expression* (Cambridge: Cambridge University Press, 1983).

7 Winthrop, *Journal*, 1:234.

8 Winthrop, *Short Story*, 262–263.

9 "The Examination of Mrs. Hutchinson at the Court at Newtown," 1637, in Hall, ed. *Antinomian Controversy*, 314.

10 Ibid., 316; Winthrop, *Short Story*, 269.

11 Nathaniel B. Shurtleff, ed., *Records of the Governor and Company of the Massachusetts Bay* (Boston, 1853), 1:189.

12 "Examination of Hutchinson," 319–326; Winthrop, *Short Story*, 269–270.

13 "Examination of Hutchinson," 326–333; Winthrop, *Short Story*, 270.

14 "Examination of Hutchinson," 332–337.

15 Ibid., 336–337; 345.

16 Ibid., 338–345; citations 343; 345. William Coddington was a magistrate and a Hutchinsonian.

17 Winthrop, *Short Story*, 274.

18 "A Report of the Trial of Mrs. Anne Hutchinson before the Church in Boston," 1638, in Hall, ed. *,Antinomian Controversy*, 350–374.

19 Winthrop, *Short Story*, 262–263; Thomas Welde, Preface to Winthrop, *Short Story*, 205–206.

20 "Church Trial of Hutchinson," 363; 372.

21 "Church Trial of Hutchinson," 374–388; citation 388.

22 Winthrop, *Journal*, 286–287.

23 Clarendon State Papers, 2:383, as cited in Keith Thomas, "Women and the Civil War Sects," *Past and Present* 13 (1958), 47.

24 Shurtleff, ed., *Records of Massachusetts Bay Company*, 4:277–278.

25 Ibid., 4:308–309; 345–346.

26 Ibid., 3:383. For Quaker accounts of persecutions, see George Bishop, *New England Judged, by the Spirit of the Lord* (1661, 1667; London: T. Sowle, 1703); [Edward Burrough], *A Declaration of the Sad and Great Persecution and*

*Martyrdom of the People of God, called Quakers, in new England* (London: for Robert Wilson, [1660]).

27  Bishop, *New England Judged*, 157; 205.
28  Shurtleff, ed., *Records of Massachusetts Bay Company*, 4:419.
29  [Burrough], *Persecution of Quakers*, 28.
30  Ibid., 29–30.
31  Dyer, Petition to General Court, 1659, Massachusetts State Archives.
32  Shurtleff, ed., *Records of Massachusetts Bay Company*, 4:346.
33  See Carla Gardina Pestana, "The City upon a Hill Under Siege: The Puritan Perception of the Quaker Threat to Massachusetts Bay, 1656–1661," *New England Quarterly* 56 (1983), 348–353, for a discussion on Puritan perception of Quakers' threat to the family.
34  See Perry Miller, "The Marrow of Puritan Divinity," in *Errand into the Wilderness* (New York: Harper & Row, 1956); Norman Pettit, *The Heart Prepared: Grace and Conversion in Puritan Spiritual Life* (New Haven: Yale University Press, 1966); Ben Barker-Benfield, "Anne Hutchinson and the Puritan Attitude Toward Women," *Feminist Studies* 1 (1972), 65–98; Marilyn J. Westerkamp, "Anne Hutchinson, Sectarian Mysticism, and the Puritan Order," *Church History* 59 (1990), 482–496.

## 4 The devil's minions

1  Anne Bradstreet, "An Epitaph on my Dear and Ever-Honoured Mother, Mrs. Dorothy Dudley, Who Deceased December 27, 1643, and of Her Age, 61" (1678), in Jeannine Hensley, ed., *The Works of Anne Bradstreet* (Cambridge: Harvard University Press, 1967), 204.
2  John Winthrop, *Winthrop's Journal "History of New England"1630–1649*, ed. James Kendall Hosmer (New York: Barnes and Noble, Inc., 1908), 1:299.
3  As Laura Thatcher Ulrich notes in *Good Wives: Image and Reality in the Lives of Women in Northern New England, 1650–1750* (New York: Oxford University Press, 1982), 168–169, Cotton Mather found in Jael a model of Puritan women. He invoked this image, however, in his praise of a woman who had already avenged herself against an Indian raid. In other words, in this case Jael was less a prescription than an analogy.
4  See, for example, William Gouge, *Of Domesticall Duties, Eight Treatises* (London, 1622), 317–319; Thomas Gataker, *A Good wife Gods Gift; and, A Wife Indeed* (London, 1623), 61; Gataker, *A Mariage Praier* (London, 1624), 14; William Hill, *A New-Years Gift for Women Being a true Looking-Glass* (London, 1660), 39; [J].S., *A Brief Anatomie of Women* (London, 1653), 1–2. See also the commentary on Jezebel in *The Geneva Bible: A Facsimile of the 1560 Edition*, Introduction by Lloyd E. Berry (Madison: University of Wisconsin Press, 1969), 1 Kings 16:31, leaf 160; 1 Kings 19:1–2, leaf 161; 1 Kings 21, leaf 163; 2 Kings 9:30–37, leaf 169.
5  Joseph Swetnam, *The Arraignment of Lewd, idle, Froward, and Unconstant Women* (1615; London, 1637), preface 2; J. S., *A Brief Anatomie of Women*, (London, 1653) 2.
6  Carol Karlsen, *The Devil in the Shape of a Woman: Witchcraft in Colonial New England* (New York: W. W. Norton, 1987), 130.
7  Swetnam, *Arraignment of Women*, 1; 2; 7; 8; 10; J. S., *Anatomie of Women*, 3; Gouge, *Of Domesticall Duties*, 26; 269.
8  Daniel Rogers, *Matrimonial Honour: or the mutuall Crowne and comfort of godly, loyall, and chaste Marriage* (London, 1642), 34; John Brinsley, *A Looking-Glasse for Good Women*(London, 1645), 4; John Elborow, *Evodias and Syntyche: or, The*

*Female Zelots of the Church of Philippi* (London, 1637), 6; *A Spirit moving in the Women-Preachers* (London, 1645), 2.

9  [J.] S., *Anatomie of Women*, 1. (London, 1653).

10 Katharine Park and Lorraine J. Daston, "Unnatural Conception: The Study of Monsters in Sixteenth-and Seventeenth-Century England and France," *Past and Present* 92 (1981), 20–54; Keith Thomas, *Religion and the Decline of Magic* (New York: Penguin, 1971), 90–132; David D. Hall, *Worlds of Wonder, Days of Judgment: Popular Religious Belief in Early New England* (Cambridge: Harvard University Press, 1990), 71–116; Anne Jacobson Schutte, " 'Such Monstrous Births': A Neglected Aspect of the Antinomian Controversy," *Renaissance Quarterly* 38 (1985), 85–106.

11 Nicholas Culpeper, *Culpepers Directory for Midwives* (London, 1675/76), 1.

12 Tessa Watt, *Cheap Print and Popular Piety, 1550–1640* (New York: Cambridge University Press, 1991), 124; 143; 165; 288.

13 *Strange Newes from Scotland* (London, 1647). Such tales were so common that a humorous broadside, *Mrs RUMP Brought to Bed of a Monster* (n.p., n.d.), used the monstrous birth (with Mrs. London as midwife) as a metaphor to criticize Parliamentary actions. See also Hall, *Worlds of Wonder*, 71–116 for examples of similar moral tales.

14 See Schutte, "Such Monstrous Births," 90–91, nn. 13, 14, for a detailed medical discussion of the Dyer and Hutchinson births. Dyer's child has been judged anencephalic with severe spina bifida, while Hutchinson is thought to have expelled a hydatidiform mole.

15 Winthrop, *Journal*, 1:267–268; John Winthrop, *A Short Story of the Rise, reign, and ruine of the Antinomians, Familists & Libertines* (London, 1642) in David D. Hall, ed. *The Antinomian Controversy, 1636–1638: A Documentary History* (Middletown, Conn., Wesleyan University Press, 1968), 281.

16 Welde, Preface to Winthrop, *Short Story*, 214.

17 Thomas Taylor, *The Works of that Faithful Servant of Jesus Christ, Dr. Thomas Taylor* (London, 1653),152–153.

18 *A Godly Forme of Household Government: For the Ordering of Private Families according to the direction of Gods Word* (London, 1598), 157; 160–161; Taylor, *Works*, 153.

19 Cotton Mather, "Memorable Providences, Relating to Witchcrafts and Possessions," in Charles Lincoln Burr, ed., *Narratives of the Witchcraft Cases, 1648–1706* (New York, 1914), 99–131. While Mather may have had no doubts about Glover's guilt and confession, alternate readings of the texts challenge the certainty of her confession. See Karlsen, *Devil in the Shape of a Woman*, 33–35. The most extensive examples of possession through the machinations of witches are found in the Salem narratives, discussed below.

20 On this sensational, moralistic literature, see Hall, *Worlds of Wonder*, 139–147. Examples include Cotton Mather, "Memorable Providences, Relating to Witchcrafts and Possessions"; Increase Mather, *An Essay for the Recording of Illustrious Providences* (Boston, 1684); Deodat Lawson, *A Brief and True Narrative of Some Remarkable Passages Relating to Sundry Persons Afflicted by Witchcraft, at Salem Village* (Boston, 1692). An additional, revealing account, not published until recently, is Samuel Willard, "Account of a Strange and Unusual Providence of God Befallen to Elizabeth Knapp of Groton," in John Demos, ed., *Remarkable Providences, 1600–1760* (New York, 1972), 358–371.

21 Willard, "Account of Elizabeth Knapp." John Demos provides an enlightening analysis of Elizabeth Knapp's possession in his *Entertaining Satan: Witchcraft and the Culture of Early New England* (New York: Oxford University Press, 1982), 97–131.

22 Willard, "Account of Elizabeth Knapp," 371.

23 Ibid., 359.

24 Ibid., 366.

25 Ibid., 371.

26 Christina Larner, *Witchcraft and Religion: The Politics of Popular Belief* (Oxford: Basil Blackwell, 1984), 84–91; 85; Thomas, *Religion and the Decline of Magic*, 620–621.

27 Of the 344, only two cannot be identified by sex. These figures come from Karlsen, *Devil in the Shape of a Woman*, 47–52. See also Demos, *Entertaining Satan*, 60–64.

28 Karlsen, *Devil in the Shape of a Woman*, 14–33; Demos, *Entertaining Satan*, Appendix, 401–409.

29 Additionally, one man was pressed to death for refusing to enter a plea, and at least six persons died in prison.

30 Karlsen, *Devil in the Shape of a Woman*, 33–45; Paul Boyer and Stephen Nissenbaum, *Salem Possessed: The Social Origins of Witchcraft* (Cambridge: Harvard University Press, 1974), 1–21.

31 See Karlsen, *Devil in the Shape of a Woman*, as opposed to Demos, *Entertaining Satan*, and Boyer and Nissenbaum, *Salem Possessed*.

32 These two paragraphs on the competing definitions of witchcraft are based upon Thomas, *Religion and the Decline of Magic*, 517–680.

33 According to Thomas, English witch trials always rose out of popular concerns and fears, while on the continent witch hunts began with the efforts of the leaders. Thus in Europe maleficium was far less important than in England. An exception to the English pattern involved professional witch hunter Matthew Hopkins, but for the most part English trials were responses to concrete problems perceived to be caused by sorcery.

34 On the statutes, see Thomas, *Religion and the Decline of Magic*, 525–527.

35 Among Puritan writings on witchcraft, one of the clearest and most detailed is William Perkins, *A Discourse of the Damned Art of Witchcraft* (Cambridge, 1608). Most of what New England theologians wrote about witchcraft was informed by Perkins' work.

36 Winthrop, *Journal*, 4 June 1649, 344.

37 Brinsley, *Looking-Glasse for Women*, 9.

38 Winthrop, *Journal*, 4 June 1649, 345.

39 Brinsley, *Looking-Glasse for Women*, 9.

40 Montague Summers, trans. and ed., *The "Malleus Maleficarum" of Heinrich Kramer and Jacob Sprenger* (New York: Dover, 1971).

41 Winthrop, *Journal*, 4 June 1649, 344.

42 Karlsen, *Devil in the Shape of a Woman*, 134–141.

43 Notes on the church trial of Ann Hibbens were recorded by Robert Keayne, *Notes on John Cotton's Sermons*, ms. in the Massachusetts Historical Society. Significant segments of these notes have been reprinted in two sources: Demos, *Remarkable Providences*, 222–239, and Nancy F. Cott., ed., *Roots of Bitterness: Documents of the Society History of American Women* (New York: Dutton, 1972), 47–58. Hibbens is discussed in Karlsen, *Devil in the Shape of a Woman*; Demos, *Entertaining Satan*, and Richard Weisman, *Witchcraft, Magic, and Religion in 17th-Century Massachusetts* (Amherst: University of Massachusetts Press, 1984).

44 Demos, *Remarkable Providences*, 224; 232; Cott, *Roots of Bitterness*, 53.

45 Demos, *Remarkable Providences*, 238.

46 Cott, *Roots of Bitterness*, 54; Karlsen, *Devil in the Shape of a Woman*, 151.

47 Karlsen, *Devil in the Shape of a Woman*, 152; Weisman, *Witchcraft*, 88.

48 Boyer and Nissenbaum, *Salem Possessed*.

49 In addition to works already cited, see Larry Gragg, *A Quest for Security: The Life of Samuel Parris, 1653–1720* (New York: Greenwood Press, 1990), and Elaine G. Breslaw, *Tituba, Reluctant Witch of Salem: Devilish Indians and Puritan Fantasies* (New York: New York University Press, 1996), for more detail on Tituba and the Parris household. Breslaw's work is an engaging historical exercise of speculation about Tituba's identity, background, and motivation.

50 Breslaw, *Tituba*, 133–170.

51 On Puritan–Amerindian relations in New England, see Neal Salisbury, *Manitou and Providence: Indians, Europeans, and the Making of New England, 1500–1643* (New York: Oxford University Press, 1982); Francis I. Jennings, *The Invasion of America: The Cant of Conquest* (New York: Norton, 1976).

52 Of Puritan histories, see Edward Johnson, *The Wonder-Working Providence of Sion's Saviour in New England*, ed. J. Franklin Jameson (1659; New York: Barnes and Noble Inc., 1959); William Hubbard, *The History of the Indians Wars in New England, From the First Settlement to the Termination of the War with King Philip in 1677* (Boston: John Foster, 1677); Increase Mather, *A Brief History of the Warr with the Indians in New England* (Boston: John Foster, 1676). On language of Puritan accounts, see Richard Slotkin's Introduction to *So Dreadfull a Judgment: Puritan Responses to King Philip's War, 1676–1677* (Middletown, Conn.: Wesleyan University Press, 1978), 3–45.

53 Breslaw, *Tituba*, 3–38, is correct in her assertion that all the records and documents indicated that Tituba was an Indian; yet at some point decades later historians wrote of her as African. This false identification reflects the simplistic, but well-founded, notion that all Caribbean slaves were African – most were. But it also reflects a connection that historians were making, whether consciously or not is unclear, between practices of voodoo and the activities in the Parris's kitchen, as if they, too, were seeking their explanation in the exotic outsider. In recent scholarship, Tituba's Indian identity has been recognized, but the exotic has been kept through the assumption that she was Carib, a native community notorious among European colonizers for their fierceness, violent resistance, and cannibalism. Breslaw challenges this conclusion as well, arguing persuasively that Tituba was one of a peaceful band of natives, an Arawak.

## 5 Witnesses to the New Light

1 An indentured servant was an individual who bound himself or herself to a labor contract for four to seven years in return for paid passage to the New World. Male servants outnumbered female approximately three to one. After their terms had ended, servants hoped for quick upward mobility.

2 Allan Kulikoff, "The Beginnings of the Afro-American Family in Maryland," in Aubrey C. Land, Lois Green Carr, and Edward C. Papenfuse, eds, *Law, Society, and Politics in Early Maryland* (Baltimore: Johns Hopkins University Press, 1977), 171–196.

3 Jon Butler, *Awash in a Sea of Faith: Christianizing the American People* (Cambridge: Harvard University Press, 1990), 42–55; 98–105.

4 Richard S. Dunn, *Sugar and Slaves: The Rise of the Planter Class in the English West Indies, 1624–1713* (New York: W. W. Norton, 1972), 103–104; 249–250; Butler, *Awash in a Sea of Faith*, 129–163.

5 Randall H. Balmer, *A Perfect Babel of Confusion: Dutch Religion and English Culture in the Middle Colonies* (New York: Oxford University Press, 1989).

6 Mary Beth Norton, *Liberty's Daughters: The Revolutionary Experience of American Women, 1750–1800* (Boston: Little, Brown, 1980), 3–151.

7 See, for example, Cotton Mather's *Ornaments for the Daughters of Zion* (Boston, 1692).

8 Patricia Bonomi, *Under the Cope of Heaven: Religion, Society, and Politics in Colonial America* (New York: Oxford University Press, 1986), 111–115.

9 Margaret Fell, *Women's Speaking Justified, Proved and Allowed of by the Scriptures* (London, 1667), 12.

10 Butler, *Awash in a Sea of Faith*, 119–120.

11 Barry Levy, *Quakers and the American Family: British Settlement in the Delaware Valley* (New York: Oxford University Press, 1988), 12–13.

12 Ibid., 193–213; citation 207.

13 Ibid., 213–215.

14 Almost all that we know of Elizabeth Ashbridge comes from her spiritual autobiography "Some Account of the Fore Part of the Life of Elizabeth Ashbridge," ed. Daniel B. Shea, in William L. Andrews, ed., *Journeys in New Worlds: Early American Women's Narratives* (Madison: University of Wisconsin Press, 1990), 147–170. This text is followed by several testimonies to her later career.

15 On the structure of the text, see Christine Levenduski, *Peculiar Power: A Quaker Woman Preacher in Eighteenth-Century America* (Washington: Smithsonian Institution Press, 1996), especially 61–108.

16 Aaron Ashbridge, an afterword in "Some Account of the Life of Elizabeth Ashbridge," 171; Aaron Ashbridge to Susy Hatton 1775, in Andrews, *Journeys in New Worlds*, 171.

17 This story of the Scots-Irish, from the 1625 revivals to the Great Awakening, is recounted in my *Triumph of the Laity: Scots-Irish Piety and the Great Awakening* (New York: Oxford University Press, 1988).

18 Religious persecutions were also cited as a reason for the emigration; but the persecution was haphazard and erratic, dependent entirely upon the attitude of the Anglican bishop overseeing the district. In my judgment, the economic factors were far more important.

19 Balmer, *Perfect Babel of Confusion*, 103–121.

20 On Edwards at Northampton, see Patricia J. Tracy, *Jonathan Edwards, Pastor: Religion and Society in Eighteenth-Century Northampton* (New York: Hill and Wang, 1979).

21 Jonathan Edwards, *A Faithful Narrative of the Surprising Work of God* (1747; Grand Rapids, Mich.: Baker Book House, 1979). All three events are recorded within this text. Tracy, *Jonathan Edwards, Pastor*, suggests that Edwards' numbers are exaggerated, since he recorded fewer than 150 names in the church membership rolls during this time. On the 1734–1735 Northampton awakening, see 109–122.

22 "The Spiritual Travels of Nathan Cole" (1741), in Richard L. Bushman, ed., *The Great Awakening: Documents on the Revival of Religion, 1740–1745* (New York: Atheneum, 1970), 67–71; Thomas Prince, *The Sovereign God Acknowledged and Blessed…A Sermon Occasioned by the Decease of Mrs. Deborah Prince* (1744), in Rosemary Radford Ruether and Rosemary Skinner Keller, eds., *Women and Religion in America* vol. 2, *The Colonial and Revolutionary Periods* (New York: Harper & Row, 1983), 342–345.

23 Prince, *Sovereign God Acknowledged*; Susan Juster, *Disorderly Women: Sexual Politics and Evangelicalism in Revolutionary New England* (Ithaca, N.Y.: Cornell University Press, 1994), 66–67; Barbara E. Lacey, "Women and the Great Awakening in Connecticut," Ph.D. Diss., Clark University, 1982, 79; 86;

145–146; Edwards, *Faithful Narrative*, 73–84; Phillis Wheatley to Arbour Tanner, 19 July 1772, in John C. Shields, ed., *The Collected Works of Phillis Wheatley* (New York: Oxford University Press, 1988), 165–166. Wheatley died at age 31.

24  Prince, *Sovereign God Acknowledged*, 343; Lacey, "Women and the Great Awakening in Connecticut," 134–135; "Obituary of Mrs. Hannah Hodge," *General Assembly's Missionary Magazine* (1806), in Ruether and Keller, eds., *Women and Religion*, 346–349; citation 346. On the woman of Sumaria, see John 4:4–42.

25  Juster, *Disorderly Women*, 65; 63; Samuel Hopkins, *Memoirs of the Life of Mrs. Sarah Osborn* (Catskill: N. Elliot, 1814), 32. See also Lacey, "Women and the Great Awakening in Connecticut," 135.

26  Diary of Benjamin Lyon, 26 December 1763 and 23 July 1765, in Juster, *Disorderly Women*, 63.

27  "Spiritual Travels of Cole," 69–70; Edwards, *Faithful Narrative*, 74–77; Prince, *Sovereign God Acknowledged*, 345; Hannah Heaton, "Experiences or Spiritual Exercises," ms., as cited in Lacey, "Women and the Great Awakening in Connecticut," 135.

28  Edwards, *Faithful Narrative*, 76.

29  Elizabeth Mixer, *An Account of some Spiritual Experiences and Rapturous and Pious Expressions of Elizabeth Mixer* (1736), as quoted in Lacey, "Women and the Great Awakening in Connecticut," 87.

30  Heaton, "Spiritual Exercises," as quoted in Lacey, "Women and the Great Awakening in Connecticut," 135.

31  Catherine Anne Brekus, "'Let Your Women Keep Silence in the Churches': Female Preaching and Evangelical Religion in America, 1740–1845," Ph.D. Diss., Yale University, 1993, 62–63.

32  Hopkins, *Memoirs of the Life of Mrs Sarah of Osborn*, 35.

33  Samuel Hopkins, ed., *The Life and Character of Miss Susanna Anthony* (1803), as quoted in Juster, *Disorderly Women*, 61. Also see Juster's discussion of the diabolical, 59–62.

34  Thomas Prince's *Christian History: Containing Accounts of the Revival and Progress of the Propagation of Religion in Great Britain and America* (Boston, 1744–1745) was supplemented by *The Christian History or General Account of the Progress of the Gospel in England, Wales, Scotland and America, as far as the Rev. Mr. Whitefield, His Fellow Labourers and Assistants are concerned* (London, 1743–1744) and *The Christian Monthly History: or An Account of the Revival and Progress of Religion, Abroad, and at Home* (Edinburgh, 1743–1746).

35  These paragraphs are largely based upon Beverly Prior Smaby, *The Transformation of Moravian Bethlehem: From Communal Mission to Family Economy* (Philadelphia: University of Pennsylvania Press, 1986), 3–36.

36  Lacey, "Women and the Great Awakening in Connecticut," 27.

37  On seventeenth-century Baptists, see Carla Gardina Pestana, *Quakers and Baptists in Colonial Massachusetts* (New York: Cambridge University Press, 1991).

38  Rhys Isaac, "Evangelical Revolt: The Nature of the Baptists' Challenge to the Traditional Order in Virginia, 1765–1775," *William and Mary Quarterly* 31 (1974), 345–368; Christine Leigh Heyrman, *Southern Cross: The Beginning of the Bible Belt* (New York: Alfred A. Knopf, 1997), 3–27.

39  Among books that address this question are Albert Raboteau, *Slave Religion: The "Invisible Institution" in the Antebellum South* (New York: Oxford University Press, 1978), 128–150; Mechal Sobel, *The World They Made Together: Black and White Values in Eighteenth-Century Virginia* (Princeton: Princeton

University Press, 1987), 178–203; Jon Butler, *Awash in a Sea of Faith*, 129–163. The Methodists, whose numbers, strength, and organization developed during the years immediately following the Revolutionary War will be discussed in some detail in Chapter 6. Characterized by a radical self-help sort of theology and an amazing penchant for organization, the emotional and experiential nature of their spirituality placed Methodists in the forefront of the evangelical movement.

40  Sobel, *The World They Made Together*, 188–198.

41  The questions of African religious continuity and African–European syncretism are addressed in Raboteau, *Slave Religion*, 44–86; John Thornton, *Africa and Africans in the Making of the Atlantic World, 1400–1680* (New York: Cambridge University Press, 1992), 239–271; Sobel, *The World They Made Together*, 188–198.

42  John Leland, *Writings of John Leland* (1845), as cited in Heyrman, *Southern Cross*, 49.

43  Samuel Davies, *Letters from the Rev. Samuel Davies, Shewing the State of Religion in Virginia, Particularly Among the Negroes* (1757), as cited in Sobel, *The World They Made Together*, 184.

44  Sobel, *The World They Made Together*, 199–203.

45  Heyrman, *Southern Cross*, 49–52; citation 50.

46  Joseph Travis, *Autobiography of Joseph Travis* (1856), in Heyrman, *Southern Cross*, 51–52; 198.

47  Heyrman, *Southern Cross*, 44.

48  Phillis Wheatley to Arbour Tanner, 19 May 1772, in *Collected Works*, 164; Carol F. Karlsen and Laurie Crumpacker, *The Journal of Esther Edwards Burr, 1754–1757* (New Haven: Yale University Press, 1984); Prince, *Sovereign God Acknowledged*, 344; "Obituary of Mrs. Hannah Hodge," 346; Lacey, "Women and the Great Awakening in Connecticut," 105; 150–153; citations 151.

49  Juster, *Disorderly Women*, 41–42.

50  Ann Dellis to Isaac Backus, 26 April 1772, as quoted in Juster, *Disorderly Women*, 83; Lois Adams, as quoted in Juster, *Disorderly Women*, 82.

51  Devereux Jarratt, *The Life of the Reverend Devereux Jarratt* (1806), in Ruether and Keller, eds., *Women and Religion*, 214–215.

52  Juster, *Disorderly Women*, 88.

53  Brekus, "Female Preaching and Evangelical Religion," 44–45; 82; 75–76.

54  Lacey, "Women and the Great Awakening in Connecticut," 152.

55  Ibid., 99–105; Hopkins, *Memoirs of Osborn*.

56  Hopkins, *Memoirs of Osborn*, 49–50; 70–74.

57  Sarah Osborn to Joseph Fish, 20 December 1760, in Lacey, "Women and the Great Awakening in Connecticut," 113.

58  Hopkins, *Memoirs of Osborn*, 81–82.

59  Lacey, "Women and the Great Awakening in Connecticut," 117–119.

60  Joseph A. Conforti, *Samuel Hopkins and the New Divinity Movement: Calvinism, the Congregational Ministry, and Reform in New England Between the Great Awakenings* (Grand Rapids, Mich.: Christian University Press, 1981), 101–106.

61  Joseph Fish to Sarah Osborn, 13 September 1761, in Lacey, "Women and the Great Awakening in Connecticut," 119.

62  Sarah Osborn to Joseph Fish, 28 February–7 March 1767, in Mary Beth Norton, ed., "'My Resting Reaping Times': Sarah Osborn's Defense of Her Unfeminine Activities, 1767," *Signs* 2 (1976), 525.

63  Ibid., 522–524.

64  Ibid., 526; 527.

65  Edwards, *Faithful Narrative*, 85–93.

66 Sarah Osborn to Joseph Fish, 28 February–7 March 1767, 528–529.
67 Lacey, "Women and the Great Awakening in Connecticut," 124.

## 6 Gender, revolution, and the Methodists

1 James Paterson to John King, 25 September 1801, in Paul Conkin, *Cane Ridge: America's Pentecost* (Madison: University of Wisconsin Press, 1990), 93.
2 Barton Warren Stone, *A Short History of the Life of Barton W. Stone Written By Himself* (1847; reprinted New York: Arno Press, 1972), 38.
3 Zilpha Elaw, *Memoirs of the Life, Religious Experience, Ministerial Travels and Labours of Mrs. Zilpha Elaw, An American Female of Colour* (1846), in William L. Andrews, ed., *Sisters of the Spirit: Three Black Women's Autobiographies of the Nineteenth Century* (Indianapolis: Indiana University Press, 1986), 64–66.
4 Ibid., 66–67.
5 James Finley, *Autobiography*, as cited in Christine Leigh Heyrman, *Southern Cross: The Beginnings of the Bible Belt*, (New York: Alfred A. Knopf, 1977) 165.
6 Stone, *Life of Stone*, 39–42.
7 Ibid., 39–42.
8 Conkin, *Cane Ridge*, 103–104.
9 Dickson D. Bruce, *And They All Sang Hallelujah: Plain-Folk Camp-Meeting Religion, 1800–1845* (Knoxville: University of Tennessee Press, 1974), 70–89; Russell E. Richey, *Early American Methodism* (Bloomington: Indiana University Press, 1991), 21–32.
10 Joseph Thomas, *The Life of the Pilgrim Joseph Thomas* (1817), as cited in Nathan O. Hatch, *The Democratization of American Christianity* (New Haven: Yale University Press, 1989), 79–80.
11 Nancy Gove Cram, *A collection of Hymns and Poems: Designed to Instruct the Inquirer...* (Schenectady, N.Y., 1815); Gilbert McMaster, *An Essay in Defence of Some Fundamental Doctrines* (1815), as cited in Hatch, *Democratization of American Christianity*, 78; Catherine Anne Brekus, "'Let Your Women Keep Silence in the Churches': Female Preaching and Evangelical Religion in America, 1740–1845," Ph.D. Diss., Yale University, 1993, 126.
12 Nancy Towle, *Vicissitudes Illustrated, in the Experiences of Nancy Towle, in Europe and America* (Portsmouth, N.H.: John Caldwell, 1833).
13 Brekus, "Female Preaching and Evangelical Religion," 98–103; 113–119.
14 C. C. Goss, *Statistical History of the First Century of American Methodism* (New York: Carlton & Porter, 1866), 109–110; Sidney E. Ahlstrom, *A Religious History of the American People* (New Haven: Yale University Press, 1972), 436–437.
15 Cited in Frank Baker, "Susannah Wesley: Puritan, Parent, Pastor, Protagonist, Pattern," in Rosemary Skinner Keller, Louise L. Queen, and Hilah F. Thomas, eds., *Women in New Worlds: Historical Perspectives on the Wesleyan Tradition* (Nashville, Tenn.: Abingdon Press, 1982), 2:125.
16 Gail Malmgreen, "Domestic Discords: Women and the Family in East Cheshire Methodism, 1750–1830," in Jim Obelkevich, Lyndal Roper, and Raphael Samuel, eds., *Disciplines of Faith: Studies in Religion, Politics, and Patriarchy* (London: Routledge & Kegan Paul, 1987), 57–58 discusses the importance of female patrons in one Methodist region. On Hastings, see John R. Tyson, "Lady Huntingdon's Reformation," *Church History* 64 (1995), 580–593.
17 Quoted in Malmgreen, "Domestic Discords," 58.
18 Henry Moore, *The Life of Mrs. Mary Fletcher*, as quoted in Christine L. Krueger, *The Reader's Repentance: Women Preachers, Women Writers, and*

*Nineteenth-Century Social Discourse* (Chicago: University of Chicago Press, 1992), 37.

19  Hester Ann Roe Rogers, *The Experience and Spiritual Letters of Mrs. Hester Ann Rogers*, as cited in Malmgreen, "Domestic Discords," 62.

20  Frederick A. Norwood, "Expanding Horizons: Women in the Methodist Movement," in Richard L. Greaves, *Triumph Over Silence: Women in Protestant History* (Westport, Conn.: Greenwood Press, 1985), 151–155; Rosemary Radford Ruether and Rosemary Skinner Keller, eds., *Women and Religion in America* vol. 2 (San Francisco: Harper & Row, 1983), 358–361; 366–367.

21  Catharine Livingston to Catharine Rutsen, December 1791, in Ruether and Keller, eds., *Women and Religion in America*, 363–364.

22  Fanny Newell's *Memoirs*, as cited in Brekus, "Female Preaching and Evangelical Religion," 122–123.

23  Abel Stevens, *The Women of Methodism* (New York: Carlton & Porter, 1866), 213–253. He, too, writes of Catharine Livingston Garretson, 256–264.

24  Heyrman, *Southern Cross*, 166–167.

25  It might be further noted that, about mid-century, when the various groups worked to reconstruct the British Methodist communion, the leadership of women would be increasingly restricted. I thank Hugh McLeod for his notes on nineteenth-century English Methodist history.

26  Richey, *Early American Methodism*, 1–20; citation 18.

27  Hatch, *Democratization of American Christianity*, 84. Quotation from Francis Asbury in *The Arminian Magazine* (1784).

28  As cited in Mary P. Ryan, *Cradle of the Middle Class: The Family in Oneida County, New York, 1790–1865* (Cambridge: Cambridge University Press, 1981), 71–73.

29  Susan Juster, *Disorderly Women: Sexual Politics and Evangelicalism in Revolutionary New England* (Ithaca, N.Y.: Cornell University Press, 1994), 122–135; citation 130. Heyrman, *Southern Cross*, 167–168 notes the same exclusion of women from Baptist positions of authority.

30  Juster, *Disorderly Women*, 128–129.

31  Gordon Wood, *The Radicalism of the American Revolution* (New York: Alfred A. Knopf, 1992). See especially "Equality," 229–243; "The Assault of Aristocracy," 271–287; and "A World Within Themselves," 305–325.

32  As quoted in Wood, *Radicalism of the Revolution*, 236.

33  Rush and Adams as quoted in Wood, *Radicalism of the Revolution*, 236; 238.

34  Winthrop Jordan, "Thomas Jefferson: Self and Society," *The White Man's Burden: Historical Origins of Racism in the United States* (New York: Oxford University Press, 1974), 165–193.

35  Stephanie McCurry, "The Two Faces of Republicanism: Gender and Proslavery Politics in South Carolina," *Journal of American History* 78 (1992), 1245–1264.

36  Linda Kerber, *Women and the Republic: Intellect and Ideology in Revolutionary America* (Chapel Hill: University of North Carolina Press, 1980); Mary Ryan, "Ceremonial Space: Public Celebration and Private Women," in *Women in Public: Between Banners and Ballots, 1825–1880* (Baltimore: Johns Hopkins University Press, 1990), 19–57.

37  Hatch, *Democratization of American Christianity*, especially 3–46; see also Juster, *Disorderly Women*, 108–144.

38  Thomas Rankin as cited in Mechal Sobel, *The World They Made Together: Black and White Values in Eighteenth-Century Virginia* (Princeton: Princeton University Press, 1987), 205. See also Sobel, 204–213; Hatch, *Democratization of American Christianity*, 103–110.

39 Both cited in Hatch, *Democratization of American Christianity*, 103.

40 As cited in Sobel, *The World They Made Together*, 206.

41 Richard Allen, *The Life Experience and Gospel Labors of the Rt. Rev. Richard Allen*, (Nashville Tenn.: Abingdon Press, 1960), 29; 30.

42 Albert J. Raboteau, *Slave Religion: The "Invisible Institution" in the Antebellum South* (New York: Oxford University Press, 1978), 149; Gary Nash, *Forging Freedom: The Formation of Philadelphia's Black Community 1720–1840* (Cambridge: Harvard University Press, 1988), 132–133.

43 Hatch, *Democratization of American Christianity*, 106–107.

44 Raboteau, *Slave Religion*, 134–144.

45 Carol V. R. George, *Segregated Sabbaths: Richard Allen and the Rise of Independent Black Churches, 1760–1840* (New York: Oxford University Press, 1973), 49–89.

46 Allen, *Life Experience*, 35.

47 Ibid., 32; George, *Segregated Sabbaths*, 128–129; Jarena Lee, *The Life and Religious Experience of Jarena Lee* (1836), in Andrews, ed. *Sisters of the Spirit*, 36; 44–45; William L. Andrews, Introduction to *Sisters of the Spirit*, 6–7.

48 Elaw, *Memoirs*, 56–57.

49 *Memoir of Old Elizabeth, A Coloured Woman* (1863), in *Six Women's Slave Narratives* (New York: Oxford University Press, 1988), 5–6.

50 Lee, *Life and Experience*, 35; Elaw, *Memoirs*, 67; 68–70; 75.

51 *Memoir of Elizabeth*, 9–10.

52 Elaw, *Memoirs*, 81–82; 87.

53 *Memoir of Elizabeth*, 10; 13; Elaw, *Memoirs*, 73–75; Lee, *Life and Experience*, 43; 45.

54 Elaw, *Memoirs*, 61.

55 Lee, *Life and Experience*, 45.

56 *Memoir of Elizabeth*, 12.

57 Ibid., 17.

58 Lee, *Life and Experience*, 45–46.

59 Elaw, *Memoirs*, 101.

60 Lee, *Life and Experience*, 36.

61 *Memoir of Elizabeth*, 15–16; Lee, *Life and Experience*, 36; Elaw, *Memoirs*, 124.

## 7 Domestic piety: mothers, misionaries, and the Holiness movement

1 "Home," *Ladies' Magazine* (1830), as cited in Nancy F. Cott, *The Bonds of Womanhood, "Woman's Sphere" in New England, 1780–1835* (New Haven: Yale University Press, 1977), 64.

2 Barbara Welter, "The Cult of True Womanhood, 1820–1860," *American Quarterly* 18 (1966), 151–174.

3 Benjamin Morgan Palmer, *The Family in its Civil and Churchly Aspects* (1876), as cited in Stephanie McCurry, *Masters of Small Worlds: Yeoman Households, Gender Relations, and the Political Culture of the Antebellum South Carolina Low Country* (New York: Oxford University Press, 1995), 217.

4 John Cosens Ogden, *The Female Guide*, as cited in Barbara Diane Loomis, "Piety and Play: Young Women's Leisure in an Era of Evangelical Religion, 1790–1840," Diss., University of California, Berkeley, 1988, 5–6.

5 Loomis, "Piety and Play," has found that many young female evangelical converts would testify against the dancing school as the center of all mischief and frivolity.

6 John Bennet[t], *Letters to a Young Lady* (1791), as cited and discussed in Loomis, "Piety and Play," 80–81.

7 T. S. Arthur, *Advice to Young Ladies* (1847), in Frances B. Cogan, *All-American Girl: The Ideal of Real Womanhood in Mid-Nineteenth-Century America* (Athens: University of Georgia, 1989), 206–207.

8 Daniel Chaplin, *A Discourse Delivered before the Charitable Female Society in Groton* (1814), as cited in Cott, *Bonds of Womanhood*, 128–129.

9 *Mother's Monthly Journal* (1836), as quoted in Mary P. Ryan, *Cradle of the Middle Class: The Family in Oneida County, New York, 1790–1865* (Cambridge: Cambridge University Press, 1981), 101.

10 John Taylor, *A History of Ten Baptist Churches* (1823), as cited in Christine Leigh Heyrman, *Southern Cross: The Beginnings of the Bible Belt* (New York: Alfred A. Knopf, 1997), 203.

11 Winthrop Jordan, *Black Over White: American Attitudes Toward the Negro, 1550–1812* (Chapel Hill: University of North Carolina Press, 1968).

12 Lori D. Ginzberg, *Women and the Work of Benevolence: Morality, Politics, and Class in the Nineteenth-Century United States* (New Haven: Yale University Press, 1990), 13–14.

13 McCurry, *Masters of Small Worlds*, 215–220.

14 Christine Stansell, *City of Women: Sex and Class in New York 1789–1860* (Urbana: University of Illinois Press, 1987), especially pages 19–30; 63–101; citation 66.

15 Charles G. Finney, *Lectures on Revivalism* (1835), as quoted in Sydney Ahlstrom, *A Religious History of the American People* (New Haven: Yale University Press, 1972), 460.

16 Hatch, Nathan, *The Democratization of American Christianity*, (New Haven: Yale University Press, 1989), 196–200; Finney quoted on 199–200.

17 H. Larry Ingle, *Quakers in Conflict: The Hicksite Reformation* (Knoxville: University of Tennessee Press, 1986).

18 As cited in Margaret Hope Bacon, *Mothers of Feminism: The Story of Quaker Women in America* (New York: Harper & Row, 1986), 95.

19 Bacon, *Mothers of Feminism*, 90–97.

20 Ryan, *Cradle of the Middle Class*, 75–80, appendices C1 and C2, 257; Cott, *Bonds of Womanhood*, 132; Sean Wilentz, *Chants Democratic: New York City and the Rise of the American Working Class, 1788–1850* (New York: Oxford University Press, 1984), 146 n. Heyrman, *Southern Cross*, 193–197 finds the same pattern among Baptists and Methodists in the south.

21 Harriet Martineau, *Society in America* (1837), as quoted in Cott, *Bonds of Womanhood*, 137.

22 Ryan, *Cradle of the Middle Class*, 81; appendix C5, 259; Beriah Green, "The Savior's Arms Open to Little Children (1836), in Ryan, 100; *Mothers Magazine* (1833), in Ryan, 98.

23 Donald G. Mathews, *Religion in the Old South* (Chicago: University of Chicago Press, 1977), 111–114; citation 112.

24 Barbara Leslie Epstein, *The Politics of Domesticity: Women, Evangelism, and Temperance in Nineteenth-Century America* (Middletown, Conn.: Wesleyan University Press, 1981), 59–61.

25 Lyman Beecher, as quoted by Epstein, *Politics of Domesticity*, 61.

26 Heyrman, *Southern Cross*, 200–202.

27 Mathews, *Religion in the Old South*, 112–113.

28 Ryan, *Cradle of the Middle Class*, 98–104; Cott, *Bonds of Womanhood*, 133–135.

29 Catherine Anne Brekus, " 'Let Your Women Keep Silence in the Churches'": Female Preaching and Evangelical Religion in America, 1740–1845," Ph.D. Diss., Yale University, 1993, 1–4; appendix, 407–412.

30 *Memorial Volume of the First Fifty Years of the American Board of Commissioners for Foreign Missions* (Boston: privately by the Board, 1861), 272; 276.

31 Dana L. Robert, *American Women in Mission: A Social History of Their Thought and Practice* (Macon, Ga.: Mercer University Press, 1996), 21.

32 James D. Knowles, *Memoir of Mrs. Ann H. Judson* (London: Wightman and Co., 1830), 31; Edward W. Hooker, *Memoir of Mrs. Sarah Lanman Smith, late of the mission in Syria* (Boston: Perkins and Marvin, 1839), 108–110.

33 Miron Winslow, *Memoir of Mrs. Harriet L. Winslow* (New York: American Tract Society, 1840), 29; 85–87.

34 Knowles, *Memoir of Judson*, 36; 37; Hooker, *Memoir of Smith*, 130–131.

35 Robert, *American Women in Mission:*, 27–28.

36 Ibid., 22–23.

37 Joan Jacobs Brumberg, *Mission for Life* (New York: The Free Press, 1980), 27–36.

38 Amanda Porterfield, *Mary Lyon and the Mount Holyoke Missionaries* (New York: Oxford University Press, 1997).

39 Winslow, *Memoir of Winslow*, 17; Knowles, *Memoir of Judson*, 18; 23.

40 Leonard Woods, *Memoirs of Mrs. Harriet Newell* (London: D. Jaques, 1818), 4; 6.

41 Winslow, *Memoir of Winslow*, 80; 90; Knowles, *Memoir of Judson*, 39; Hooker, *Memoir of Smith*, 132–133; 135.

42 Robert, *American Women in Mission*, 43–46.

43 Fanny Forester, *Memoir of Sarah B. Judson* (1848), as cited in Robert, *American Women in Mission*, 53.

44 Robert, *American Women in Mission*, 52–55.

45 Hooker, *Memoir of Smith*, 187; 167.

46 Knowles, *Memoir of Judson*, 149; Hooker, *Memoir of Smith*, 158–165; citation 165.

47 Hooker, *Memoir of Smith*, 228–229.

48 Ibid., 134–135.

49 The title on the spine of Daniel C. Eddy, *Heroines of the Missionary Enterprise* (Boston: Ticknor, Reed, and Fields, 1850).

50 On the transformation of the camp meeting, see Russell E. Richey, *Early American Methodism* (Bloomington: Indiana University Press, 1991), 21–32.

51 Harold E. Rasur, *Phoebe Palmer: Her Life and Thought* (Lewiston, N.Y.: Edward Mellen Press, 1987), 44.

52 Ibid., 45.

53 Phoebe Palmer, *Memoirs*, as cited in Thomas C. Oden, ed., *Phoebe Palmer Selected Writings* (New York: Paulist Press, 1988), 116.

54 Phoebe Palmer, *Faith and Its Effects: Or, Fragments from my Portfolio*, facsimile edition (New York: Garland Publishing, Inc., 1985), 64–67.

55 Ibid., 71; 72.

56 Palmer's better-known works include *The Way of Holiness, With Notes by the Way* (1843), *Entire Devotion to God: A Present to A Christian Friend* (1845), *Faith and Its Effects* (1845), *Incidental Illustrations of the Economy of Salvation* (1855), and *The Promise of the Father, or, A Neglected Specialty of the Last Days* (1859). *The Guide to Christian Perfection/Holiness* became a journal of central importance for the Holiness movement during the last two-thirds of the nineteenth century.

57 On the dynamics of the meeting, see Rasur, *Phoebe Palmer*, 79–81.

58 Thomas C. Oden, Introduction to *Phoebe Palmer Selected Writings*, 1–5 for his estimate of her centrality to the Methodist Holiness movement.

59 Phoebe Palmer, *Tongues of Fire on the Daughters of the Lord* (1869), was a significantly shortened version of her *Promise of the Father*. The text cited here is found in Oden, ed., *Phoebe Palmer Selected Writings*, 33–49.
60 Palmer, *Tongues of Fire*, 46.
61 Palmer, *Promise of the Father*, as cited in Nancy Hardesty, "Minister As Prophet? or As Mother? Two Nineteenth-Century Models," in Hilah F. Thomas and Rosemary Skinner Keller, eds., *Women in New Worlds* (Nashville, Tenn.: Abingdon Press, 1981), 96.

## 8 The reformer's pulpit

1 Lori D. Ginzberg, *Women and the Work of Benevolence: Morality, Politics, and Class in the Nineteenth-Century United States* (New Haven: Yale University Press, 1990), 36–66.
2 Elias Cornelius, *Sermon before the Salem Society for the Moral and Religious Instruction of the Poor* (1824), as cited in Ginzberg, *Women and the Work of Benevolence*, 36.
3 On temperance and other reform movements, see Ronald G. Walters, *American Reformers, 1815–1860* (New York: Hill and Wang, 1978).
4 Carroll Smith-Rosenberg, "Beauty, the Beast, and the Militant Woman: A Case Study in Sex Roles and Social Stress in Jacksonian America," in *Disorderly Conduct: Visions of Gender in Victorian America* (New York: Oxford University Press, 1985), 109–128.
5 As cited in Smith-Rosenberg, "Beauty, the Beast, and the Militant Woman," 117; 116. See also Ginzberg, *Women and the Work of Benevolence*, 19–23.
6 Smith-Rosenberg, "Beauty, the Beast, and the Militant Woman," 118–119.
7 Nancy A. Hardesty, *Your Daughters Shall Prophesy: Revivalism and Feminism in the Age of Finney* (Brooklyn: Carlson Publishing, Inc., 1991).
8 As cited in Hardesty, *Your Daughters Shall Prophesy*, 20.
9 Elizabeth Cady Stanton, *Eighty Years and More* (1898; New York: Schocken Books, 1971), 43.
10 John R. McKivigan, *The War against Proslavery Religion: Abolitionism and the Northern Churches, 1830–1865* (Ithaca, N.Y.: Cornell University Press, 1984), 44.
11 Ibid., 105–106.
12 Margaret Hope Bacon, *Mothers of Feminism: The Story of Quaker Women in America* (San Francisco: Harper & Row, 1986), 102–104.
13 Margaret Hope Bacon, *Valiant Friend: The Life of Lucretia Mott* (New York: Walker, 1980).
14 Ronald G. Walters, *The Antislavery Appeal: American Abolitionism After 1830* (1978; New York: Norton, 1984), 39–42.
15 McKivigan, *War against Proslavery Religion*, especially 74–127.
16 AFASS, *Remonstrance against the Course Pursued by the Evangelical Alliance on the Subject of American Slavery* (1847), 12, as cited in McKivigan, *War against Proslavery Religion*, 126; see 125–127.
17 Hardesty, *Your Daughters Shall Prophesy*, 16. See Luke 10:1–12.
18 Shirley J. Yee, *Black Women Abolitionists: A Study in Activism, 1828–1860* (Knoxville: University of Tennessee Press, 1992), 22–24; 113.
19 Ibid., 111.
20 Maria W. Stewart, "Productions" (1835), in Sue E. Houchins, *Spiritual Narratives* (New York: Oxford University Press, 1988), 54–55; 64.
21 Ibid., 73.
22 Ibid., 5; 6; 18.
23 Idid., 10; 16.

24 Stewart, as cited in Jean Fagan Yellin, *Women and Sisters: The Antislavery Feminists in American Culture* (New Haven: Yale University Press, 1989), 47.

25 Stewart, "Productions," 74–78; citations 75; 82.

26 On the creation of this image, see Nell Irvin Painter, *Sojourner Truth: A Life, A Symbol* (New York: W. W. Norton, 1996), 151–178.

27 *Narrative of Sojourner Truth*, ed. Margaret Washington (New York: Vintage Books, 1993), 30–40.

28 Ibid., 49–52.

29 Painter, *Sojourner Truth*, 43–44; *Narrative of Sojourner Truth*, 62–68.

30 *Narrative of Sojourner Truth*, 69–80.

31 Painter, *Sojourner Truth*, 125–126; 136; 138.

32 *Liberator* (1851), in Painter, *Sojourner Truth*, 128.

## 9 Voices and silence: women, the Spirit, and the Enlightenment

1 Ben Barker-Benfield, "Anne Hutchinson and the Puritan Attitude Toward Women," *Feminist Studies* 1 (1972), 65–98.

2 Barbara Welter, "The Feminization of American Religion, 1800–1860," in *Dimity Convictions: The American Woman in the Nineteenth Century* (Athens: Ohio University Press, 1976), citation 89; Barbara Epstein, *Politics of Domesticity: Women, Evangelicalism, and Temperance in Nineteenth-Century America* (Middletown, Conn.: Wesleyan University Press, 1981), 45–64; Susan Juster, *Disorderly Women: Sexual Politics and Evangelical Politics in Revolutionary New England* (Ithaca, N.Y.: Cornell University Press, 1994), 180–208.

3 Sarah Grimke, *Letters on the Equality of the Sexes and the Condition of Women* (1838; New York: Source Book Press, 1970); Phoebe Palmer, *The Promise of the Father, or a Neglected Speciality of the Last Days* (1859; New York: Garland Press, 1985).

# Bibliographic essay
## Further reading and research projects

When I began this project seven years ago, the subject of women and religion represented relatively uncharted waters. With the possible exception of studies on the relationship between Church and State, the history of American religion has, until recently, remained the province of denominational historians, primarily apologist and celebratory, primarily concerned with theology and institutions, theologians and clergymen. As such, this scholarship stood squarely outside the standard historiography of U.S. history. Over the past three decades U.S. historians, among others, have become deeply interested in the behavior and ideas of ordinary people. For historians of religion, this interest translated into studies of the "people in the pews." Of course, despite such promise, the majority of persons sitting in the pews, women, were generally ignored. During these same three decades, new generations of historians of women explored the leadership and lives of women; yet despite the fact that a significant number of American women who lived during the seventeenth, eighteenth, and nineteenth centuries were devoted to God, religion, and churchgoing, women's historians, with a few notable exceptions, ignored religion.

Since the mid-1980s, however, three important developments have worked to ignite historical interest in religion generally and in women's place within religion specifically. First, the new cultural history, with its focus upon ideology as the product as well as producer of power politics, social structures, and ordinary people's lives, has moved early American historians toward the study of religions as central cultural systems. Second, historians of women have discovered that religion, far from acting solely as a force of oppression, actually opened up some avenues of authority and power to women. In a community that valued holiness, piety, and virtue, the high achievers in religion could well hold moral authority even without explicit political, economic, or social power. Finally, the relatively new direction, heralded by the publication of Joan Scott's now famous "Gender: A Useful Category of Historical Analysis" (1986), that some historians have taken toward gender history has excited renewed interest in the subject of women and religion. Granting that religion was of exceptional importance in determining the national identity of the United States, and knowing that the majority of practitioners were women, the exploration of religious systems as gendered systems has held extraordinary promise.

The truly eccentric historiography of this field represents its newness. There are some areas, such as Anne Hutchinson and the Antinomian controversy, witchcraft and witch trials, women reformers, and domestic piety, that have been deeply researched and revisited – frequently with new insight. There are other areas of early American religious history, such as Puritan studies and the first and second Great Awakenings, that have been extensively researched, but little of the resulting scholarship engages questions of women's experiences. Finally there are some topics, such as African-American Christianity and pre-1860 missionary efforts, that are just beginning to receive the attention deserved. Because these latter have been pursued in the past decade, many as a matter of course incorporate women's experiences and gender politics. Generally speaking, the field is still so new that many dissertations have provided some primary research data and interpretive possibilities for my study. Due to this new enthusiasm for women and religion and the production of transformative scholarship, this book, published in 1999, is a radically different volume from the one imagined in 1992.

In contextualizing the Reformation faiths and the gender dynamics of early modern religion, I was inspired by an early essay written by Eleanor McLaughlin, "Women, Power, and the Pursuit of Holiness in Medieval Christianity" (1979). McLaughlin argues for the real power lodged in holiness within a society that highly regards virtuous performance and spiritual charisma. In this same vein, I have found the work of Caroline Walker Bynum particularly enlightening. The essays in her *Fragmentation and Redemption* (1992) articulate the component parts of a Christian theology and ritual system within the highly gendered, mystical world of early modern religious orders. Most important to my own thinking have been her discussions of body–mind–spirit relationships and her call for early modern historians to recognize that the construction of gender and sexuality cannot be understood as constants, or universals; rather, historians must begin explorations of medieval women and spirituality with an investigation into the changing ideological parameters of that particular world.

Of course, historians of the United States are not the only scholars who have turned to the investigation of women and religion. Historians of Tudor and Stuart England have also recognized the need to examine this subject. The outpouring of essays and books has greatly furthered my own study because of my need to place colonizing women within their transatlantic worlds. Susan Amussen's *An Ordered Society* (1988) provides an excellent introduction to the culture and society of early modern England. Mary Prior and Sherrin Marshall have both edited collections of essays that touch upon key moments, individuals, and themes in the history of Reformation women. Retha M. Warnicke's *Women of the English Renaissance and Reformation* (1983) remains a valuable resource for anyone exploring English women in this period, while Phillis Mack's *Visionary Women* (1992) provides an enlightening introduction to English perceptions of gender in the seventeenth century, along with an excellent analysis of women within the nascent Quaker community. Finally, I have found invaluable Patricia Crawford's masterly synthesis, *Women and Religion in England 1500–1720* (1993). Crawford recognizes the extraordinary diversity of English religious culture during this era, incorporates women who participate in a comprehensive range of communities, and brings a perceptive interpretation to the entire subject as she analyzes women and religion within the context of a politics, society, and culture highly unstable and transformative.

In turning to Puritan women in New England, any beginning reader is advised to turn to Edmund S. Morgan's elegant *Puritan Family* (1956), a lucid discussion of New England family structure and dynamics based largely in the prescriptive literature. Twenty-five years later, Laura Thatcher Ulrich's *Good Wives* (1980) focuses upon the experiences of women. Finding her evidence in private letters and diaries, as well as the public evidence of court records and published writings, Ulrich presents a fairly positive picture of women who find unofficial authority as settlers within a frontier society. Mary Beth Norton's *Founding Mothers & Fathers* (1996), in its emphasis upon legal and political authority, finds the Puritans far less supportive of women's power. Patricia Caldwell's excellent study of *The Puritan Conversion Narrative* (1983) should be consulted by anyone seeking to decode the spiritual testimonies of Puritan believers. Amanda Porterfield's *Female Piety in Puritan New England* (1992) stands among the first to explore the Puritanism of old and New England as a gendered religious system, and, while I agree that Puritan spirituality held enormous possibilities for women, I challenge her conclusion that Puritans were particularly supportive of women's power. My own reading is that the strength women found posed problems for men, who worked to redirect women's energy into domestic enterprise. Surprisingly little has been written on Anne Bradstreet. Two good approaches are Wendy Martin's *American Triptych* (1984), engaging Bradstreet, Emily Dickinson, and Adrienne Rich, and Rosamond Rosenmeier's *Anne Bradstreet Revisited* (1991). Moreover, Bradstreet's poetry is available in several republications, all of which include her personal poetry.

Unsurprisingly, disturbers of the peace are far more popular as subjects, with Anne Hutchinson and her followers among the most frequently explored topics. Emery Battis's *Saints and Sectaries* (1962) tries to understand the crisis in terms of Bostonian politics and, less successfully, Hutchinson, through the parameters of psychohistory. Aside from

Battis, the very paucity of sources (publishable within a single volume, David Hall's 1968 documentary history, *The Antinomian Controversy*) has led most scholars to write essays. Many of the most accessible were gathered into an excellent collection by Francis J. Bremer (1981), and these make up an identifiable historiography that either blames Hutchinson as a potentially fatal deviant or blames the magistrates as overreactive, unjust magistrates exercising enormous authority. Philip F. Gura's *Glimpse of Sion's Glory* (1984), devoting an entire chapter to Antinomianism, provides a great service in introducing his readers to the diversity of a colony that many historians have assumed was homogeneous. With the exception of Battis's problematic interpretation of Hutchinson as menopausal neurotic, gender does not figure prominently in these studies. Recently, following the lead of Ben Barker-Benfield's inspired "Anne Hutchinson and the Puritan Attitude Toward Women" (1972), Amy Schrager Lang's *Prophetic Woman* (1987) and my own essay, "Anne Hutchinson, Sectarian Mysticism, and the Puritan Order" (1990), focus upon gender as a primary factor in the analysis. Readers seeking a solid, readable biography that takes gender seriously should consider Selma Williams's *Divine Rebel* (1981). Although the Quaker persecutions have drawn some attention from historians, significantly less has been written. Jonathan Chu's *Neighbors, Friends, or Madmen* (1985) and, especially, Carla Gardina Pestana's *Quakers and Baptists in Colonial Massachusetts* (1991) are both worthy of attention. But Hutchinsonian/Quaker Mary Dyer remains a subject to be explored.

As witchcraft in New England has long remained among the most popular subjects of historical writing at all levels, from fiction and drama to high-powered scholarship, it is impossible to provide a comprehensive introduction to the field. Any investigation of witch hunting should begin with the British background, including Christina Larner's *Witchcraft and Religion* (1984) and Keith Thomas's incomparable *Religion and the Decline of Magic* (1971). Early New England histories tend to distinguish between the massive outbreak at Salem and earlier efforts to rid the colony of witches. John Demos's *Entertaining Satan* (1982) explores the dynamics of ideology, accusation, and trial through a range of methods, including sociology, anthropology, and psychohistory, concentrating upon all cases *except* Salem, while Paul Boyer and Stephen Nissenbaum in *Salem Possessed* (1974) provide a perceptive exploration of the Salem phenomena through the long history of social conflict there. In the past ten years, historians have focused more directly upon gender as a primary analytical category, and Carol Karlsen's transformative *Devil in the Shape of a Woman* (1987) has been followed by Richard Godbeer's *The Devil's Dominion* (1992) and Elizabeth Reis's exciting and provocative cultural analysis *Damned Women: Sinners and Witches in Puritan New England* (1997). Those readers interested in either biography or the problems of reconstructing life histories without boxes of family papers should take up Elaine G. Breslaw's impressive *Tituba, Reluctant Witch of Salem* (1996).

In turning to the entire colonial landscape, I have been greatly assisted by two works of synthesis. Patricia Bonomi's *Under the Cope of Heaven* (1986) takes a careful look at the expanding and changing institutional structures defining churches during the eighteenth century. Her insights into the inner works of denominations as well as the relationships among denominations and the relationship between churches and the State informed much of my discussion. So, too, Jon Butler's *Awash in a Sea of Faith* (1990) includes a wealth of information and evidence along with its provocative interpretation of the first two and a half centuries of American religious history as a slow accommodation to the demands of formal, institutional religion. In addition to warning us away from over-arching generalizations, Butler has reminded us that European colonizers were believers in magic as well as Christ. My brief exploration of mid-Atlantic Quakers owes much to Barry Levy's illuminating *Quakers and the American Family* (1988), while Daniel B. Shea's introduction to Elizabeth Ashbridge's narrative in *Journeys in New Worlds* (ed. Andrews; 1990) and Christine Levenduski's *Peculiar Power: A Quaker Woman Preacher in Eighteenth-Century America* (1996) are useful introductions for anyone interested in Quaker spiritual biography from this period.

In moving to the Great Awakening one finds many books examining the revivalism movement: most focused upon New England, a few on the mid-Atlantic and Chesapeake regions, but almost none directly engaging women's support. Here, two dissertations have provided engaging discussions: Barbara Lacey's "Women and the Great Awakening in Connecticut" (1982) and Catherine Anne Brekus's "'Let Your Women Keep Silence in the Churches': Female Preaching and Evangelical Religion in America, 1740–1845" (1993). Moreover, in her *World They Made Together* (1987), Mechal Sobel incorporates extensive source materials from colonial Virginia within a perceptive reconstruction of Chesapeake culture, including the rise of evangelical religion in the south. Finally, Susan Juster's impressive study of New England Baptist women, *Disorderly Women* (1994), delineates a useful framework for making sense of women's active involvement in the pre-Revolutionary Baptist community and accounts for the decline of women's authority following the war. Her book's significance lies not only in its focus upon women and its perceptive reconstruction of evangelical piety as a gendered piety, but also in its bridging the divider of the Revolution. Traditionally, historians have seen the a pre-Revolution Awakening and a post-Revolution *Second* Great Awakening. Juster demonstrates the extensive continuities even as she argues that the evangelicals did change over this century of revivalism, primarily as a result of the political changes of the nation.

The rise of Methodism in the United States is, like the Great

Awakening, thoroughly documented, but the consideration of women is quite scarce. When investigating the English background to Methodist women, I found Frank Baker's essay, "Susannah Wesley" (1982) and Gail Malmgreen's "Domestic Discords: Women and the Family in East Cheshire Methodism, 1750–1830" (1987) extremely helpful. On the American side, among the best overviews of this era is Russell E. Richey's *Early American Methodism* (1991), a collection of his own lectures that synthesizes much of his previous work. To identify women, however, I was dependent again upon Catherine Brekus's comprehensive coverage, as well as Nancy Hardesty's *Your Daughters Shall Prophesy* (1991). With the exception of Donald Mathews' *Religion in the Old South* (1977), most history of early nineteenth-century American evangelicalism has been centered in the northeast. Christine Leigh Heyrman's *Southern Cross: The Beginning of the Bible Belt* (1997) accepts the regional challenge and provides an excellent survey of the religious culture of the early south, dedicating equitable space and analysis to the majority of members, women, and, like Juster, bridging the artificial divide of the revolution.

Heyrman also, like Mathews and Sobel, takes seriously the task of investigating a community that includes African Americans as well as Anglo-Americans. All three examine the similarities and differences between white and black evangelicalism, and all three take seriously the question of the attraction of evangelical Christianity for African-American slaves. For me, Albert J. Raboteau's *Slave Religion* (1978) has remained the best exposition of slave religion. His consideration of African continuities, his estimate of the number of slaves converting (and when), and his analysis of the components of slave theology and religious practice as an integrated and politicized religious culture have set comprehensible foundations from which to consider these questions. On evangelical religion within the free black community, readers should turn to Carol George's *Segregated Sabbaths* (1973) on Richard Allen and the independent black churches. The more recent discovery of African-American women preachers, growing primarily out of the separate African Methodist Episcopal church overlaps other historical efforts to recover women's voices. William Andrews' (1986, 1988, 1990) editorial efforts to recover the voices of African-American women have borne extraordinary fruit, and it is through his efforts that Jarena Lee and especially Zilpha Elaw have come to be known. Just like the subfield of Methodist women's history, in the realm of African-American Christianity before emancipation, there is much work to be done.

The field of U.S. women's history has flourished for the nineteenth century. In an effort to uncover women's culture, historians have dedicated extensive attention to domesticity. Barbara Welter's "Cult of True Womanhood, 1820–1860" (1966) laid out, via the prescriptive literature, a framework within which to examine women's experiences. The impact of evangelical culture upon women's lives was further developed by Barbara Diane Loomis in her dissertation "Piety and Play: Young Women's Leisure in an Era of Evangelical Religion, 1790–1840" (1988). Nancy F. Cott's *Bonds of Womanhood* (1977) first articulated a model of a woman's world as headquartered within domesticity, while the path-breaking essays of Carroll Smith-Rosenberg, collected in her *Disorderly Conduct* (1985), have developed a highly sophisticated portrait of the world of white, bourgeois women during the Victorian period. In the same vein, Karen Halttunen's *Confidence Men and Painted Women* (1982) considers the impact of industrial capitalist culture upon a culture in transition. Two historians almost simultaneously added to the under-standing of domesticity by taking seriously the performance of piety and the significance of women within church communities. Mary P. Ryan's *Cradle of the Middle Class* (1981) showed the impact of domestic piety upon one county, Oneida, in upstate New York. Barbara Epstein's *Politics of Domesticity* (1981) traversed a wider scope, beginning in the Great Awakening itself and carrying the story through to the end of the nine-teenth-century. Unfortunately, this scholarship has generally been limited by class and region, though two scholars have sought to broaden the range. Christine Stansell's study of working women in New York, *City of Women* (1987), pulls poor, urban women into the equation, while Stephanie McCurry's *Masters of Small Worlds* (1995) addresses similar questions among yeoman households in South Carolina.

Historians interested in women following some sort of public reli-gious career have generally looked in three directions. Since no woman was ordained until the 1850s, women following a ministerial calling were either lay preachers, missionaries, or reformers. Women preachers were usually outside the primary evangelical denominations, and might be found in the African Methodist Episcopal church, the Christian move-ment, and the Holiness movement among the Methodists. Nancy Hardesty has done an excellent job reclaiming many of these women for the history of evangelicalism, pointing out the surprising lack of renown enjoyed by Holiness leader Phoebe Palmer. Early nineteenth-century missionary women, primarily devoted believers who married in order to serve overseas, are just now appearing in the scholarship. Dana L. Robert's *American Women in Mission* (1996) provides a comprehensive introduction to women in the mission field across two centuries, while Amanda Porterfield's *Mary Lyon and the Mount Holyoke Missionaries* (1997) focuses more directly upon the earlier group, the romanticization of mission, and the dedicated efforts to train women for such vocations. Both books depend in key ways upon an early in-depth exploration of one missionary network, Joan Jacobs Brumberg's *Mission for Life* (1980), an illuminating examination of the famous Judson family.

Books on religion and reform are numerous and voluminous, begin-ning with Timothy L. Smith's *Revivalism and Social Reform* (1957), arguing that the reform movement of the early nineteenth century arose out of the evangelical impulses of the era. While this interpretation dominated American religious history for several decades, I, along with Ronald G. Walters' *American Reformers, 1815–1860* (1978) and Lori D. Ginzberg's *Women and the Work of Benevolence* (1990), am less enthusiastic. The record of evangelicals in relationship with reform is not monolithic and, in many cases, parallels that of other denominations. What are of particular interest are the possibilities that many benevolence and reform movements, such as sabbatarianism, temperance, and the Sunday-school movement offered to evangelicals pursuing personal and family holiness as well as the attraction that reform movements held for evangelical women. Mary Ryan, Barbara Epstein, Carroll Smith-Rosenberg, and Lori Ginzberg have all been struck by the extraordinary public opportunities offered to female church members and the alacrity with which women took up those challenges.

In the case of abolitionism, evangelical ambivalence as well as the attraction of the movement for women is particularly striking. John R. McKivigan's *The War Against Proslavery Religion* (1984) makes a strong case for abolitionism standing as a strident, single issue that divided evangelicals. While Quakers seemed a dominant force in the abolitionist movement, they, too, heavily influenced by the evangelical movement, were not unilateral supporters. Although themselves refusing to own slaves and, in many cases, purchase products made by slaves, many Quakers were opposed to involving themselves in affairs of society. Exceptions to this were often at odds with their Meetings, but individuals like Lucretia Mott, memorialized in Margaret Hope Bacon's biography *Valiant Friend* (1980), managed to maintain her status as leader even as she promoted abolitionism. Because abolitionism was a particularly public area of reform, prominent female activists were criticized for their involvement; but women found abolitionism to be a moral reform and as such a natural cause for women. Of course, the commitment of the strongest white women could not match the intensity of black women abolitionists, for, as Shirley J. Yee's *Black Women Abolitionists* (1992) and Jean Fagan Yellin's *Women & Sisters* (1989) point out, black women were more directly impacted by slavery and the battle for emancipation.

However, lest students of reform are inclined to find in the righteousness and the political rhetoric of abolitionism the forces that empowered women as well as men in its service, the example of Sojourner Truth stands as a reminder of the importance of evangelical religion as a source of strength. In her *Sojourner Truth: A Life, A Symbol* (1996), Nell Irvin Painter searches for the key to Truth's powerful political presence within the abolitionist and women's rights movement. What she discovered was a woman who directly encountered God, had once been the member of a small Christian cult, and later found herself called to preach on the itinerant circuit of camp meetings and millennialist gatherings. Her rhetorical power was first there, yet it soon spread to the political causes. This biography, along with Nancy Hardesty's scholarship, and Ann Braude's *Radical Spirits* (1989), an examination of spiritualists and their connection to political activism, should be only the beginning of work to connect religious leadership with political leadership.

Historians have argued, sometimes too strongly, for the connection between an evangelical ethos and the reform impulse, perhaps because they hope, through such a connection, to argue for the importance of evangelicalism. However, current scholarship indicates to me that we may be taking the wrong tack. Instead of trying to connect ideas, perhaps we should also be working seriously upon behaviors – that is, upon voices. When the first woman to address publicly an American audience did so in 1829, how can it be assumed that any woman came to the platform "naturally"? In the current interest in questions of culture, gender, and voice, we can at last begin to understand the importance of religious participation and leadership in providing an arena in which women can hone their speaking skills, build their confidence, and claim some authority to exercise their own voices. Along with confirming (or challenging) some interpretations of specific moments in women's religious history, this book engages the question of women's authority as demonstrated in her expressive voice. The question is not whether evangelicals are inclined toward specific political or social visions, but whether evangelical women, by virtue of their spiritual authority and participation in churches, have empowered themselves to act upon a political or social vision. This question of woman's voice, its character, its power, and its appearance, will, I think, dominate research on women and religion for the upcoming decade.

## Works cited in bibliographic essay and key primary source reprints

Amussen, Susan Dwyer. *An Ordered Society: Gender and Class in Early Modern England.* Oxford: Basil Blackwell, 1988.

Andrews, William L., ed. *Sisters of the Spirit: Three Black Women's Autobiographies of the Nineteenth Century.* Indianapolis: Indiana University Press, 1986.

——, ed. *Six Women's Slave Narratives.* New York: Oxford University Press, 1988.

—— , ed. *Journeys in New Worlds: Early American Women's Narratives.* Madison: University of Wisconsin Press, 1990.

Bacon, Margaret Hope. *Mothers of Feminism: The Story of Quaker Women in America.* New York: Harper & Row, 1986.

—— *Valiant Friend: The Life of Lucretia Mott.* New York: Walker, 1980.

Baker, Frank. "Susannah Wesley: Puritan, Parent, Pastor, Protagonist, Pattern," in Keller, Rosemary Skinner, Queen, Louise L., and Thomas, Hilah F., eds. *Women in New Worlds: Historical Perspectives on the Wesleyan Tradition.* Nashville, Tenn.: Abingdon Press, 1982.

Barker-Benfield, Ben. "Anne Hutchinson and the Puritan Attitude Toward Women." *Feminist Studies* 1 (1972), 65–98.

Battis, Emery. *Saints and Sectaries: Anne Hutchinson and the Antinomian Controversy in the Massachusetts Bay Colony*. Chapel Hill: University of North Carolina Press, 1962.

Bonomi, Patricia. *Under the Cope of Heaven: Religion, Society, and Politics in Colonial America*. New York: Oxford University Press, 1986.

Boyer, Paul and Nissenbaum, Stephen. *Salem Possessed: The Social Origins of Witchcraft*. Cambridge: Harvard University Press, 1974.

——, eds. *Salem Witchcraft: A Documentary Record of Local Conflict in Colonial New England*. Belmont, Calif: Wadsworth Publishing Co., 1972.

Bradstreet, Anne. *The Works of Anne Bradstreet*, ed. Jeannine Hensley. Cambridge: Harvard University Press, 1967.

Braude, Ann. *Radical Spirits: Spiritualism and Women's Rights in Nineteenth-Century America*. Boston: Beacon Press, 1989.

Brekus, Catherine Anne. "'Let Your Women Keep Silence in the Churches': Female Preaching and Evangelical Religion in America, 1740–1845," Ph.D. Diss., Yale University, 1993.

Bremer, Francis J. *Anne Hutchinson: Troubler of the Puritan Zion*. Huntington, N.Y.: R. E. Krieger Pub. Co., 1981.

Breslaw, Elaine G. *Tituba, Reluctant Witch of Salem: Devilish Indians and Puritan Fantasies*. New York: New York University Press, 1996.

Brumberg, Joan Jacobs. *Mission for Life*. New York: The Free Press, 1980.

Butler, Jon. *Awash in a Sea of Faith: Christianizing the American People*. Cambridge: Harvard University Press, 1990.

Bynum, Caroline Walker. *Fragmentation and Redemption: Essays on Gender and the Human Body in Medieval Religion*. New York: Zone Books, 1992.

Caldwell, Patricia. *The Puritan Conversion Narrative: The Beginnings of American Expression*. Cambridge: Cambridge University Press, 1983.

Chu, Jonathan M. *Neighbors, Friends, or Madmen: The Puritan Adjustment to Quakerism in Seventeenth-Century Massachusetts Bay*. Westport, Conn.: Greenwood Press, 1985.

Cott, Nancy F. *The Bonds of Womanhood, "Woman's Sphere" in New England, 1780–1835*. New Haven: Yale University Press, 1977.

Crawford, Patricia. *Women and Religion in England 1500–1720*. London: Routledge, 1993.

Demos, John. *Entertaining Satan: Witchcraft and the Culture of Early New England*. New York: Oxford University Press, 1982.

Epstein, Barbara Leslie. *The Politics of Domesticity: Women, Evangelism, and Temperance in Nineteenth-Century America*. Middletown, Conn.: Wesleyan University Press, 1981.

George, Carol V. R., *Segregated Sabbaths: Richard Allen and the Rise of Independent Black Churches, 1760–1840*. New York: Oxford University Press, 1973.

Ginzberg, Lori D. *Women and the Work of Benevolence: Morality, Politics, and Class in the Nineteenth-Century United States*. New Haven: Yale University Press, 1990.

Godbeer, Richard. *The Devil's Dominion: Magic and Religion in Early New England*. New York: Cambridge University Press, 1992.

Greaves, Richard L., ed. *Triumph Over Silence: Women in Protestant History*. Westport, Conn.: Greenwood Press, 1985.

Gura, Philip F. *A Glimpse of Sion's Glory: Puritan Radicalism in New England, 1620–1660*. Middletown, Conn.: Wesleyan University Press, 1984.

Hall, David D., ed. *The Antinomian Controversy, 1636–1638: A Documentary History*. Middletown, Conn.: Wesleyan University Press, 1968.

Halttunen, Karen. *Confidence Men and Painted Women: A Study of Middle-Class Culture in America, 1830–1870*. New Haven: Yale University Press, 1982.

Hardesty, Nancy A. *Your Daughters Shall Prophesy: Revivalism and Feminism in the Age of Finney*. Brooklyn: Carlson Publishing, Inc., 1991.

Hatch, Nathan O. *The Democratization of American Christianity*. New Haven: Yale University Press, 1989.

Heyrman, Christine Leigh. *Southern Cross: The Beginning of the Bible Belt*. New York: Alfred Knopf, 1997.

Houchins, Sue E. *Spiritual Narratives*. New York: Oxford University Press, 1988.

Juster, Susan. *Disorderly Women: Sexual Politics and Evangelicalism in Revolutionary New England*. Ithaca, N.Y.: Cornell University Press, 1994.

Karlsen, Carol. *The Devil in the Shape of a Woman: Witchcraft in Colonial New England*. New York: W. W. Norton, 1987.

Keller, Rosemary Skinner, Queen, Louise L., and Thomas, Hilah F., eds. *Women in New Worlds: Historical Perspectives on the Wesleyan Tradition*. Nashville, Tenn.: Abingdon Press, 1982.

Lacey, Barbara E. "Women and the Great Awakening in Connecticut," Ph.D. Diss., Clark University, 1982.

Lang, Amy Schrager. *Prophetic Woman: Anne Hutchinson and the Problem of Dissent in the Literature of New England*. Berkeley: University of California Press, 1987.

Larner, Christina. *Witchcraft and Religion: The Politics of Popular Belief*. Oxford: Basil Blackwell, 1984.

Levenduski, Christine. *Peculiar Power: A Quaker Woman Preacher in Eighteenth-Century America*. Washington: Smithsonian Institution Press, 1996.

Levy, Barry. *Quakers and the American Family: British Settlement in the Delaware Valley*. New York: Oxford University Press, 1988.

Loomis, Barbara Diane. "Piety and Play: Young Women's Leisure in an Era of Evangelical Religion, 1790–1840," Diss., University of California, Berkeley, 1988.

McCurry, Stephanie. *Masters of Small Worlds: Yeoman Households, Gender Relations, and the Political Culture of the Antebellum South Carolina Low Country*. New York: Oxford University Press, 1995.

McKivigan, John R. *The War Against Proslavery Religion: Abolitionism and the Northern Churches, 1830–1865*. Ithaca, N.Y.: Cornell University Press, 1984.

McLaughlin, Eleanor. "Women, Power, and the Pursuit of Holiness in Medieval Christianity," in McLaughlin, Eleanor and Ruether, Rosemary, eds. *Women of Spirit: Female Leadership in the Jewish and Christian Traditions*. New York: Simon and Schuster, 1979.

Mack, Phyllis. *Visionary Women: Ecstatic Prophecy in Seventeenth-Century England*. Berkeley: University of California Press, 1992.

Malmgreen, Gail. "Domestic Discords: Women and the Family in East Cheshire Methodism, 1750–1830," in Obelkevich, Jim, Roper, Lyndal, and Samuel, Raphael, eds. *Disciplines of Faith: Studies in Religion, Politics, and Patriarchy*. London: Routledge & Kegan Paul, 1987.

Marshall, Sherrin, ed. *Women in Reformation and Counter-Reformation Europe: Public and Private Worlds*. Bloomington: University of Indiana Press, 1989.

Martin, Wendy. *An American Triptych: Anne Bradstreet, Emily Dickinson, Adrienne Rich*. Chapel Hill: University of North Carolina Press, 1984.

Mathews, Donald G. *Religion in the Old South*. Chicago: University of Chicago Press, 1977.

Morgan, Edmund S. *The Puritan Family*. New York: Harper & Row, 1956.

Norton, Mary Beth *Founding Mothers & Fathers: Gendered Power and the Forming of American Society*. New York: Alfred A. Knopf, 1996.

Obelkevich, Jim, Roper, Lyndal, and Samuel, Raphael, eds. *Disciplines of Faith: Studies in Religion, Politics, and Patriarchy*. London: Routledge & Kegan Paul, 1987.

Painter, Nell Irvin. *Sojourner Truth: A Life, A Symbol*. New York: W. W. Norton, 1996.

Palmer, Phoebe. *Phoebe Palmer Selected Writings*, ed. Thomas C. Oden. New York: Paulist Press, 1988.

Pestana, Carla Gardina. *Quakers and Baptists in Colonial Massachusetts*. New York: Cambridge University Press, 1991.

Porterfield, Amanda. *Female Piety in Puritan New England: The Emergence of Religious Humanism*. New York: Oxford University Press, 1992.

—— *Mary Lyon and the Mount Holyoke Missionaries*. New York: Oxford University Press, 1997.

Prior, Mary, ed. *Women in English Society, 1500–1800*. London: Methuen, 1985.

Raboteau, Albert J. *Slave Religion: The "Invisible Institution" in the Antebellum South*. New York: Oxford University Press, 1978.

Reis, Elizabeth. *Damned Women: Sinners and Witches in Puritan New England*. Ithaca, N.Y.: Cornell University Press, 1997.

Richey, Russell E. *Early American Methodism*. Bloomington: Indiana University Press, 1991.

Robert, Dana L. *American Women in Mission: A Social History of Their Thought and Practice*. Macon, Ga.: Mercer University Press, 1996.

Rosenmeier, Rosamond. *Anne Bradstreet Revisited*. Boston: Twayne Publishers, 1991.

Ruether, Rosemary Radford and Keller, Rosemary Skinner, eds. *Women and Religion in America*. Vol. 2, *The Colonial and Revolutionary Periods*. New York: Harper & Row, 1983.

Ryan, Mary P. *Cradle of the Middle Class: The Family in Oneida County, New York, 1790–1865*. Cambridge: Cambridge University Press, 1981.

Scott, Joan Wallach. "Gender: A Useful Category of Historical Analysis," *American Historical Review* 91 (1986).

Smith, Timothy L. *Revivalism and Social Reform: American Protestantism on the Eve of the Civil War*. New York: Harper & Row, 1957.

Smith-Rosenberg, Carroll. *Disorderly Conduct: Visions of Gender in Victorian America*. New York: Oxford University Press, 1985.

Sobel, Mechal. *The World They Made Together: Black and White Values in Eighteenth-Century Virginia*. Princeton: Princeton University Press, 1987.

Stansell, Christine. *City of Women: Sex and Class in New York 1789–1860*. Urbana: University of Illinois Press, 1987.

Thomas, Hilah F. and Keller, Rosemary Skinner, eds. *Women in New Worlds*. Nashville, Tenn.: Abingdon Press, 1981.

Thomas, Keith. *Religion and the Decline of Magic: Studies in Popular Beliefs in Sixteenth and Seventeenth Century England*. New York: Penguin, 1971.

Truth, Sojourner. *Narrative of Sojourner Truth*, ed. Margaret Washington. New York: Vintage Books, 1993.

Ulrich, Laura Thatcher. *Good Wives: Image and Reality in the Lives of Women in Northern New England, 1650–1750*. New York: Oxford University Press, 1980.

Walters, Ronald G. *American Reformers, 1815–1860*. New York: Hill and Wang, 1978.

Warnicke, Retha M. *Women of the English Renaissance and Reformation*. Westport, Conn.: Greenwood Press, 1983.

Weisman, Richard. *Witchcraft, Magic, and Religion in Seventeenth-Century Massachusetts*. Amherst: University of Massachusetts Press, 1984.

Welter, Barbara. "The Cult of True Womanhood, 1820–1860," *American Quarterly* 18 (1966), 151–174.

Westerkamp, Marilyn J. "Anne Hutchinson, Sectarian Mysticism, and the Puritan Order," *Church History* 59 (1990), 482–496.

Williams, Selma. *Divine Rebel: The Life of Anne Marbury Hutchinson*. New York: Holt, Rinehart and Winston, 1981.

Yee, Shirley J. *Black Women Abolitionists: A Study in Activism, 1828–1860*. Knoxville: University of Tennessee Press, 1992.

Yellin, Jean Fagan. *Women & Sisters: The Antislavery Feminists in American Culture*. New Haven: Yale University Press, 1989.

# Index